The Novels and Tales of Henry James: The Turn of the Screw, The Liar, The Two Faces

Henry James

THE ASPERN PAPERS
THE TURN OF THE SCREW
THE LIAR
THE TWO FACES

BY

HENRY JAMES

NEW YORK
CHARLES SCRIBNER'S SONS
1908

PREFACE

I NOT only recover with ease, but I delight to recall, the first impulse given to the idea of "The Aspern Papers." It is at the same time true that my present mention of it may perhaps too effectually dispose of any complacent claim to my having "found" the situation. Not that I quite know indeed what situations the seeking fabulist does "find"; he seeks them enough assuredly, but his discoveries are, like those of the navigator, the chemist, the biologist, scarce more than alert recognitions. He *comes upon* the interesting thing as Columbus came upon the isle of San Salvador, because he had moved in the right direction for it — also because he knew, with the encounter, what "making land" then and there represented. Nature had so placed it, to profit — if as profit we may measure the matter! — by his fine unrest, just as history, "literary history" we in this connexion call it, had in an out-of-the-way corner of the great garden of life thrown off a curious flower that I was to feel worth gathering as soon as I saw it. I got wind of my positive fact, I followed the scent. It was in Florence years ago; which is precisely, of the whole matter, what I like most to remember. The air of the old-time Italy invests it, a mixture that on the faintest invitation I rejoice again to inhale — and this in spite of the mere cold renewal, ever, of the infirm side of that felicity, the sense, in the whole element, of things too numerous, too deep, too obscure, too strange, or even simply too beautiful, for any ease of intellectual relation. One must pay one's self largely with words, I think, one must induce almost any "Italian subject" to *make believe* it gives up its secret, in order to keep at all on working — or call them perhaps rather playing — terms with the general impression. We entertain it thus, the impression, by the aid of a merciful convention which

v

PREFACE

resembles the fashion of our intercourse with Iberians or Orientals whose form of courtesy places everything they have at our disposal. We thank them and call upon them, but without acting on their professions. The offer has been too large and our assurance is too small; we peep at most into two or three of the chambers of their hospitality, with the rest of the case stretching beyond our ken and escaping our penetration. The pious fiction suffices; we have entered, we have seen, we are charmed. So, right and left, in Italy—before the great historic complexity at least—penetration fails; we scratch at the extensive surface, we meet the perfunctory smile, we hang about in the golden air. But we exaggerate our gathered values only if we are eminently witless. It is fortunately the exhibition in all the world before which, as admirers, we can most remain superficial without feeling silly.

All of which I note, however, perhaps with too scant relevance to the inexhaustible charm of Roman and Florentine memories. Off the ground, at a distance, our fond indifference to being " silly " grows fonder still; the working convention, as I have called it — the convention of the real revelations and surrenders on one side and the real immersions and appreciations on the other — has not only nothing to keep it down, but every glimpse of contrast, every pang of exile and every nostalgic twinge to keep it up. These latter haunting presences in fact, let me note, almost reduce at first to a mere blurred, sad, scarcely consolable vision this present revisiting, re-appropriating impulse. There are parts of one's past, evidently, that bask consentingly and serenely enough in the light of other days — which is but the intensity of thought; and there are other parts that take it as with agitation and pain, a troubled consciousness that heaves as with the disorder of drinking it deeply in. So it is at any rate, fairly in too thick and rich a retrospect, that I see my old Venice of " The Aspern Papers," that I see the still earlier one of Jeffrey Aspern himself, and that I see even the comparatively recent Florence that was to drop into my ear the solicitation of these things. I would fain

PREFACE

" lay it on " thick for the very love of them — that at least I may profess; and, with the ground of this desire frankly admitted, something that somehow makes, in the whole story, for a romantic harmony. I have had occasion in the course of these remarks to define my sense of the romantic, and am glad to encounter again here an instance of that virtue as I understand it. I shall presently say why this small case so ranges itself, but must first refer more exactly to the thrill of appreciation it was immediately to excite in me. I saw it somehow at the very first blush as romantic — for the use, of course I mean, I should certainly have had to make of it — that Jane Clairmont, the half-sister of Mary Godwin, Shelley's second wife and for a while the intimate friend of Byron and the mother of his daughter Allegra, should have been living on in Florence, where she had long lived, up to our own day, and that in fact, had I happened to hear of her but a little sooner, I might have seen her in the flesh. The question of whether I should have wished to do so was another matter — the question of whether I should n't have preferred to keep her preciously unseen, to run no risk, in other words, by too rude a choice, of depreciating that romance-value which, as I say, it was instantly inevitable to attach (through association above all, with another signal circumstance) to her long survival.

I had luckily not had to deal with the difficult option; difficult in such a case by reason of that odd law which somehow always makes the minimum of valid suggestion serve the man of imagination better than the maximum. The historian, essentially, wants more documents than he can really use; the dramatist only wants more liberties than he can really take. Nothing, fortunately, however, had, as the case stood, depended on my delicacy; I might have " looked up " Miss Clairmont in previous years had I been earlier informed — the silence about her seemed full of the " irony of fate "; but I felt myself more concerned with the mere strong fact of her having testified for the reality and the closeness of our relation to the past than with any question of the particular sort of person I might have flattered myself I "found." I had certainly at the very least been saved the undue simplicity of pretending to read meanings into things absolutely sealed and beyond test or proof — to tap a fount of waters that could n't possibly not have run dry. The thrill of learning that she had "overlapped," and by so much, and the wonder of my having doubtless at several earlier seasons passed again and again, all unknowing, the door of her house, where she sat above, within call and in her habit as she lived, these things gave me all I wanted; I seem to remember in fact that my more or less immediately recognising that I positively ought n't — "for anything to come of it" — to have wanted more. I saw, quickly, how something might come of it *thus*; whereas a fine instinct told me that the effect of a nearer view of the case (the case of the overlapping) would probably have had to be quite differently calculable. It was really with another item of knowledge, however, that I measured the mistake I should have made in waking up sooner to the question of opportunity. That item consisted of the action taken on the premises by a person who *had* waked up in time, and the legend of whose consequent adventure, as a few spoken words put it before me, at once kindled a flame. This gentleman, an American of long ago, an ardent Shelleyite, a singularly marked figure and himself in the highest degree a subject for a free sketch — I had known him a little, but there is not a reflected glint of him in "The Aspern Papers" — was named to me as having made interest with Miss Clairmont to be accepted as a lodger on the calculation that she would have Shelley documents for which, in the possibly not remote event of her death, he would thus enjoy priority of chance to treat with her representatives. He had at any rate, according to the legend, become, on earnest Shelley grounds, her yearning, though also her highly diplomatic, *pensionnaire* — but without gathering, as was to befall, the fruit of his design.

Legend here dropped to another key; it remained in a manner interesting, but became to my ear a trifle coarse, or at least rather vague and obscure. It mentioned a younger female relative of the ancient woman as a person who, for a queer climax, had had to be dealt with; it flickered so for a moment and then, as a light, to my great relief, quite went out. It had flickered indeed but at the best — yet had flickered enough to give me my " facts," bare facts of intimation; which, scant handful though they were, were more distinct and more numerous than I mostly *like* facts: like them, that is, as we say of an etcher's progressive subject, in an early " state." Nine tenths of the artist's interest in them is that of what he shall add to them and how he shall turn them. Mine, however, in the connexion I speak of, had fortunately got away from me, and quite of their own movement, in time not to crush me. So it was, at all events, that my imagination preserved power to react under the mere essential charm — that, I mean, of a final scene of the rich dim Shelley drama played out in the very theatre of our own " modernity." This was the beauty that appealed to me; there had been, so to speak, a forward continuity, from the actual man, the divine poet, on; and the curious, the ingenious, the admirable thing would be to throw it backward again, to compress — squeezing it hard! — the connexion that had drawn itself out, and convert so the stretched relation into a value of nearness on our own part. In short I saw my chance as admirable, and one reason, when the direction is right, may serve as well as fifty; but if I " took over," as I say, everything that was of the essence, I stayed my hand for the rest. The Italian side of the legend closely clung; if only because the so possible terms of my Juliana's life in the Italy of other days could make conceivable for her the fortunate privacy, the long uninvaded and uninterviewed state on which I represent her situation as founded. Yes, a surviving unexploited unparagraphed Juliana was up to a quarter of a century since still supposeable — as much so as any such buried treasure, any such grave unprofaned, would defy probability now. And then the case had the air of the past just in the degree in which that air, I confess, most appeals to me — when the region over which it hangs is far enough away without being too far.

PREFACE

I delight in a palpable imaginable *visitable* past — in the
nearer distances and the clearer mysteries, the marks and signs
of a world we may reach over to as by making a long arm we
grasp an object at the other end of our own table. The
table is the one, the common expanse, and where we lean,
so stretching, we find it firm and continuous. That, to my
imagination, is the past fragrant of all, or of almost all, the
poetry of the thing outlived and lost and gone, and yet in
which the precious element of closeness, telling so of connexions but tasting so of differences, remains appreciable.
With more moves back the element of the appreciable
shrinks — just as the charm of looking over a garden-wall
into another garden breaks down when successions of walls
appear. The other gardens, those still beyond, may be there,
but even by use of our longest ladder we are baffled and bewildered — the view is mainly a view of barriers. The one
partition makes the place we have wondered about *other*, both
richly and recogniseably so ; but who shall pretend to im-
pute an effect of composition to the twenty ? We are divided of course between liking to feel the past strange and
liking to feel it familiar ; the difficulty is, for intensity, to
catch it at the moment when the scales of the balance hang
with the right evenness. I say for intensity, for we may
profit by them in other aspects enough if we are content to
measure or to feel loosely. It would take me too far, however, to tell why the particular afternoon light that I thus
call intense rests clearer to my sense on the Byronic age,
as I conveniently name it, than on periods more protected by
the " dignity " of history. With the times beyond, intrinsic-
ally more " strange," the tender grace, for the backward
vision, has faded, the afternoon darkened ; for any time
nearer to us the special effect has n't begun. So there, to
put the matter crudely, is the appeal I fondly recognise, an
appeal residing doubtless more in the " special effect," in
some deep associational force, than in a virtue more intrinsic.
I am afraid I must add, since I allow myself so much to fan-
tasticate, that the impulse had more than once taken me to
project the Byronic age and the afternoon light across the

great sea, to see in short whether association would carry so far and what the young century might pass for on that side of the modern world where it was not only itself so irremediably youngest, but was bound up with youth in everything else. There was a refinement of curiosity in this imputation of a golden strangeness to American social facts — though I cannot pretend, I fear, that there was any greater wisdom.

Since what it had come to then was, harmlessly enough, cultivating a sense of the past under that close protection, it was natural, it was fond and filial, to wonder if a few of the distilled drops might n't be gathered from some vision of, say, " old " New York. Would that human congeries, to aid obligingly in the production of a fable, be conceivable as " taking " the afternoon light with the right happy slant? — or could a recogniseable reflexion of the Byronic age, in other words, be picked up on the banks of the Hudson? (Only just there, beyond the great sea, if anywhere: in no other connexion would the question so much as raise its head. I admit that Jeffrey Aspern is n't even feebly localised, but I *thought* New York as I projected him.) It was " amusing," in any case, always, to try experiments; and the experiment for the right *transposition* of my Juliana would be to fit her out with an immortalising poet as transposed as herself. Delicacy had demanded, I felt, that my appropriation of the Florentine legend should purge it, first of all, of references too obvious; so that, to begin with, I shifted the scene of the adventure. Juliana, as I saw her, was thinkable only in Byronic and more or less immediately post-Byronic Italy; but there were conditions in which she was ideally arrangeable, as happened, especially in respect to the later time and the long undetected survival; there being absolutely no refinement of the mouldy rococo, in human or whatever other form, that you may not disembark at the dislocated water-steps of almost any decayed monument of Venetian greatness in auspicious quest of. It was a question, in fine, of covering one's tracks — though with no great elaboration I am bound to admit; and I felt I could n't cover mine more than in postulating a comparative American Byron to match an American Miss Clairmont — she as absolute as she would. I scarce know whether best to say for this device to-day that it cost me little or that it cost me much; it was "cheap" or expensive according to the degree of verisimilitude artfully obtained. If that degree appears *nil* the "art," such as it was, is wasted, and my remembrance of the contention, on the part of a highly critical friend who at that time and later on often had my ear, that it had been simply foredoomed to be wasted, puts before me the passage in the private history of "The Aspern Papers" that I now find, I confess, most interesting. I comfort myself for the needful brevity of a present glance at it by the sense that the general question involved, under criticism, can't but come up for us again at higher pressure.

My friend's argument bore then — at the time and afterward — on my vicious practice, as he maintained, of postulating for the purpose of my fable celebrities who not only *had n't* existed in the conditions I imputed to them, but who for the most part (and in no case more markedly than in that of Jeffrey Aspern) could n't possibly have done so. The stricture was to apply itself to a whole group of short fictions in which I had, with whatever ingenuity, assigned to several so-called eminent figures positions absolutely unthinkable in our actual encompassing air, an air definitely unfavourable to certain forms of eminence. It was vicious, my critic contended, to flourish forth on one's page "great people," public persons, who should n't more or less square with our quite definite and calculable array of such notabilities; and by this rule I was heavily incriminated. The rule demanded that the "public person" portrayed should be at least of the tradition, of the general complexion, of the face-value, exactly, of some past or present producible counterfoil. Mere private figures, under one's hand, might correspond with nobody, it being of their essence to be but narrowly known; the represented state of being conspicuous, on the other hand, involved before anything else a recognition — and none of my eminent folk were recogniseable. It was all very well for instance to have put one's self at such pains for Miriam Rooth in " The Tragic Muse " ; but *there* was misapplied zeal, there a case of pitiful waste, crying aloud to be denounced. Miriam is offered not as a young person passing unnoticed by her age — like the Biddy Dormers and Julia Dallows, say, of the same book, but as a high rarity, a time-figure of the scope inevitably attended by other commemorations. Where on earth would be then Miriam's inscribed " counterfoil," and in what conditions of the contemporary English theatre, in what conditions of criticism, of appreciation, under what conceivable Anglo-Saxon star, might we take an artistic value of this order either for produced or for recognised ? We are, as a " public," chalk-marked by nothing, more unmistakeably, than by the truth that we know nothing of such values — any more than, as my friend was to impress on me, we are susceptible of consciousness of such others (these in the sphere of literary eminence) as my Neil Paraday in " The Death of the Lion," as my Hugh Vereker in " The Figure in the Carpet," as my Ralph Limbert, above all, in " The Next Time," as sundry unprecedented and unmatched heroes and martyrs of the artistic ideal, in short, elsewhere exemplified in my pages. We shall come to these objects of animadversion in another hour, when I shall have no difficulty in producing the defence I found for them — since, obviously, I had n't cast them into the world *all* naked and ashamed ; and I deal for the moment but with the stigma in general as Jeffrey Aspern carries it.

The charge being that I foist upon our early American annals a distinguished presence for which they yield me absolutely no warrant — " Where, within them, gracious heaven, were we to look for so much as an approach to the social elements of habitat and climate of birds of that note and plumage ? " — I find his link with reality then just in the tone of the picture wrought round him. What was that tone but exactly, but exquisitely, calculated, the harmless hocus-pocus under cover of which we might suppose him to have existed ? This tone is the tone, artistically speaking, of " amusement," the current floating that precious influence

PREFACE

home quite as one of those high tides watched by the smugglers of old might, in case of their boat's being boarded, be trusted to wash far up the strand the cask of foreign liquor expertly committed to it. If through our lean prime Western period no dim and charming ghost of an adventurous lyric genius might by a stretch of fancy flit, if the time was really too hard to "take," in the light form proposed, the elegant reflexion, then so much the worse for the time — it was all one could say! The retort to that of course was that such a plea represented no "link" with reality — which was what was under discussion — but only a link, and flimsy enough too, with the deepest depths of the artificial: the restrictive truth exactly contended for, which may embody my critic's last word rather of course than my own. My own, so far as I shall pretend in that especial connexion to report it, was that one's warrant, in such a case, hangs essentially on the question of whether or no the false element imputed would have borne that test of further development which so exposes the wrong and so consecrates the right. My last word was, heaven forgive me, that, occasion favouring, I could have perfectly "worked out" Jeffrey Aspern. The boast remains indeed to be verified when we shall arrive at the other challenged cases.

That particular challenge at least "The Turn of the Screw" does n't incur; and this perfectly independent and irresponsible little fiction rejoices, beyond any rival on a like ground, in a conscious provision of prompt retort to the sharpest question that may be addressed to it. For it has the small strength — if I should n't say rather the unattackable ease — of a perfect homogeneity, of being, to the very last grain of its virtue, all of a kind; the very kind, as happens, least apt to be baited by earnest criticism, the only sort of criticism of which account need be taken. To have handled again this so full-blown flower of high fancy is to be led back by it to easy and happy recognitions. Let the first of these be that of the starting-point itself — the sense, all charming again, of the circle, one winter afternoon, round the hall-fire of a grave old country-house where (for all the world as if to resolve itself promptly and obligingly into convertible, into "literary" stuff) the talk turned, on I forget what homely pretext, to apparitions and night-fears, to the marked and sad drop in the general supply, and still more in the general quality, of such commodities. The good, the really effective and heart-shaking ghost-stories (roughly so to term them) appeared all to have been told, and neither new crop nor new type in any quarter awaited us. The new type indeed, the mere modern " psychical " case, washed clean of all queerness as by exposure to a flowing laboratory tap, and equipped with credentials vouching for this — the new type clearly promised little, for the more it was respectably certified the less it seemed of a nature to rouse the dear old sacred terror. Thus it was, I remember, that amid our lament for a beautiful lost form, our distinguished host expressed the wish that he might but have recovered for us one of the scantest of fragments of this form at its best. He had never forgotten the impression made on him as a young man by the withheld glimpse, as it were, of a dreadful matter that had been reported years before, and with as few particulars, to a lady with whom he had youthfully talked. The story would have been thrilling could she but have found herself in better possession of it, dealing as it did with a couple of small children in an out-of-the way place, to whom the spirits of certain " bad " servants, dead in the employ of the house, were believed to have appeared with the design of " getting hold" of them. This was all, but there had been more, which my friend's old converser had lost the thread of: she could only assure him of the wonder of the allegations as she had anciently heard them made. He himself could give us but this shadow of a shadow — my own appreciation of which, I need scarcely say, was exactly wrapped up in that thinness. On the surface there wasn't much, but another grain, none the less, would have spoiled the precious pinch addressed to its end as neatly as some modicum extracted from an old silver snuff-box and held between finger and thumb. I was to remember the haunted children and the prowling servile spirits as a "value," of the disquieting sort, in all conscience sufficient; so that when, after an interval, I was asked for something seasonable by the promoters of a periodical dealing in the time-honoured Christmas-tide toy, I bethought myself at once of the vividest little note for sinister romance that I had ever jotted down.

Such was the private source of " The Turn of the Screw "; and I wondered, I confess, why so fine a germ, gleaming there in the wayside dust of life, had never been deftly picked up. The thing had for me the immense merit of allowing the imagination absolute freedom of hand, of inviting it to act on a perfectly clear field, with no " outside " control involved, no pattern of the usual or the true or the terrible " pleasant " (save always of course the high pleasantry of one's very form) to consort with. This makes in fact the charm of my second reference, that I find here a perfect example of an exercise of the imagination unassisted, unassociated — playing the game, making the score, in the phrase of our sporting day, off its own bat. To what degree the game was worth playing I need n't attempt to say : the exercise I have noted strikes me now, I confess, as the interesting thing, the imaginative faculty acting with the *whole* of the case on its hands. The exhibition involved is in other words a fairy-tale pure and simple — save indeed as to its springing not from an artless and measureless, but from a conscious and cultivated credulity. Yet the fairy-tale belongs mainly to either of two classes, the short and sharp and single, charged more or less with the compactness of anecdote (as to which let the familiars of our childhood, Cinderella and Blue-Beard and Hop o' my Thumb and Little Red Riding Hood and many of the gems of the Brothers Grimm directly testify), or else the long and loose, the copious, the various, the endless, where, dramatically speaking, roundness is quite sacrificed — sacrificed to fulness, sacrificed to exuberance, if one will : witness at hazard almost any one of the Arabian Nights. The charm of all these things for the distracted modern mind is in the clear field of experience, as I call it, over which we are thus led to roam ; an annexed but independent world in which nothing is right

PREFACE

save as we rightly imagine it. We have to do *that*, and we do it happily for the short spurt and in the smaller piece, achieving so perhaps beauty and lucidity; we flounder, we lose breath, on the other hand — that is we fail, not of continuity, but of an agreeable unity, of the " roundness " in which beauty and lucidity largely reside — when we go in, as they say, for great lengths and breadths. And this, oddly enough, not because " keeping it up " isn't abundantly within the compass of the imagination appealed to in certain conditions, but because the finer interest depends just on *how* it is kept up.

Nothing is so easy as improvisation, the running on and on of invention; it is sadly compromised, however, from the moment its stream breaks bounds and gets into flood. Then the waters may spread indeed, gathering houses and herds and crops and cities into their arms and wrenching off, for our amusement, the whole face of the land — only violating by the same stroke our sense of the course and the channel, which is our sense of the uses of a stream and the virtue of a story. Improvisation, as in the Arabian Nights, may keep on terms with encountered objects by sweeping them in and floating them on its breast; but the great effect it so loses — that of keeping on terms with itself. This is ever, I intimate, the hard thing for the fairy-tale; but by just so much as it struck me as hard did it in " The Turn of the Screw " affect me as irresistibly prescribed. To improvise with extreme freedom and yet at the same time without the possibility of ravage, without the hint of a flood; to keep the stream, in a word, on something like ideal terms with itself: that was here my definite business. The thing was to aim at absolute singleness, clearness and roundness, and yet to depend on an imagination working freely, working (call it) with extravagance; by which law it would n't be thinkable except as free and would n't be amusing except as controlled. The merit of the tale, as it stands, is accordingly, I judge, that it has struggled successfully with its dangers. It is an excursion into chaos while remaining, like Blue-Beard and Cinderella, but an anecdote — though an anecdote amplified

xvii

PREFACE

and highly emphasised and returning upon itself; as, for that matter, Cinderella and Blue-Beard return. I need scarcely add after this that it is a piece of ingenuity pure and simple, of cold artistic calculation, an *amusette* to catch those not easily caught (the "fun" of the capture of the merely witless being ever but small), the jaded, the disillusioned, the fastidious. Otherwise expressed, the study is of a conceived "tone," the tone of suspected and felt trouble, of an inordinate and incalculable sort — the tone of tragic, yet of exquisite, mystification. To knead the subject of my young friend's, the supposititious narrator's, mystification thick, and yet strain the expression of it so clear and fine that beauty would result: no side of the matter so revives for me as that endeavour. Indeed if the artistic value of such an experiment be measured by the intellectual echoes it may again, long after, set in motion, the case would make in favour of this little firm fantasy — which I seem to see draw behind it to-day a train of associations. I ought doubtless to blush for thus confessing them so numerous that I can but pick among them for reference. I recall for instance a reproach made me by a reader capable evidently, for the time, of some attention, but not quite capable of enough, who complained that I hadn't sufficiently "characterised" my young woman engaged in her labyrinth; hadn't endowed her with signs and marks, features and humours, hadn't in a word invited her to deal with her own mystery as well as with that of Peter Quint, Miss Jessel and the hapless children. I remember well, whatever the absurdity of its now coming back to me, my reply to that criticism — under which one's artistic, one's ironic heart shook for the instant almost to breaking. "You indulge in that stricture at your ease, and I don't mind confiding to you that — strange as it may appear! — one has to choose ever so delicately among one's difficulties, attaching one's self to the greatest, bearing hard on those and intelligently neglecting the others. If one attempts to tackle them all one is certain to deal completely with none; whereas the effectual dealing with a few casts a blest golden haze under cover of which, like wanton mocking goddesses

xviii

in clouds, the others find prudent to retire. It was 'déjà
très-joli,' in 'The Turn of the Screw,' please believe, the
general proposition of our young woman's keeping crystal-
line her record of so many intense anomalies and obscur-
ities — by which I don't of course mean her explanation of
them, a different matter; and I saw no way, I feebly grant
(fighting, at the best too, periodically, for every grudged inch
of my space) to exhibit her in relations other than those;
one of which, precisely, would have been her relation to her
own nature. We have surely as much of her own nature as
we can swallow in watching it reflect her anxieties and inductions. It constitutes no little of a character indeed, in
such conditions, for a young person, as she says, 'privately
bred,' that she is able to make her particular credible statement of such strange matters. She has 'authority,' which
is a good deal to have given her, and I could n't have arrived
at so much had I clumsily tried for more."

For which truth I claim part of the charm latent on occasion in the extracted reasons of beautiful things — putting for the beautiful always, in a work of art, the close,
the curious, the deep. Let me place above all, however,
under the protection of that presence the side by which this
fiction appeals most to consideration: its choice of its way
of meeting its gravest difficulty. There were difficulties not
so grave: I had for instance simply to renounce all attempt
to keep the kind and degree of impression I wished to produce on terms with the to-day so copious psychical record
of cases of apparitions. Different signs and circumstances,
in the reports, mark these cases; different things are done
— though on the whole very little appears to be — by the
persons appearing; the point is, however, that some things
are never done at all: this negative quantity is large — certain reserves and proprieties and immobilities consistently
impose themselves. Recorded and attested "ghosts" are in
other words as little expressive, as little dramatic, above all
as little continuous and conscious and responsive, as is consistent with their taking the trouble — and an immense
trouble they find it, we gather — to appear at all. Wonder-

PREFACE

ful and interesting therefore at a given moment, they are inconceivable figures in an *action*—and "The Turn of the Screw" was an action, desperately, or it was nothing. I had to decide in fine between having my apparitions correct and having my story "good"—that is producing my impression of the dreadful, my designed horror. Good ghosts, speaking by book, make poor subjects, and it was clear that from the first my hovering prowling blighting presences, my pair of abnormal agents, would have to depart altogether from the rules. They would be agents in fact; there would be laid on them the dire duty of causing the situation to reek with the air of Evil. Their desire and their ability to do so, visibly measuring meanwhile their effect, together with their observed and described success—this was exactly my central idea; so that, briefly, I cast my lot with pure romance, the appearances conforming to the true type being so little romantic.

This is to say, I recognise again, that Peter Quint and Miss Jessel are not "ghosts" at all, as we now know the ghost, but goblins, elves, imps, demons as loosely constructed as those of the old trials for witchcraft; if not, more pleasingly, fairies of the legendary order, wooing their victims forth to see them dance under the moon. Not indeed that I suggest their reducibility to any form of the pleasing pure and simple; they please at the best but through having helped me to express my subject all directly and intensely. Here it was—in the use made of them—that I felt a high degree of art really required; and here it is that, on reading the tale over, I find my precautions justified. The essence of the matter was the villainy of motive in the evoked predatory creatures; so that the result would be ignoble—by which I mean would be trivial—were this element of evil but feebly or inanely suggested. Thus arose on behalf of my idea the lively interest of a possible suggestion and process of *adumbration;* the question of how best to convey that sense of the depths of the sinister without which my fable would so woefully limp. Portentous evil— how was I to save that, as an intention on the part of my demon-spirits, from the drop, the comparative vulgarity, inevitably attending, throughout the whole range of possible brief illustration, the offered example, the imputed vice, the cited act, the limited deplorable presentable instance ? To bring the bad dead back to life for a second round of badness is to warrant them as indeed prodigious, and to become hence as shy of specifications as of a waiting anti-climax. One had seen, in fiction, some grand form of wrong-doing, or better still of wrong-being, imputed, seen it promised and announced as by the hot breath of the Pit — and then, all lamentably, shrink to the compass of some particular brutality, some particular immorality, some particular infamy portrayed : with the result, alas, of the demonstration's falling sadly short. If *my* bad things, for " The Turn of the Screw," I felt, should succumb to this danger, if they should n't seem sufficiently bad, there would be nothing for me but to hang my artistic head lower than I had ever known occasion to do.

The view of that discomfort and the fear of that dishonour, it accordingly must have been, that struck the proper light for my right, though by no means easy, short cut. What, in the last analysis, had I to give the sense of ? Of their being, the haunting pair, capable, as the phrase is, of everything — that is of exerting, in respect to the children, the very worst action small victims so conditioned might be conceived as subject to. What would *be* then, on reflexion, this utmost conceivability ? — a question to which the answer all admirably came. There is for such a case no eligible *absolute* of the wrong; it remains relative to fifty other elements, a matter of appreciation, speculation, imagination — these things moreover quite exactly in the light of the spectator's, the critic's, the reader's experience. Only make the reader's general vision of evil intense enough, I said to myself — and that already is a charming job — and his own experience, his own imagination, his own sympathy (with the children) and horror (of their false friends) will supply him quite sufficiently with all the particulars. Make him *think* the evil, make him think it for himself, and you are released from weak specifications. This ingenuity I took pains — as indeed great pains were required — to apply; and with a success apparently beyond my liveliest hope. Droll enough at the same time, I must add, some of the evidence — even when most convincing — of this success. How can I feel my calculation to have failed, my wrought suggestion not to have worked, that is, on my being assailed, as has befallen me, with the charge of a monstrous emphasis, the charge of all indecently expatiating? There is not only from beginning to end of the matter not an inch of expatiation, but my values are positively all blanks save so far as an excited horror, a promoted pity, a created expertness — on which punctual effects of strong causes no writer can ever fail to plume himself — proceed to read into them more or less fantastic figures. Of high interest to the author meanwhile — and by the same stroke a theme for the moralist — the artless resentful reaction of the entertained person who has abounded in the sense of the situation. He visits his abundance, morally, on the artist — who has but clung to an ideal of faultlessness. Such indeed, for this latter, are some of the observations by which the prolonged strain of that clinging may be enlivened!

I arrive with "The Liar" (1888) and "The Two Faces" (1900) at the first members of the considerable group of shorter, of shortest tales here republished; though I should perhaps place quite in the forefront "The Chaperon" and "The Pupil," at which we have already glanced. I am conscious of much to say of these numerous small productions as a family — a family indeed quite organised as such, with its proper representatives, its "heads," its subdivisions and its branches, its poor relations perhaps not least: its unmistakeable train of poor relations in fact, the very poorer, the poorest of whom I am, in family parlance, for this formal appearance in society, "cutting" without a scruple. These repudiated members, some of them, for that matter, well-nourished and substantial presences enough, with their compromising rustiness plausibly, almost touchingly dissimulated, I fondly figure as standing wistful

PREFACE

but excluded, after the fashion of the outer fringe of the connected whom there are not carriages enough to convey from the church — whether (for we have our choice of similes) to the wedding-feast or to the interment! Great for me from far back had been the interest of the whole "question of the short story," roundabout which our age has, for lamentable reasons, heard so vain a babble; but I foresee occasions yet to come when it will abundantly waylay me. Then it will insist on presenting itself but in too many lights. Little else perhaps meanwhile is more relevant as to "The Liar" than the small fact of its having, when its hour came, quite especially conformed to that custom of shooting straight from the planted seed, of responding at once to the touched spring, of which my fond appeal here to "origins" and evolutions so depicts the sway. When it shall come to fitting, historically, anything like *all* my small children of fancy with their pair of progenitors, and all my reproductive unions with their inevitable fruit, I shall seem to offer my backward consciousness in the image of a shell charged and recharged by the Fates with some patent and infallible explosive. Never would there seem to have been a pretence to such economy of ammunition!

However this may be, I come back, for "The Liar," as for so many of its fellows, to holding my personal experience, poor thing though it may have been, immediately accountable. For by what else in the world but by fatal design had I been placed at dinner one autumn evening of old London days face to face with a gentleman, met for the first time, though favourably known to me by name and fame, in whom I recognised the most unbridled colloquial romancer the "joy of life" had ever found occasion to envy? Under what other conceivable coercion had I been invited to reckon, through the evening, with the type, with the character, with the countenance, of this magnificent master's wife, who, veracious, serene and charming, yet not once meeting straight the eyes of one of us, did her duty by each, and by her husband most of all, without so much as, in the vulgar phrase, turning a hair? It was long ago, but

PREFACE

I have never, to this hour, forgotten the evening itself—embalmed for me now in an old-time sweetness beyond any aspect of my reproduction. I made but a fifth person, the other couple our host and hostess; between whom and one of the company, while we listened to the woven wonders of a summer holiday, the exploits of a salamander, among Mediterranean isles, were exchanged, dimly and discreetly, ever so guardedly, but all expressively, imperceptible lingering looks. It was exquisite, it *could* but become, inevitably, some " short story " or other, which it clearly pre-fitted as the hand the glove. I must reserve " The Two Faces " till I come to speak of the thrilling question of the poor painter's tormented acceptance, in advance, of the scanted canvas; of the writer's rueful hopeful assent to the conditions known to him as " *too little room to turn round.*" Of the liveliest interest then — or so at least I could luckily always project the case — to see how he may nevertheless, in the event, effectively manœuvre. The value of " The Two Faces " — by reason of which I have not hesitated to gather it in — is thus peculiarly an economic one. It may conceal rather than exhale its intense little principle of calculation; but the neat evolution, as I call it, the example of the turn of the *whole* coach and pair in the contracted court, without the " spill " of a single passenger or the derangement of a single parcel, is only in three or four cases (where the coach is fuller still) more appreciable.

HENRY JAMES.

CONTENTS

THE ASPERN PAPERS

I

I HAD taken Mrs. Prest into my confidence; without her in truth I should have made but little advance, for the fruitful idea in the whole business dropped from her friendly lips. It was she who found the short cut and loosed the Gordian knot. It is not supposed easy for women to rise to the large free view of anything, anything to be done; but they sometimes throw off a bold conception—such as a man would n't have risen to—with singular serenity. "Simply make them take you in on the footing of a lodger" — I don't think that unaided I should have risen to that. I was beating about the bush, trying to be ingenious, wondering by what combination of arts I might become an acquaintance, when she offered this happy suggestion that the way to become an acquaintance was first to become an intimate. Her actual knowledge of the Misses Bordereau was scarcely larger than mine, and indeed I had brought with me from England some definite facts that were new to her. Their name had been mixed up ages before with one of the greatest names of the century, and they now lived obscurely in Venice, lived on very small means, unvisited, unapproachable, in a sequestered and dilapidated old palace: this was the substance of my friend's impression of them. She herself had been established in Venice some fifteen years and

had done a great deal of good there; but the circle of
her benevolence had never embraced the two shy,
mysterious and, as was somehow supposed, scarcely
respectable Americans—they were believed to have
lost in their long exile all national quality, besides
being as their name implied of some remoter French
affiliation—who asked no favours and desired no attention. In the early years of her residence she had
made an attempt to see them, but this had been successful only as regards the little one, as Mrs. Prest
called the niece; though in fact I afterwards found
her the bigger of the two in inches. She had heard
Miss Bordereau was ill and had a suspicion she was
in want, and had gone to the house to offer aid, so
that if there were suffering, American suffering in
particular, she should n't have it on her conscience.
The "little one" had received her in the great cold
tarnished Venetian *sala*, the central hall of the house,
paved with marble and roofed with dim cross-beams,
and had n't even asked her to sit down. This was
not encouraging for me, who wished to sit so fast,
and I remarked as much to Mrs. Prest. She replied
however with profundity "Ah, but there's all the
difference: I went to confer a favour and you 'll go
to ask one. If they 're proud you 'll be on the right
side." And she offered to show me their house to
begin with — to row me thither in her gondola. I
let her know I had already been to look at it half a
dozen times; but I accepted her invitation, for it
charmed me to hover about the place. I had made
my way to it the day after my arrival in Venice —
it had been described to me in advance by the friend

4

in England to whom I owed definite information as
to their possession of the papers—laying siege to it
with my eyes while I considered my plan of cam-
paign. Jeffrey Aspern had never been in it that I
knew of, but some note of his voice seemed to abide
there by a roundabout implication and in a "dying
fall."

Mrs. Prest knew nothing about the papers, but
was interested in my curiosity, as always in the joys
and sorrows of her friends. As we went, however,
in her gondola, gliding there under the sociable hood
with the bright Venetian picture framed on either
side by the moveable window, I saw how my eagerness
amused her and that she found my interest in my
possible spoil a fine case of monomania. "One would
think you expected from it the answer to the riddle
of the universe," she said; and I denied the impeachment only by replying that if I had to choose between
that precious solution and a bundle of Jeffrey Aspern's letters I knew indeed which would appear to
me the greater boon. She pretended to make light
of his genius and I took no pains to defend him. One
does n't defend one's god : one's god is in himself a
defence. Besides, to-day, after his long comparative
obscuration, he hangs high in the heaven of our literature for all the world to see; he's a part of the
light by which we walk. The most I said was that
he was no doubt not a woman's poet; to which she
rejoined aptly enough that he had been at least Miss
Bordereau's. The strange thing had been for me to
discover in England that she was still alive: it was
as if I had been told Mrs. Siddons was, or Queen

Caroline, or the famous Lady Hamilton, for it seemed
to me that she belonged to a generation as extinct.
"Why she must be tremendously old — at least a
hundred," I had said; but on coming to consider
dates I saw it not strictly involved that she should
have far exceeded the common span. None the less
she was of venerable age and her relations with Jeffrey
Aspern had occurred in her early womanhood.
"That's her excuse," said Mrs. Prest half-senten-
tiously and yet also somewhat as if she were ashamed
of making a speech so little in the real tone of Venice.
As if a woman needed an excuse for having loved the
divine poet! He had been not only one of the most
brilliant minds of his day — and in those years, when
the century was young, there were, as every one
knows, many — but one of the most genial men and
one of the handsomest.

The niece, according to Mrs. Prest, was of minor
antiquity, and the conjecture was risked that she was
only a grand-niece. This was possible; I had nothing
but my share in the very limited knowledge of my
English fellow worshipper John Cumnor, who had
never seen the couple. The world, as I say, had recognised Jeffrey Aspern, but Cumnor and I had recognised him most. The multitude to-day flocked
to his temple, but of that temple he and I regarded
ourselves as the appointed ministers. We held, justly,
as I think, that we had done more for his memory
than any one else, and had done it simply by opening
lights into his life. He had nothing to fear from us
because he had nothing to fear from the truth, which
alone at such a distance of time we could be inter-

ested in establishing. His early death had been the
only dark spot, as it were, on his fame, unless the
papers in Miss Bordereau's hands should perversely
bring out others. There had been an impression
about 1825 that he had "treated her badly," just as
there had been an impression that he had "served,"
as the London populace says, several other ladies in
the same masterful way. Each of these cases Cumnor
and I had been able to investigate, and we had never
failed to acquit him conscientiously of any grossness.
I judged him perhaps more indulgently than my
friend; certainly, at any rate, it appeared to me that
no man could have walked straighter in the given
circumstances. These had been almost always difficult and dangerous. Half the women of his time, to
speak liberally, had flung themselves at his head, and
while the fury raged — the more that it was very
catching — accidents, some of them grave, had not
failed to occur. He was not a woman's poet, as I had
said to Mrs. Prest, in the modern phase of his reputation; but the situation had been different when the
man's own voice was mingled with his song. That
voice, by every testimony, was one of the most charming ever heard. "Orpheus and the Mænads!" had
been of course my foreseen judgement when first I
turned over his correspondence. Almost all the
Mænads were unreasonable and many of them un-
bearable; it struck me that he had been kinder and
more considerate than in his place — if I could imagine myself in any such box — I should have found
the trick of.

It was certainly strange beyond all strangeness,

and I shall not take up space with attempting to explain it, that whereas among all these other relations
and in these other directions of research we had to
deal with phantoms and dust, the mere echoes of
echoes, the one living source of information that had
lingered on into our time had been unheeded by us.
Every one of Aspern's contemporaries had, according
to our belief, passed away; we had not been able to
look into a single pair of eyes into which his had
looked or to feel a transmitted contact in any aged
hand that his had touched. Most dead of all did poor
Miss Bordereau appear, and yet she alone had survived. We exhausted in the course of months our
wonder that we had not found her out sooner, and
the substance of our explanation was that she had
kept so quiet. The poor lady on the whole had had
reason for doing so. But it was a revelation to us that
self-effacement on such a scale had been possible in
the latter half of the nineteenth century—the age of
newspapers and telegrams and photographs and in-
terviewers. She had taken no great trouble for it
either — had n't hidden herself away in an undis-
coverable hole, had boldly settled down in a city of
exhibition. The one apparent secret of her safety
had been that Venice contained so many much greater
curiosities. And then accident had somehow favoured her, as was shown for example in the fact that
Mrs. Prest had never happened to name her to me,
though I had spent three weeks in Venice — under
her nose, as it were — five years before. My friend
indeed had not named her much to any one; she appeared almost to have forgotten the fact of her con-

tinuance. Of course Mrs. Prest had n't the nerves of an editor. It was meanwhile no explanation of the old woman's having eluded us to say that she lived abroad, for our researches had again and again taken us — not only by correspondence but by personal enquiry — to France, to Germany, to Italy, in which countries, not counting his important stay in England, so many of the too few years of Aspern's career had been spent. We were glad to think at least that in all our promulgations — some people now consider I believe that we have overdone them — we had only touched in passing and in the most discreet manner on Miss Bordereau's connexion. Oddly enough, even if we had had the material — and we had often wondered what could have become of it — this would have been the most difficult episode to handle.

The gondola stopped, the old palace was there; it was a house of the class which in Venice carries even in extreme dilapidation the dignified name. "How charming! It's grey and pink!" my companion exclaimed; and that is the most comprehensive description of it. It was not particularly old, only two or three centuries; and it had an air not so much of decay as of quiet discouragement, as if it had rather missed its career. But its wide front, with a stone balcony from end to end of the *piano nobile* or most important floor, was architectural enough, with the aid of various pilasters and arches; and the stucco with which in the intervals it had long ago been endued was rosy in the April afternoon. It overlooked a clean melancholy rather lonely canal, which had a narrow *riva* or convenient footway on either side.

"I don't know why — there are no brick gables," said Mrs. Prest, "but this corner has seemed to me before more Dutch than Italian, more like Amsterdam than like Venice. It's eccentrically neat, for reasons of its own; and though you may pass on foot scarcely any one ever thinks of doing so. It's as negative — considering *where* it is — as a Protestant Sunday. Perhaps the people are afraid of the Misses Bordereau. I·dare say they have the reputation of witches."

I forget what answer I made to this — I was given up to two other reflexions. The first of these was that if the old lady lived in such a big and imposing house she could n't be in any sort of misery and therefore would n't be tempted by a chance to let a couple of rooms. I expressed this fear to Mrs. Prest, who gave me a very straight answer. "If she did n't live in a big house how could it be a question of her having rooms to spare? If she were not amply lodged you'd lack ground to approach her. Besides, a big house here, and especially in this *quartier perdu*, proves nothing at all: it's perfectly consistent with a state of penury. Dilapidated old palazzi, if you'll go out of the way for them, are to be had for five shillings a year. And as for the people who live in them — no, until you've explored Venice socially as much as I have, you can form no idea of their domestic desolation. They live on nothing, for they've nothing to live on." The other idea that had come into my head was connected with a high blank wall which appeared to confine an expanse of ground on one side of the house. Blank I call it, but it was figured over with the patches that please a painter, repaired breaches, crumblings of plaster, extrusions of brick that had turned pink with time; while a few thin trees, with the poles of certain rickety trellises, were visible over the top. The place was a garden and apparently attached to the house. I suddenly felt that so attached it gave me my pretext.

I sat looking out on all this with Mrs. Prest (it was covered with the golden glow of Venice) from the shade of our *felze*, and she asked me if I would go in then, while she waited for me, or come back another time. At first I could n't decide — it was doubtless very weak of me. I wanted still to think I *might* get a footing, and was afraid to meet failure, for it would leave me, as I remarked to my companion, without another arrow for my bow. "Why not another?" she enquired as I sat there hesitating and thinking it over; and she wished to know why even now and before taking the trouble of becoming an inmate — which might be wretchedly uncomfortable after all, even if it succeeded — I had n't the resource of simply offering them a sum of money down. In that way I might get what I wanted without bad nights.

"Dearest lady," I exclaimed, "excuse the impatience of my tone when I suggest that you must have forgotten the very fact — surely I communicated it to you — which threw me on your ingenuity. The old woman won't have her relics and tokens so much as spoken of; they're personal, delicate, intimate, and she has n't the feelings of the day, God bless her! If I should sound that note first I should certainly spoil the game. I can arrive at my spoils only by putting her off her guard, and I can put her off her guard only by ingratiating diplomatic arts. Hypocrisy, duplicity are my only chance. I'm sorry. for it, but there's no baseness I would n't commit for Jeffrey Aspern's sake. First I must take tea with her — then tackle the main job." And I told over what had happened to John Cumnor on his respectfully writing to her. No notice whatever had been taken of his first letter, and the second had been answered very sharply, in six lines, by the niece. "Miss Bordereau requested her to say that she could n't imagine what he meant by troubling them. They had none of Mr. Aspern's 'literary remains,' and if they *had* had would n't have dreamed of showing them to any one on any account whatever. She could n't imagine what he was talking about and begged he would let her alone." I certainly did n't want to be met that way.

"Well," said Mrs. Prest after a moment and all provokingly, "perhaps they really have n't anything. If they deny it flat how are you sure?"

"John Cumnor's sure, and it would take me long to tell you how his conviction, or his very strong presumption — strong enough to stand against the old lady's not unnatural fib — has built itself up. Besides, he makes much of the internal evidence of the niece's letter."

"The internal evidence?"

"Her calling him 'Mr. Aspern.'"

"I don't see what that proves."

"It proves familiarity, and familiarity implies the possession of mementoes, of tangible objects. I can't tell you how that 'Mr.' affects me — how it bridges over the gulf of time and brings our hero near to me — nor what an edge it gives to my desire to see Juliana. You don't say 'Mr.' Shakespeare."

"Would I, any more, if I had a box full of his letters?"

"Yes, if he had been your lover and some one wanted them." And I added that John Cumnor was so convinced, and so all the more convinced by Miss Bordereau's tone, that he would have come himself to Venice on the undertaking were it not for the obstacle of his having, for any confidence, to disprove his identity with the person who had written to them, which the old ladies would be sure to suspect in spite of dissimulation and a change of name. If they were to ask him point-blank if he were not their snubbed correspondent it would be too awkward for him to lie; whereas I was fortunately not tied in that way. I was a fresh hand — I could protest without lying.

"But you 'll have to take a false name," said Mrs. Prest. "Juliana lives out of the world as much as it is possible to live, but she has none the less probably heard of Mr. Aspern's editors. She perhaps possesses what you 've published."

"I 've thought of that," I returned; and I drew out of my pocket-book a visiting-card neatly engraved with a well-chosen *nom de guerre*.

"You 're very extravagant — it adds to your immorality. You might have done it in pencil or ink," said my companion.

"This looks more genuine."

"Certainly you 've the courage of your curiosity.

But it will be awkward about your letters; they won't come to you in that mask."

"My banker will take them in and I shall go every day to get them. It will give me a little walk."

"Shall you depend all on that?" asked Mrs. Prest. "Are n't you coming to see me?"

"Oh you 'll have left Venice for the hot months long before there are any results. I 'm prepared to roast all summer — as well as through the long hereafter perhaps you 'll say! Meanwhile John Cumnor will bombard me with letters addressed, in my feigned name, to the care of the padrona."

"She 'll recognise his hand," my companion suggested.

"On the envelope he can disguise it."

"Well, you 're a precious pair! Does n't it occur to you that even if you 're able to say you 're not Mr. Cumnor in person they may still suspect you of being his emissary?"

"Certainly, and I see only one way to parry that."

"And what may that be?"

I hesitated a moment. "To make love to the niece."

"Ah," cried my friend, "wait till you see her!"

II

"I MUST work the garden — I must work the garden,"
I said to myself five minutes later and while I waited,
upstairs, in the long, dusky sala, where the bare
scagliola floor gleamed vaguely in a chink of the
closed shutters. The place was impressive, yet looked
somehow cold and cautious. Mrs. Prest had floated
away, giving me a rendezvous at the end of half an
hour by some neighbouring water-steps; and I had
been let into the house, after pulling the rusty bell-
wire, by a small red-headed and white-faced maid-
servant, who was very young and not ugly and wore
clicking pattens and a shawl in the fashion of a hood.
She had not contented herself with opening the door
from above by the usual arrangement of a creaking
pulley, though she had looked down at me first from
an upper window, dropping the cautious challenge
which in Italy precedes the act of admission. I was
irritated as a general thing by this survival of medi-
æval manners, though as so fond, if yet so special, an
antiquarian I suppose I ought to have liked it; but,
with my resolve to be genial from the threshold at
any price, I took my false card out of my pocket and
held it up to her, smiling as if it were a magic token.
It had the effect of one indeed, for it brought her, as I
say, all the way down. I begged her to hand it to her
mistress, having first written on it in Italian the words:
"Could you very kindly see a gentleman, a travelling
American, for a moment?" The little maid was n't

hostile — even that was perhaps something gained. She coloured, she smiled and looked both frightened and pleased. I could see that my arrival was a great affair, that visits in such a house were rare and that she was a person who would have liked a bustling place. When she pushed forward the heavy door behind me I felt my foot in the citadel and promised myself ever so firmly to keep it there. She pattered across the damp stony lower hall and I followed her up the high staircase — stonier still, as it seemed — without an invitation. I think she had meant I should wait for her below, but such was not my idea, and I took up my station in the sala. She flitted, at the far end of it, into impenetrable regions, and I looked at the place with my heart beating as I had known it to do in dentists' parlours. It had a gloomy grandeur, but owed its character almost all to its noble shape and to the fine architectural doors, as high as those of grand frontages, which, leading into the various rooms, repeated themselves on either side at intervals. They were surmounted with old faded painted escutcheons, and here and there in the spaces between them hung brown pictures, which I noted as speciously bad, in battered and tarnished frames that were yet more desirable than the canvases themselves. With the exception of several straw-bottomed chairs that kept their backs to the wall the grand obscure vista contained little else to minister to effect. It was evidently never used save as a passage, and scantly even as that. I may add that by the time the door through which the maid-servant had escaped opened again my eyes had grown used to the want of light.

I had n't meanwhile meant by my private ejaculation that I must myself cultivate the soil of the tangled enclosure which lay beneath the windows, but the lady who came toward me from the distance over the hard shining floor might have supposed as much from the way in which, as I went rapidly to meet her, I exclaimed, taking care to speak Italian: "The garden, the garden — do me the pleasure to tell me if it's yours!"

She stopped short, looking at me with wonder; and then, "Nothing here is mine," she answered in English, coldly and sadly.

"Oh you're English; how delightful!" I ingenuously cried. "But surely the garden belongs to the house?"

"Yes, but the house does n't belong to me." She was a long lean pale person, habited apparently in a dull-coloured dressing-gown, and she spoke very simply and mildly. She did n't ask me to sit down, any more than years before — if she were the niece — she had asked Mrs. Prest, and we stood face to face in the empty pompous hall.

"Well then, would you kindly tell me to whom I must address myself? I'm afraid you'll think me horribly intrusive, but you know I *must* have a garden — upon my honour I must!"

Her face was not young, but it was candid; it was not fresh, but it was clear. She had large eyes which were not bright, and a great deal of hair which was not "dressed," and long fine hands which were — possibly — not clean. She clasped these members almost convulsively as, with a confused alarmed look, she broke out: "Oh don't take it away from us; we like it ourselves!"

"You have the use of it then?"

"Oh yes. If it was n't for that —!" And she gave a wan vague smile.

"Is n't it a luxury, precisely? That's why, intending to be in Venice some weeks, possibly all summer, and having some literary work, some reading and writing to do, so that I must be quiet and yet if possible a great deal in the open air — that's why I've felt a garden to be really indispensable. I appeal to your own experience," I went on with as sociable a smile as I could risk. "Now can't I look at yours?"

"I don't know, I don't understand," the poor woman murmured, planted there and letting her weak wonder deal — helplessly enough, as I felt — with my strangeness.

"I mean only from one of those windows — such grand ones as you have here — if you'll let me open the shutters." And I walked toward the back of the house. When I had advanced halfway I stopped and waited as in the belief she would accompany me. I had been of necessity quite abrupt, but I strove at the same time to give her the impression of extreme courtesy. "I've looked at furnished rooms all over the place, and it seems impossible to find any with a garden attached. Naturally in a place like Venice gardens are rare. It's absurd if you like, for a man, but I can't live without flowers."

"There are none to speak of down there." She came nearer, as if, though she mistrusted me, I had drawn her by an invisible thread. I went on again, and she continued as she followed me: "We've a few, but they're very common. It costs too much to cultivate them; one has to have a man."

"Why should n't I be the man?" I asked. "I'll work without wages; or rather I'll put in a gardener. You shall have the sweetest flowers in Venice."

She protested against this with a small quaver of sound that might have been at the same time a gush of rapture for my free sketch. Then she gasped: "We don't know you — we don't know you."

"You know me as much as I know you; or rather much more, because you know my name. And if you're English I'm almost a countryman."

"We're not English," said my companion, watching me in practical submission while I threw open the shutters of one of the divisions of the wide high window.

"You speak the language so beautifully: might I ask what you are?" Seen from above the garden was in truth shabby, yet I felt at a glance that it had great capabilities. She made no rejoinder, she was so lost in her blankness and gentleness, and I exclaimed: "You don't mean to say you're also by chance American?"

"I don't know. We used to be."

"Used to be? Surely you have n't changed?"

"It's so many years ago. We don't seem to be anything now."

"So many years that you've been living here? Well, I don't wonder at that; it's a grand old house. I suppose you all use the garden," I went on, "but I assure you I should n't be in your way. I'd be very quiet and stay quite in one corner."

"We all use it?" she repeated after me vaguely, not coming close to the window but looking at my shoes. She appeared to think me capable of throwing her out.

"I mean all your family — as many as you are."

"There's only one other than me. She's very old. She never goes down."

I feel again my thrill at this close identification of Juliana; in spite of which, however, I kept my head. "Only one other in all this great house!" I feigned to be not only amazed but almost scandalised. "Dear lady, you must have space then to spare!"

"To spare?" she repeated — almost as for the rich unwonted joy to her of spoken words.

"Why you surely don't live (two quiet women — I see *you* are quiet, at any rate) in fifty rooms!" Then with a burst of hope and cheer I put the question straight. "Could n't you for a good rent *let* me two or three? That would set me up!"

I had now struck the note that translated my purpose, and I need n't reproduce the whole of the tune I played. I ended by making my entertainer believe me an undesigning person, though of course I did n't even attempt to persuade her I was not an eccentric one. I repeated that I had studies to pursue; that I wanted quiet; that I delighted in a garden and had vainly sought one up and down the city: that I would undertake that before another month was over the dear old house should be smothered in flowers. I think it was the flowers that won my suit, for I afterwards found that Miss Tina — for such the name of this high tremulous spinster proved somewhat incongruously to be — had an insatiable appetite for them.

When I speak of my suit as won I mean that before I left her she had promised me she would refer the question to her aunt. I invited information as to who her aunt might be and she answered "Why Miss Bordereau!" with an air of surprise, as if I might have been expected to know. There were contradictions like this in Miss Tina which, as I observed later, contributed to make her rather pleasingly incalculable and interesting. It was the study of the two ladies to live so that the world should n't talk of them or touch them, and yet they had never altogether accepted the idea that it did n't hear of them. In Miss Tina at any rate a grateful susceptibility to human contact had not died out, and contact of a limited order there would be if I should come to live in the house.

"We 've never done anything of the sort; we 've never had a lodger or any kind of inmate." So much as this she made a point of saying to me. "We 're very poor, we live very badly — almost on nothing. The rooms are very bare — those you might take; they 've nothing at all in them. I don't know how you 'd sleep, how you 'd eat."

"With your permission I could easily put in a bed and a few tables and chairs. *C'est la moindre des choses* and the affair of an hour or two. I know a little man from whom I can hire for a trifle what I should so briefly want, what I should use; my gondolier can bring the things round in his boat. Of course in this great house you must have a second kitchen, and my servant, who 's a wonderfully handy fellow" — this personage was an evocation of the moment — "can easily cook me a chop there. My tastes and habits

are of the simplest: I live on flowers!" And then I
ventured to add that if they were very poor it was all
the more reason they should let their rooms. They
were bad economists — I had never heard of such a
waste of material.

I saw in a moment my good lady had never before
been spoken to in any such fashion — with a humorous firmness that did n't exclude sympathy, that was
quite founded on it. She might easily have told me
that my sympathy was impertinent, but this by good
fortune did n't occur to her. I left her with the understanding that she would submit the question to her
aunt and that I might come back the next day for their
decision.

"The aunt will refuse; she'll think the whole proceeding very *louche!*" Mrs. Prest declared shortly
after this, when I had resumed my place in her gondola. She had put the idea into my head and now —
so little are women to be counted on — she appeared
to take a despondent view of it. Her pessimism provoked me and I pretended to have the best hopes; I
went so far as to boast of a distinct prevision of success. Upon this Mrs. Prest broke out: "Oh I see
what's in your head! You fancy you've made such
an impression in five minutes that she's dying for you
to come and can be depended on to bring the old one
round. If you do get in you'll count it as a triumph."

I did count it as a triumph, but only for the commentator — in the last analysis — not for the man,
who had not the tradition of personal conquest. When
I went back on the morrow the little maid-servant
conducted me straight through the long sala — it

opened there as before in large perspective and was
lighter now, which I thought a good omen — into the
apartment from which the recipient of my former visit
had emerged on that occasion. It was a spacious
shabby parlour with a fine old painted ceiling under
which a strange figure sat alone at one of the windows.
They come back to me now almost with the palpitation they caused, the successive states marking my
consciousness that as the door of the room closed
behind me I was really face to face with the Juliana of
some of Aspern's most exquisite and most renowned
lyrics. I grew used to her afterwards, though never
completely; but as she sat there before me my heart
beat as fast as if the miracle of resurrection had taken
place for my benefit. Her presence seemed somehow
to contain and express his own, and I felt nearer to
him at that first moment of seeing her than I ever had
been before or ever have been since. Yes, I remember
my emotions in their order, even including a curious
little tremor that took me when I saw the niece not to
be there. With her, the day before, I had become sufficiently familiar, but it almost exceeded my courage
— much as I had longed for the event — to be left
alone with so terrible a relic as the aunt. She was too
strange, too literally resurgent. Then came a check
from the perception that we were n't really face to face,
inasmuch as she had over her eyes a horrible green
shade which served for her almost as a mask. I believed for the instant that she had put it on expressly,
so that from underneath it she might take me all in
without my getting at herself. At the same time it created a presumption of some ghastly death's-head lurk-

23

ing behind it. The divine Juliana as a grinning skull — the vision hung there until it passed. Then it came to me that she *was* tremendously old — so old that death might take her at any moment, before I should have time to compass my end. The next thought was a correction to that; it lighted up the situation. She would die next week, she would die to-morrow — then I could pounce on her possessions and ransack her drawers. Meanwhile she sat there neither moving nor speaking. She was very small and shrunken, bent forward with her hands in her lap. She was dressed in black and her head was wrapped in a piece of old black lace which showed no hair.

My emotion keeping me silent she spoke first, and the remark she made was exactly the most unexpected.

III

"Our house is very far from the centre, but the little canal is very *comme il faut*."

"It's the sweetest corner of Venice and I can imagine nothing more charming," I hastened to reply. The old lady's voice was very thin and weak, but it had an agreeable, cultivated murmur and there was wonder in the thought that that individual note had been in Jeffrey Aspern's ear.

"Please to sit down there. I hear very well," she said quietly, as if perhaps I had been shouting; and the chair she pointed to was at a certain distance. I took possession of it, assuring her I was perfectly aware of my intrusion and of my not having been properly introduced, and that I could but throw myself on her indulgence. Perhaps the other lady, the one I had had the honour of seeing the day before, would have explained to her about the garden. That was literally what had given me courage to take a step so unconventional. I had fallen in love at sight with the whole place — she herself was probably so used to it that she did n't know the impression it was capable of making on a stranger — and I had felt it really a case to risk something. Was her own kindness in receiving me a sign that I was not wholly out in my calculation? It would make me extremely happy to think so. I could give her my word of honour that I was a most respectable inoffensive person and that as

25

a co-tenant of the palace, so to speak, they would be barely conscious of my existence. I would conform to any regulations, any restrictions, if they would only let me enjoy the garden. Moreover I should be delighted to give her references, guarantees; they would be of the very best, both in Venice and in England, as well as in America.

She listened to me in perfect stillness and I felt her look at me with great penetration, though I could see only the lower part of her bleached and shrivelled face. Independently of the refining process of old age it had a delicacy which once must have been great. She had been very fair, she had had a wonderful complexion. She was silent a little after I had ceased speaking; then she began: "If you're so fond of a garden why don't you go to *terra firma,* where there are so many far better than this?"

"Oh it's the combination!" I answered, smiling; and then with rather a flight of fancy: "It's the idea of a garden in the middle of the sea."

"This is n't the middle of the sea; you can't so much as see the water."

I stared a moment, wondering if she wished to convict me of fraud. "Can't see the water? Why, dear madam, I can come up to the very gate in my boat."

She appeared inconsequent, for she said vaguely in reply to this: "Yes, if you've got a boat. I have n't any; it's many years since I've been in one of the *gondole.*" She uttered these words as if they designed a curious far-away craft known to her only by hearsay.

"Let me assure you of the pleasure with which I would put mine at your service!" I returned. I had

26

scarcely said this however before I became aware that the speech was in questionable taste and might also do me the injury of making me appear too eager, too possessed of a hidden motive. But the old woman remained impenetrable and her attitude worried me by suggesting that she had a fuller vision of me than I had of her. She gave me no thanks for my some-what extravagant offer, but remarked that the lady I had seen the day before was her niece; she would presently come in. She had asked her to stay away a little on purpose — had had her reasons for seeing me first alone. She relapsed into silence and I turned over the fact of these unmentioned reasons and the question of what might come yet; also that of whether I might venture on some judicious remark in praise of her companion. I went so far as to say I should be delighted to see our absent friend again: she had been so very patient with me, considering how odd she must have thought me — a declaration which drew from Miss Bordereau another of her whimsical speeches.

"She has very good manners; I bred her up my-self!" I was on the point of saying that that ac-counted for the easy grace of the niece, but I arrested myself in time, and the next moment the old woman went on: "I don't care who you may be — I don't want to know: it signifies very little to-day." This had all the air of being a formula of dismissal, as if her next words would be that I might take myself off now that she had had the amusement of looking on the face of such a monster of indiscretion. Therefore I was all the more surprised when she added in her soft venerable quaver: "You may have as many rooms as you like — if you'll pay me a good deal of money."

I hesitated but an instant, long enough to measure what she meant in particular by this condition. First it struck me that she must have really a large sum in her mind; then I reasoned quickly that her idea of a large sum would probably not correspond to my own. My deliberation, I think, was not so visible as to diminish the promptitude with which I replied: "I will pay with pleasure and of course in advance whatever you may think it proper to ask me."

"Well then, a thousand francs a month," she said instantly, while her baffling green shade continued to cover her attitude.

The figure, as they say, was startling and my logic had been at fault. The sum she had mentioned was, by the Venetian measure of such matters, exceedingly large; there was many an old palace in an out-of-the-way corner that I might on such terms have enjoyed the whole of by the year. But so far as my resources allowed I was prepared to spend money, and my decision was quickly taken. I would pay her with a smiling face what she asked, but in that case I would make it up by getting hold of my "spoils" for nothing. Moreover if she had asked five times as much I should have risen to the occasion, so odious would it have seemed to me to stand chaffering with Aspern's Juliana. It was queer enough to have a question of money with her at all. I assured her that her views perfectly met my own and that on the morrow I should have the pleasure of putting three months'

rent into her hand. She received this announcement
with apparent complacency and with no discoverable
sense that after all it would become her to say that I
ought to see the rooms first. This did n't occur to
her, and indeed her serenity was mainly what I
wanted. Our little agreement was just concluded
when the door opened and the younger lady appeared
on the threshold. As soon as Miss Bordereau saw
her niece she cried out almost gaily: "He'll give
three thousand — three thousand to-morrow!"

Miss Tina stood still, her patient eyes turning
from one of us to the other; then she brought out,
scarcely above her breath: "Do you mean francs?"

"Did you mean francs or dollars?" the old woman
asked of me at this.

"I think francs were what you said," I sturdily
smiled.

"That's very good," said Miss Tina, as if she had
felt how overreaching her own question might have
looked.

"What do *you* know? You're ignorant," Miss
Bordereau remarked; not with acerbity but with a
strange soft coldness.

"Yes, of money — certainly of money!" Miss
Tina hastened to concede.

"I'm sure you've your own fine branches of knowledge," I took the liberty of saying genially. There
was something painful to me, somehow, in the turn
the conversation had taken, in the discussion of
dollars and francs.

"She had a very good education when she was
young. I looked into that myself," said Miss Bor-

dereau. Then she added: "But she has learned nothing since."

"I've always been with *you*," Miss Tina rejoined very mildly, and of a certainty with no intention of an epigram.

"Yes, but for that —!" her aunt declared with more satirical force. She evidently meant that but for this her niece would never have got on at all; the point of the observation however being lost on Miss Tina, though she blushed at hearing her history revealed to a stranger. Miss Bordereau went on, addressing herself to me: "And what time will you come to-morrow with the money?"

"The sooner the better. If it suits you I'll come at noon."

"I'm always here, but I have my hours," said the old woman as if her convenience were not to be taken for granted.

"You mean the times when you receive?"

"I never receive. But I'll see you at noon, when you come with the money."

"Very good, I shall be punctual." To which I added: "May I shake hands with you on our contract?" I thought there ought to be some little form; it would make me really feel easier, for I was sure there would be no other. Besides, though Miss Bordereau could n't to-day be called personally attractive and there was something even in her wasted antiquity that bade one stand at one's distance, I felt an irresistible desire to hold in my own for a moment the hand Jeffrey Aspern had pressed.

For a minute she made no answer, and I saw that

my proposal failed to meet with her approbation. She indulged in no movement of withdrawal, which I half-expected; she only said coldly: "I belong to a time when that was not the custom."

I felt rather snubbed but I exclaimed good-humouredly to Miss Tina "Oh you'll do as well!" I shook hands with her while she assented with a small flutter. "Yes, yes, to show it's all arranged!"

"Shall you bring the money in gold?" Miss Bordereau demanded as I was turning to the door.

I looked at her a moment. "Are n't you a little afraid, after all, of keeping such a sum as that in the house?" It was not that I was annoyed at her avidity, but was truly struck with the disparity between such a treasure and such scanty means of guarding it.

"Whom should I be afraid of if I'm not afraid of you?" she asked with her shrunken grimness.

"Ah well," I laughed, "I shall be in point of fact a protector and I'll bring gold if you prefer."

"Thank you," the old woman returned with dignity and with an inclination of her head which evidently signified my dismissal. I passed out of the room, thinking how hard it would be to circumvent her. As I stood in the sala again I saw that Miss Tina had followed me, and I supposed that as her aunt had neglected to suggest I should take a look at my quarters it was her purpose to repair the omission. But she made no such overture; she only stood there with a dim, though not a languid smile, and with an effect of irresponsible incompetent youth almost comically at variance with the faded facts of her person. She was not infirm, like her aunt, but she struck me as more deeply futile, because her inefficiency was inward, which was not the case with Miss Bordereau's. I waited to see if she would offer to show me the rest of the house, but I did n't precipitate the question, inasmuch as my plan was from this moment to spend as much of my time as possible in her society. A minute indeed elapsed before I committed myself.

"I've had better fortune than I hoped. It was very kind of her to see me. Perhaps you said a good word for me."

"It was the idea of the money," said Miss Tina.

"And did you suggest that?"

"I told her you'd perhaps pay largely."

"What made you think that?"

"I told her I thought you were rich."

"And what put that into your head?"

"I don't know; the way you talked."

"Dear me, I must talk differently now," I returned. "I'm sorry to say it's not the case."

"Well," said Miss Tina, "I think that in Venice the *forestieri* in general often give a great deal for something that after all is n't much." She appeared to make this remark with a comforting intention, to wish to remind me that if I had been extravagant I was n't foolishly singular. We walked together along the sala, and as I took its magnificent measure I observed that I was afraid it would n't form a part of my *quartiere*. Were my rooms by chance to be among those that opened into it? "Not if you go above — to the second floor," she answered as if she had rather taken for granted I would know my proper place.

32

"And I infer that that's where your aunt would like me to be."

"She said your apartments ought to be very distinct."

"That certainly would be best." And I listened with respect while she told me that above I should be free to take whatever I might like; that there was another staircase, but only from the floor on which we stood, and that to pass from it to the garden-level or to come up to my lodging I should have in effect to cross the great hall. This was an immense point gained; I foresaw that it would constitute my whole leverage in my relations with the two ladies. When I asked Miss Tina how I was to manage at present to find my way up she replied with an access of that sociable shyness which constantly marked her manner:

"Perhaps you can't. I don't see — unless I should go with you." She evidently had n't thought of this before.

We ascended to the upper floor and visited a long succession of empty rooms. The best of them looked over the garden; some of the others had above. the opposite rough-tiled house-tops a view of the blue lagoon. They were all dusty and even a little disfigured with long neglect, but I saw that by spending a few hundred francs I should be able to make three or four of them habitable enough. My experiment was turning out costly, yet now that I had all but taken possession I ceased to allow this to trouble me. I mentioned to my companion a few of the things I should put in, but she replied rather more precipitately than usual that I might do exactly what I liked:

she seemed to wish to notify me that the Misses Bordereau would take none but the most veiled interest in my proceedings. I guessed that her aunt had instructed her to adopt this tone, and I may as well say now that I came afterwards to distinguish perfectly (as I believed) between the speeches she made on her own responsibility and those the old woman imposed upon her. She took no notice of the unswept condition of the rooms and indulged neither in explanations nor in apologies. I said to myself that this was a sign Juliana and her niece — disenchanting idea! — were untidy persons with a low Italian standard; but I afterwards recognised that a lodger who had forced an entrance had no *locus standi* as a critic. We looked out of a good many windows, for there was nothing within the rooms to look at, and still I wanted to linger. I asked her what several different objects in the prospect might be, but in no case did she appear to know. She was evidently not familiar with the view —it was as if she had not looked at it for years — and I presently saw that she was too preoccupied with something else to pretend to care for it. Suddenly she said — the remark was not suggested:

"I don't know whether it will make any difference to you, but the money is for me."

"The money — ?"

"The money you're going to bring."

"Why you'll make me wish to stay here two or three years!" I spoke as benevolently as possible, though it had begun to act on my nerves that these women so associated with Aspern should so constantly bring the pecuniary question back.

"That would be very good for me," she answered almost gaily.

"You put me on my honour!"

She looked as if she failed to understand this, but went on: "She wants me to have more. She thinks she's going to die."

"Ah not soon I hope!" I cried with genuine feeling. I had perfectly considered the possibility of her destroying her documents on the day she should feel her end at hand. I believed that she would cling to them till then, and I was as convinced of her reading Aspern's letters over every night or at least pressing them to her withered lips. I would have given a good deal for some view of those solemnities. I asked Miss Tina if her venerable relative were seriously ill, and she replied that she was only very tired — she had lived so extraordinarily long. That was what she said herself — she wanted to die for a change. Besides, all her friends had been dead for ages; either they ought to have remained or she ought to have gone. That was another thing her aunt often said: she was not at all resigned — resigned, that is, to life.

"But people don't die when they like, do they?" Miss Tina enquired. I took the liberty of asking why, if there was actually enough money to maintain both of them, there would not be more than enough in case of her being left alone. She considered this difficult problem a moment and then said: "Oh well, you know, she takes care of me. She thinks that when I'm alone I shall be a great fool and shan't know how to manage."

"I should have supposed rather that you took care of *her*. I'm afraid she's very proud."

"Why, have you discovered that already?" Miss Tina cried with a dimness of glad surprise.

"I was shut up with her there for a considerable time and she struck me, she interested me extremely. It did n't take me long to make my discovery. She won't have much to say to me while I'm here."

"No, I don't think she will," my companion averred.

"Do you suppose she has some suspicion of me?"

Miss Tina's honest eyes gave me no sign I had touched a mark. "I should n't think so — letting you in after all so easily."

"You call it easily? She has covered her risk," I said. "But where is it one could take an advantage of her?"

"I ought n't to tell you if I knew, ought I?" And Miss Tina added, before I had time to reply to this, smiling dolefully: "Do you think we've any weak points?"

"That's exactly what I'm asking. You'd only have to mention them for me to respect them religiously."

She looked at me hereupon with that air of timid but candid and even gratified curiosity with which she had confronted me from the first; after which she said: "There's nothing to tell. We're terribly quiet. I don't know how the days pass. We've no life."

"I wish I might think I should bring you a little."

"Oh we know what we want," she went on. "It's all right."

There were twenty things I desired to ask her: how in the world they did live; whether they had any friends or visitors, any relations in America or in other countries. But I judged such probings premature; I must leave it to a later chance. "Well, don't *you* be proud," I contented myself with saying. "Don't hide from me altogether."

"Oh I must stay with my aunt," she returned without looking at me. And at the same moment, abruptly, without any ceremony of parting, she quitted me and disappeared, leaving me to make my own way downstairs. I stayed a while longer, wandering about the bright desert — the sun was pouring in — of the old house, thinking the situation over on the spot. Not even the pattering little *serva* came to look after me, and I reflected that after all this treatment showed confidence.

IV

PERHAPS it did, but all the same, six weeks later, towards the middle of June, the moment when Mrs. Prest undertook her annual migration, I had made no measurable advance. I was obliged to confess to her that I had no results to speak of. My first step had been unexpectedly rapid, but there was no appearance it would be followed by a second. I was a thousand miles from taking tea with my hostesses — that privilege of which, as I reminded my good friend, we both had had a vision. She reproached me with lacking boldness and I answered that even to be bold you must have an opportunity: you may push on through a breach, but you can't batter down a dead wall. She returned that the breach I had already made was big enough to admit an army and accused me of wasting precious hours in whimpering in her salon when I ought to have been carrying on the struggle in the field. It is true that I went to see her very often — all on the theory that it would console me (I freely expressed my discouragement) for my want of success on my own premises. But I began to feel that it did n't console me to be perpetually chaffed for my scruples, especially since I was really so vigilant; and I was rather glad when my ironic friend closed her house for the summer. She had expected to draw amusement from the drama of my intercourse with the Misses Bordereau, and was disappointed that the intercourse, and consequently the drama, had not come off. "They'll lead you on to your ruin," she said before she left Venice. "They'll get all your money without showing you a scrap." I think I settled down to my business with more concentration after her departure.

It was a fact that up to that time I had not, save on a single brief occasion, had even a moment's contact with my queer hostesses. The exception had occurred when I carried them according to my promise the terrible three thousand francs. Then I found Miss Tina awaiting me in the hall, and she took the money from my hand with a promptitude that prevented my seeing her aunt. The old lady had promised to receive me, yet apparently thought nothing of breaking that vow. The money was contained in a bag of chamois leather, of respectable dimensions, which my banker had given me, and Miss Tina had to make a big fist to receive it. This she did with extreme solemnity, though I tried to treat the affair a little as a joke. It was in no jocular strain, yet it was with a clearness akin to a brightness that she enquired, weighing the money in her two palms: "Don't you think it's too much?" To which I replied that this would depend on the amount of pleasure I should get for it. Hereupon she turned away from me quickly, as she had done the day before, murmuring in a tone different from any she had used hitherto: "Oh pleasure, pleasure — there's no pleasure in this house!"

After that, for a long time, I never saw her, and I wondered the common chances of the day should n't

have helped us to meet. It could only be evident that
she was immensely on her guard against them; and
in addition to this the house was so big that for each
other we were lost in it. I used to look out for her
hopefully as I crossed the sala in my comings and
goings, but I was not rewarded with a glimpse of the
tail of her dress. It was as if she never peeped out of
her aunt's apartment. I used to wonder what she
did there week after week and year after year. I had
never met so stiff a policy of seclusion; it was more
than keeping quiet — it was like hunted creatures
feigning death. The two ladies appeared to have no
visitors whatever and no sort of contact with the
world. I judged at least that people could n't have
come to the house and that Miss Tina could n't have
gone out without my catching some view of it. I
did what I disliked myself for doing — considering
it but as once in a way: I questioned my servant about
their habits and let him infer that I should be interested in any information he might glean. But he
gleaned amazingly little for a knowing Venetian: it
must be added that where there is a perpetual fast
there are very few crumbs on the floor. His ability
in other ways was sufficient, if not quite all I had
attributed to him on the occasion of my first interview with Miss Tina. He had helped my gondolier
to bring me round a boat-load of furniture; and when
these articles had been carried to the top of the palace
and distributed according to our associated wisdom
he organised my household with such dignity as
answered to its being composed exclusively of himself.
He made me in short as comfortable as I could be

with my indifferent prospects. I should have been
glad if he had fallen in love with Miss Bordereau's
maid or, failing this, had taken her in aversion: either
event might have brought about some catastrophe,
and a catastrophe might have led to some parley. It
was my idea that she would have been sociable, and
I myself on various occasions saw her flit to and fro
on domestic errands, so that I was sure she was accessible. But I tasted of no gossip from that fountain,
and I afterwards learned that Pasquale's affections
were fixed upon an object that made him heedless of
other women. This was a young lady with a pow-
dered face, a yellow cotton gown and much leisure,
who used often to come to see him. She practised,
at her convenience, the art of a stringer of beads —
these ornaments are made in Venice to profusion;
she had her pocket full of them and I used to find
them on the floor of my apartment — and kept an
eye on the possible rival in the house. It was not for
me of course to make the domestics tattle, and I
never said a word to Miss Bordereau's cook.

It struck me as a proof of the old woman's resolve
to have nothing to do with me that she should never
have sent me a receipt for my three months' rent. For
some days I looked out for it and then, when I had
given it up, wasted a good deal of time in wondering
what her reason had been for neglecting so indispensable and familiar a form. At first I was tempted to
send her a reminder; after which I put by the idea —
against my judgement as to what was right in the particular case — on the general ground of wishing to
keep quiet. If Miss Bordereau suspected me of ulte-

rior aims she would suspect me less if I should be busi-
nesslike, and yet I consented not to be. It was possible she intended her omission as an impertinence, a
visible irony, to show how she could overreach people
who attempted to overreach her. On that hypothesis
it was well to let her see that one did n't notice her
little tricks. The real reading of the matter, I afterwards gathered, was simply the poor lady's desire to
emphasise the fact that I was in the enjoyment of a
favour as rigidly limited as it had been liberally be-
stowed. She had given me part of her house, but she
would n't add to that so much as a morsel of paper
with her name on it. Let me say that even at first this
did n't make me too miserable, for the whole situation
had the charm of its oddity. I foresaw that I should
have a summer after my own literary heart, and the
sense of playing with my opportunity was much
greater after all than any sense of being played with.
There could be no Venetian business without patience,
and since I adored the place I was much more in the
spirit of it for having laid in a large provision. That
spirit kept me perpetual company and seemed to look
out at me from the revived immortal face — in which
all his genius shone — of the great poet who was my
prompter. I had invoked him and he had come; he
hovered before me half the time; it was as if his bright
ghost had returned to earth to assure me he regarded
the affair as his own no less than as mine and that we
should see it fraternally and fondly to a conclusion.
It was as if he had said: "Poor dear, be easy with her;
she has some natural prejudices; only give her time.
Strange as it may appear to you she was very attract-

ive in 1820. Meanwhile are n't we in Venice together, and what better place is there for the meeting of dear friends? See how it glows with the advancing summer; how the sky and the sea and the rosy air and the marble of the palaces all shimmer and melt together." My eccentric private errand became a part of the general romance and the general glory — I felt even a mystic companionship, a moral fraternity with all those who in the past had been in the service of art. They had worked for beauty, for a devotion; and what else was I doing? That element was in everything that Jeffrey Aspern had written, and I was only bringing it to light.

I lingered in the sala when I went to and fro; I used to watch — as long as I thought decent — the door that led to Miss Bordereau's part of the house. A person observing me might have supposed I was trying to cast a spell on it or attempting some odd experiment in hypnotism. But I was only praying it might open or thinking what treasure probably lurked behind it. I hold it singular, as I look back, that I should never have doubted for a moment that the sacred relics were there; never have failed to know the joy of being beneath the same roof with them. After all they were under my hand — they had not escaped me yet; and they made my life continuous, in a fashion, with the illustrious life they had touched at the other end. I lost myself in this satisfaction to the point of assuming — in my quiet extravagance — that poor Miss Tina also went back, and still went back, as I used to phrase it. She did indeed, the gentle spinster, but not quite so far as Jeffrey Aspern, who was simple

43

hearsay to her quite as he was to me. Only she had
lived for years with Juliana, she had seen and handled
all mementoes and — even though she was stupid —
some esoteric knowledge had rubbed off on her. That
was what the old woman represented — esoteric
knowledge; and this was the idea with which my
critical heart used to thrill. It literally beat faster
often, of an evening when I had been out, as I stopped
with my candle in the re-echoing hall on my way up
to bed. It was as if at such a moment as that, in the
stillness and after the long contradiction of the day,
Miss Bordereau's secrets were in the air, the wonder
of her survival more vivid. These were the acute
impressions. I had them in another form, with more
of a certain shade of reciprocity, during the hours I sat
in the garden looking up over the top of my book at
the closed windows of my hostess. In these windows
no sign of life ever appeared; it was as if, for fear of
my catching a glimpse of them, the two ladies passed
their days in the dark. But this only emphasised their
having matters to conceal; which was what I had
wished to prove. Their motionless shutters became as
expressive as eyes consciously closed, and I took comfort in the probability that, though invisible themselves, they kept me in view between the lashes.

I made a point of spending as much time as possible in the garden, to justify the picture I had originally given of my horticultural passion. And I not only
spent time, but (hang it! as I said) spent precious
money. As soon as I had got my rooms arranged and
could give the question proper thought I surveyed the
place with a clever expert and made terms for having

it put in order. I was sorry to do this, for personally I liked it better as it was, with its weeds and its wild rich tangle, its sweet characteristic Venetian shabbiness. I had to be consistent, to keep my promise that I would smother the house in flowers. Moreover I clung to the fond fancy that by flowers I should make my way — I should succeed by big nosegays. I would batter the old women with lilies — I would bombard their citadel with roses. Their door would have to yield to the pressure when a mound of fragrance should be heaped against it. The place in truth had been brutally neglected. The Venetian capacity for dawdling is of the largest, and for a good many days unlimited litter was all my gardener had to show for his ministrations. There was a great digging of holes and carting about of earth, and after a while I grew so impatient that I had thoughts of sending for my "results" to the nearest stand. But I felt sure my friends would see through the chinks of their shutters where such tribute could n't have been gathered, and might so make up their minds against my veracity. I possessed my soul and finally, though the delay was long, perceived some appearances of bloom. This encouraged me and I waited serenely enough till they multiplied. Meanwhile the real summer days arrived and began to pass, and as I look back upon them they seem to me almost the happiest of my life. I took more and more care to be in the garden whenever it was not too hot. I had an arbour arranged and a low table and an armchair put into it; and I carried out books and portfolios — I had always some business of writing in hand — and worked and waited and mused and hoped, while the golden hours elapsed and the plants drank in the light and the inscrutable old palace turned pale and then, as the day waned, began to recover and flush and my papers rustled in the wandering breeze of the Adriatic.

Considering how little satisfaction I got from it at first it is wonderful I should n't have grown more tired of trying to guess what mystic rites of ennui the Misses Bordereau celebrated in their darkened rooms; whether this had always been the tenor of their life and how in previous years they had escaped elbowing their neighbours. It was supposable they had then had other habits, forms and resources; that they must once have been young or at least middle-aged. There was no end to the questions it was possible to ask about them and no end to the answers it was not possible to frame. I had known many of my country-people in Europe and was familiar with the strange ways they were liable to take up there; but the Misses Bordereau formed altogether a new type of the American absentee. Indeed it was clear the American name had ceased to have any application to them — I had seen this in the ten minutes I spent in the old woman's room. You could never have said whence they came from the appearance of either of them; wherever it was they had long ago shed and unlearned all native marks and notes. There was nothing in them one recognised or fitted, and, putting the question of speech aside, they might have been Norwegians or Spaniards. Miss Bordereau, after all, had been in Europe nearly three quarters of a century; it appeared by some verses addressed to her by Aspern on the

occasion of his own second absence from America —
verses of which Cumnor and I had after infinite conjecture established solidly enough the date — that she
was even then, as a girl of twenty, on the foreign side
of the sea. There was a profession in the poem — I
hope not just for the phrase — that he had come back
for her sake. We had no real light on her circumstances at that moment, any more than we had upon
her origin, which we believed to be of the sort usually
spoken of as modest. Cumnor had a theory that she
had been a governess in some family in which the poet
visited and that, in consequence of her position, there
was from the first something unavowed, or rather
something quite clandestine, in their relations. I on
the other hand had hatched a little romance according to which she was the daughter of an artist, a
painter or a sculptor, who had left the Western world,
when the century was fresh, to study in the ancient
schools. It was essential to my hypothesis that this
amiable man should have lost his wife, should have
been poor and unsuccessful and should have had
a second daughter of a disposition quite different
from Juliana's. It was also indispensable that he
should have been accompanied to Europe by these
young ladies and should have established himself
there for the remainder of a struggling saddened life.
There was a further implication that Miss Bordereau had had in her youth a perverse and reckless,
albeit a generous and fascinating character, and that
she had braved some wondrous chances. By what
passions had she been ravaged, by what adventures
and sufferings had she been blanched, what store of

memories had she laid away for the monotonous
future ?

I asked myself these things as I sat spinning theories
about her in my arbour and the bees droned in the
flowers. It was incontestable that, whether for right
or for wrong, most readers of certain of Aspern's
poems (poems not as ambiguous as the sonnets —
scarcely more divine, I think — of Shakespeare) had
taken for granted that Juliana had not always ad-
hered to the steep footway of renunciation. There
hovered about her name a perfume of impenitent passion, an intimation that she had not been exactly as
the respectable young person in general. Was this a
sign that her singer had betrayed her, had given her
away, as we say nowadays, to posterity ? Certain it
is that it would have been difficult to put one's finger
on the passage in which her fair fame suffered injury.
Moreover was not any fame fair enough that was so
sure of duration and was associated with works immortal through their beauty ? It was a part of my
idea that the young lady had had a foreign lover —
and say an unedifying tragical rupture — before her
meeting with Jeffrey Aspern. She had lived with her
father and sister in a queer old-fashioned expatriated
artistic Bohemia of the days when the æsthetic was
only the academic and the painters who knew the best
models for *contadina* and *pifferaro* wore peaked hats
and long hair. It was a society less awake than the
coteries of to-day — in its ignorance of the wonderful
chances, the opportunities of the early bird, with
which its path was strewn — to tatters of old stuff
and fragments of old crockery; so that Miss Bordereau

appeared not to have picked up or have inherited many
objects of importance. There was no enviable *bric-à-
brac*, with its provoking legend of cheapness, in the
room in which I had seen her. Such a fact as that suggested bareness, but none the less it worked happily
into the sentimental interest I had always taken in the
early movements of my countrymen as visitors to
Europe. When Americans went abroad in 1820 there
was something romantic, almost heroic in it, as compared with the perpetual ferryings of the present hour,
the hour at which photography and other conveniences have annihilated surprise. Miss Bordereau had
sailed with her family on a tossing brig in the days of
long voyages and sharp differences; she had had her
emotions on the top of yellow diligences, passed the
night at inns where she dreamed of travellers' tales,
and was most struck, on reaching the Eternal City,
with the elegance of Roman pearls and scarfs and
mosaic brooches. There was something touching to
me in all that, and my imagination frequently went
back to the period. If Miss Bordereau carried it there
of course Jeffrey Aspern had at other times done so
with greater force. It was a much more important
fact, if one was looking at his genius critically, that
he had lived in the days before the general transfusion.
It had happened to me to regret that he had known
Europe at all; I should have liked to see what he would
have written without that experience, by which he had
incontestably been enriched. But as his fate had ruled
otherwise I went with him — I tried to judge how the
general old order would have struck him. It was not
only there, however, I watched him; the relations he

49

had entertained with the special new had even a livelier interest. His own country after all had had most
of his life, and his muse, as they said at that time, was
essentially American. That was originally what I had
prized him for: that at a period when our native land
was nude and crude and provincial, when the famous
"atmosphere" it is supposed to lack was not even
missed, when literature was lonely there and art and
form almost impossible, he had found means to live
and write like one of the first; to be free and general
and not at all afraid; to feel, understand and express
everything.

V

I WAS seldom at home in the evening, for when I attempted to occupy myself in my apartments the lamplight brought in a swarm of noxious insects, and it was too hot for closed windows. Accordingly I spent the late hours either on the water — the moonlights of Venice are famous — or in the splendid square which serves as a vast forecourt to the strange old church of Saint Mark. I sat in front of Florian's café eating ices, listening to music, talking with acquaintances: the traveller will remember how the immense cluster of tables and little chairs stretches like a promontory into the smooth lake of the Piazza. The whole place, of a summer's evening, under the stars and with all the lamps, all the voices and light footsteps on marble — the only sounds of the immense arcade that encloses it — is an open-air saloon dedicated to cooling drinks and to a still finer degustation, that of the splendid impressions received during the day. When I didn't prefer to keep mine to myself there was always a stray tourist, disencumbered of his Bädeker, to discuss them with, or some domesticated painter rejoicing in the return of the season of strong effects. The great basilica, with its low domes and bristling embroideries, the mystery of its mosaic and sculpture, looked ghostly in the tempered gloom, and the sea-breeze passed between the twin columns of the Piazzetta, the lintels of a door no longer guarded,

as gently as if a rich curtain swayed there. I used
sometimes on these occasions to think of the Misses
Bordereau and of the pity of their being shut up in
apartments which in the Venetian July even Venetian
vastness could n't relieve of some stuffiness. Their life
seemed miles away from the life of the Piazza, and no
doubt it was really too late to make the austere Juliana change her habits. But poor Miss Tina would
have enjoyed one of Florian's ices, I was sure; sometimes I even had thoughts of carrying one home to her.
Fortunately my patience bore fruit and I was not
obliged to do anything so ridiculous.

One evening about the middle of July I came in
earlier than usual — I forget what chance had led to
this — and instead of going up to my quarters made
my way into the garden. The temperature was very
high; it was such a night as one would gladly have
spent in the open air, and I was in no hurry to go to
bed. I had floated home in my gondola, listening to
the slow splash of the oar in the dark narrow canals,
and now the only thought that occupied me was that it
would be good to recline at one's length in the fragrant
darkness on a garden-bench. The odour of the canal
was doubtless at the bottom of that aspiration, and the
breath of the garden, as I entered it, gave consistency
to my purpose. It was delicious — just such an air
as must have trembled with Romeo's vows when he
stood among the thick flowers and raised his arms to
his mistress's balcony. I looked at the windows of the
palace to see if by chance the example of Verona —
Verona being not far off — had been followed; but
everything was dim, as usual, and everything was

still. Juliana might on the summer nights of her youth have murmured down from open windows at Jeffrey Aspern, but Miss Tina was not a poet's mistress any more than I was a poet. This however did n't prevent my gratification from being great as I became aware on reaching the end of the garden that my younger padrona was seated in one of the bowers. At first I made out but an indistinct figure, not in the least counting on such an overture from one of my hostesses; it even occurred to me that some enamoured maid-servant had stolen in to keep a tryst with her sweet-heart. I was going to turn away, not to frighten her, when the figure rose to its height and I recognised Miss Bordereau's niece. I must do myself the justice that I did n't wish to frighten her either, and much as I had longed for some such accident I should have been capable of retreating. It was as if I had laid a trap for her by coming home earlier than usual and by adding to that oddity my invasion of the garden. As she rose she spoke to me, and then I guessed that perhaps, secure in my almost inveterate absence, it was her nightly practice to take a lonely airing. There was no trap in truth, because I had had no suspicion. At first I took the words she uttered for an impatience of my arrival; but as she repeated them — I had n't caught them clearly — I had the surprise of hearing her say: "Oh dear, I'm so glad you've come!" She and her aunt had in common the property of unex-pected speeches. She came out of the arbour almost as if to throw herself in my arms.

I hasten to add that I escaped this ordeal and that she did n't even then shake hands with me. It was an

53

ease to her to see me and presently she told me why —
because she was nervous when out-of-doors at night
alone. The plants and shrubs looked so strange in the
dark, and there were all sorts of queer sounds — she
could n't tell what they were — like the noises of animals. She stood close to me, looking about her with an
air of greater security but without any demonstration
of interest in me as an individual. Then I felt how
little nocturnal prowlings could have been her habit,
and I was also reminded — I had been afflicted by the
same in talking with her before I took possession —
that it was impossible to allow too much for her
simplicity.

"You speak as if you were lost in the backwoods,"
I cheeringly laughed. "How you manage to keep out
of this charming place when you've only three steps
to take to get into it is more than I've yet been able
to discover. You hide away amazingly so long as I'm
on the premises, I know; but I had a hope you peeped
out a little at other times. You and your poor aunt
are worse off than Carmelite nuns in their cells.
Should you mind telling me how you exist without air,
without exercise, without any sort of human contact?
I don't see how you carry on the common business of
life."

She looked at me as if I had spoken a strange tongue,
and her answer was so little of one that I felt it make
for irritation. "We go to bed very early — earlier
than you'd believe." I was on the point of saying that
this only deepened the mystery, but she gave me some
relief by adding: "Before you came we were n't so
private. But I've never been out at night."

"Never in these fragrant alleys, blooming here under your nose?"

"Ah," said Miss Tina, "they were never nice till now!" There was a finer sense in this and a flattering comparison, so that it seemed to me I had gained some advantage. As I might follow that further by establishing a good grievance I asked her why, since she thought my garden nice, she had never thanked me in any way for the flowers I had been sending up in such quantities for the previous three weeks. I had not been discouraged — there had been, as she would have observed, a daily armful; but I had been brought up in the common forms and a word of recognition now and then would have touched me in the right place.

"Why I did n't know they were for me!"

"They were for both of you. Why should I make a difference?"

Miss Tina reflected as if she might be thinking of a reason for that, but she failed to produce one. Instead of this she asked abruptly: "Why in the world do you want so much to know us?"

"I ought after all to make a difference," I replied. "That question 's your aunt's; it is n't yours. You would n't ask it if you had n't been put up to it."

"She did n't tell me to ask you," Miss Tina replied without confusion. She was indeed the oddest mixture of shyness and straightness.

"Well, she has often wondered about it herself and expressed her wonder to you. She has insisted on it, so that she has put the idea into your head that I 'm insufferably pushing. Upon my word I think

I've been very discreet. And how completely your aunt must have lost every tradition of sociability, to see anything out of the way in the idea that respectable intelligent people, living as we do under the same roof, should occasionally exchange a remark! What could be more natural? We're of the same country and have at least some of the same tastes, since, like you, I'm intensely fond of Venice."

My friend seemed incapable of grasping more than one clause in any proposition, and she now spoke quickly, eagerly, as if she were answering my whole speech. "I'm not in the least fond of Venice. I should like to go far away!"

"Has she always kept you back so?" I went on, to show her I could be as irrelevant as herself.

"She told me to come out to-night; she has told me very often," said Miss Tina. "It is I who would n't come. I don't like to leave her."

"Is she too weak, is she really failing?" I demanded, with more emotion, I think, than I meant to betray. I measured this by the way her eyes rested on me in the darkness. It embarrassed me a little, and to turn the matter off I continued genially: "Do let us sit down together comfortably somewhere — while you tell me all about her."

Miss Tina made no resistance to this. We found a bench less secluded, less confidential, as it were, than the one in the arbour; and we were still sitting there when I heard midnight ring out from those clear bells of Venice which vibrate with a solemnity of their own over the lagoon and hold the air so much more than the chimes of other places. We were to-

gether more than an hour, and our interview gave,
as it struck me, a great lift to my undertaking. Miss
Tina accepted the situation without a protest; she
had avoided me for three months, yet now she treated
me almost as if these three months had made me an
old friend. If I had chosen I might have gathered
from this that though she had avoided me she had
given a good deal of consideration to doing so. She
paid no attention to the flight of time — never worried at my keeping her so long away from her aunt.
She talked freely, answering questions and asking
them and not even taking advantage of certain long-
ish pauses by which they were naturally broken to say
she thought she had better go in. It was almost as
if she were waiting for something — something I
might say to her — and intended to give me my
opportunity. I was the more struck by this as she
told me how much less well her aunt had been for a
good many days, and in a way that was rather new.
She was markedly weaker; at moments she showed
no strength at all; yet more than ever before she
wished to be left alone. That was why she had told
her to come out — not even to remain in her own
room, which was alongside; she pronounced poor
Miss Tina "a worry, a bore and a source of aggravation." She sat still for hours together, as if for long
sleep; she had always done that, musing and dozing;
but at such times formerly she gave, in breaks, some
small sign of life, of interest, liking her companion
to be near her with her work. This sad personage
confided to me that at present her aunt was so motionless as to create the fear she was dead; moreover

she scarce ate or drank — one could n't see what she lived on. The great thing was that she still on most days got up; the serious job was to dress her, to wheel her out of her bedroom. She clung to as many of her old habits as possible and had always, little company as they had received for years, made a point of sitting in the great parlour.

I scarce knew what to think of all this — of Miss Tina's sudden conversion to sociability and of the strange fact that the more the old woman appeared to decline to her end the less she should desire to be looked after. The story hung indifferently together, and I even asked myself if it might n't be a trap laid for me, the result of a design to make me show my hand. I could n't have told why my companions (as they could only by courtesy be called) should have this purpose — why they should try to trip up so lucrative a lodger. But at any hazard I kept on my guard, so that Miss Tina should n't have occasion again to ask me what I might really be "up to." Poor woman, before we parted for the night my mind was at rest as to what *she* might be. She was up to nothing at all.

She told me more about their affairs than I had hoped; there was no need to be prying, for it evidently drew her out simply to feel me listen and care. She ceased wondering why I *should*, and at last, while describing the brilliant life they had led years before, she almost chattered. It was Miss Tina who judged it brilliant; she said that when they first came to live in Venice, years and years back — I found her essentially vague about dates and the order in which

events had occurred — there was never a week they
had n't some visitor or did n't make some pleasant
passeggio in the town. They had seen all the curiosities; they had even been to the Lido in a boat — she
spoke as if I might think there was a way on foot;
they had had a collation there, brought in three
baskets and spread out on the grass. I asked her
what people they had known and she said Oh very
nice ones — the Cavaliere Bombicci and the Con-
tessa Altemura, with whom they had had a great
friendship! Also English people — the Churtons
and the Goldies and Mrs. Stock-Stock, whom they
had loved dearly; she was dead and gone, poor dear.
That was the case with most of their kind circle —
this expression was Miss Tina's own; though a few
were left, which was a wonder considering how they
had neglected them. She mentioned the names of
two or three Venetian old women; of a certain doctor,
very clever, who was so attentive — he came as a
friend, he had really given up practice; of the *avvocato* Pochintesta, who wrote beautiful poems and had
addressed one to her aunt. These people came to see
them without fail every year, usually at the *capo
d'anno*, and of old her aunt used to make them some
little present — her aunt and she together: small
things that she, Miss Tina, turned out with her own
hand, paper lamp-shades, or mats for the decanters
of wine at dinner, or those woollen things that in
cold weather are worn on the wrists. The last few
years there had n't been many presents; she could n't
think what to make and her aunt had lost interest
and never suggested. But the people came all the

same; if the good Venetians liked you once they liked you for ever.

There was affecting matter enough in the good faith of this sketch of former social glories; the picnic at the Lido had remained vivid through the ages and poor Miss Tina evidently was of the impression that she had had a dashing youth. She had in fact had a glimpse of the Venetian world in its gossiping home-keeping parsimonious professional walks; for I noted for the first time how nearly she had acquired by contact the trick of the familiar soft-sounding almost infantile prattle of the place. I judged her to have imbibed this invertebrate dialect from the natural way the names of things and people — mostly purely local — rose to her lips. If she knew little of what they represented she knew still less of anything else. Her aunt had drawn in — the failure of interest in the table-mats and lamp-shades was a sign of that — and she had n't been able to mingle in society or to entertain it alone; so that her range of reminiscence struck one as an old world altogether. Her tone, had n't it been so decent, would have seemed to carry one back to the queer rococo Venice of Goldoni and Casanova. I found myself mistakenly think of her too as one of Jeffrey Aspern's contemporaries; this came from her having so little in common with my own. It was possible, I indeed reasoned, that she had n't even heard of him; it might very well be that Juliana had forborne to lift for innocent eyes the veil that covered the temple of her glory. In this case she perhaps would n't know of the existence of the papers, and I welcomed that presumption — it made me feel more safe with her — till I remembered we had believed the letter of disavowal received by Cumnor to be in the hand-writing of the niece. If it had been dictated to her she had of course to know what it was about; though the effect of it withal was to repudiate the idea of any connexion with the poet. I held it probable at all events that Miss Tina had n't read a word of his poetry. Moreover if, with her companion, she had always escaped invasion and research, there was little occasion for her having got it into her head that people were "after" the letters. People had not been after them, for people had n't heard of them. Cumnor's fruitless feeler would have been a solitary accident.

When midnight sounded Miss Tina got up; but she stopped at the door of the house only after she had wandered two or three times with me round the garden. "When shall I see you again?" I asked before she went in; to which she replied with prompt-ness that she should like to come out the next night. She added however that she should n't come — she was so far from doing everything she liked.

"You might do a few things *I* like," I quite sin-cerely sighed.

"Oh you — I don't believe you!" she murmured at this, facing me with her simple solemnity.

"Why don't you believe me?"

"Because I don't understand you."

"That's just the sort of occasion to have faith." I could n't say more, though I should have liked to, as I saw I only mystified her; for I had no wish to

have it on my conscience that I might pass for having
made love to her. Nothing less should I have seemed
to do had I continued to beg a lady to "believe in me"
in an Italian garden on a midsummer night. There
was some merit in my scruples, for Miss Tina lingered and lingered: I made out in her the conviction
that she should n't really soon come down again and
the wish therefore to protract the present. She insisted too on making the talk between us personal to
ourselves; and altogether her behaviour was such as
would have been possible only to a perfectly artless
and a considerably witless woman.

"I shall like the flowers better now that I know
them also meant for me."

"How could you have doubted it? If you 'll tell
me the kind you like best I 'll send a double lot."

"Oh I like them all best!" Then she went on
familiarly: "Shall you study — shall you read and
write — when you go up to your rooms?"

"I don't do that at night — at this season. The
lamplight brings in the animals."

"You might have known that when you came."

"I did know it!"

"And in winter do you work at night?"

"I read a good deal, but I don't often write." She
listened as if these details had a rare interest, and suddenly a temptation quite at odds with all the prudence
I had been teaching myself glimmered at me in her
plain mild face. Ah yes, she was safe and I could make
her safer! It seemed to me from one moment to another that I could n't wait longer — that I really must
take a sounding. So I went on: "In general before I

go to sleep (very often in bed; it's a bad habit, but I confess to it) I read some great poet. In nine cases out of ten it's a volume of Jeffrey Aspern."

I watched her well as I pronounced that name, but I saw nothing wonderful. Why should I indeed? Was n't Jeffrey Aspern the property of the human race?

"Oh *we* read him — we *have* read him," she quietly replied.

"He's my poet of poets — I know him almost by heart."

For an instant Miss Tina hesitated; then her sociability was too much for her. "Oh by heart — that's nothing;" and, though dimly, she quite lighted. "My aunt used to know him, to know him" — she paused an instant and I wondered what she was going to say — "to know him as a visitor."

"As a visitor?" I guarded my tone.

"He used to call on her and take her out."

I continued to stare. "My dear lady, he died a hundred years ago!"

"Well," she said amusingly, "my aunt's a hundred and fifty."

"Mercy on us!" I cried; "why did n't you tell me before? I should like so to ask her about him."

"She would n't care for that — she would n't tell you," Miss Tina returned.

"I don't care what she cares for! She *must* tell me — it's not a chance to be lost."

"Oh you should have come twenty years ago. Then she still talked about him."

"And what did she say?" I eagerly asked.

"I don't know — that he liked her immensely."

"And she — did n't she like *him?*"

"She said he was a god." Miss Tina gave me this information flatly, without expression; her tone might have made it a piece of trivial gossip. But it stirred me deeply as she dropped the words into the summer night; their sound might have been the light rustle of an old unfolded love-letter.

"Fancy, fancy!" I murmured. And then: "Tell me this, please — has she got a portrait of him? They're distressingly rare."

"A portrait? I don't know," said Miss Tina; and now there was discomfiture in her face. "Well, good-night!" she added; and she turned into the house.

I accompanied her into the wide dusky stone-paved passage that corresponded on the ground floor with our great sala. It opened at one end into the garden, at the other upon the canal, and was lighted now only by the small lamp always left for me to take up as I went to bed. An extinguished candle which Miss Tina apparently had brought down with her stood on the same table with it. "Good-night, good-night!" I replied, keeping beside her as she went to get her light. "Surely you 'd know, should n't you, if she had one?"

"If she had what?" the poor lady asked, looking at me queerly over the flame of her candle.

"A portrait of the god. I don't know what I would n't give to see it."

"I don't know what she has got. She keeps her things locked up." And Miss Tina went away toward the staircase with the sense evidently of having said too much.

I let her go — I wished not to frighten her — and I contented myself with remarking that Miss Bordereau would n't have locked up such a glorious possession as that: a thing a person would be proud of and hang up in a prominent place on the parlour-wall. Therefore of course she had n't any portrait. Miss Tina made no direct answer to this and, candle in hand, with her back to me, mounted two or three degrees. Then she stopped short and turned round, looking at me across the dusky space.

"Do you write — do you write?" There was a shake in her voice — she could scarcely bring it out.

"Do I write? Oh don't speak of my writing on the same day with Aspern's!"

"Do you write about *him* — do you pry into his life?"

"Ah that's your aunt's question; it can't be yours!" I said in a tone of slightly wounded sensibility.

"All the more reason then that you should answer it. Do you, please?"

I thought I had allowed for the falsehoods I should have to tell, but I found that in fact when it came to the point I had n't. Besides, now that I had an opening there was a kind of relief in being frank. Lastly — it was perhaps fanciful, even fatuous — I guessed that Miss Tina personally would n't in the last resort be less my friend. So after a moment's hesitation I answered: "Yes, I 've written about him and I 'm looking for more material. In heaven's name have you got any?"

"*Santo Dio!*" she exclaimed without heeding my

question; and she hurried upstairs and out of sight. I might count upon her in the last resort, but for the present she was visibly alarmed. The proof of it was that she began to hide again, so that for a fortnight I kept missing her. I found my patience ebbing and after four or five days of this I told the gardener to stop the "floral tributes."

VI

ONE afternoon, at last, however, as I came down from my quarters to go out, I found her in the sala: it was our first encounter on that ground since I had come to the house. She put on no air of being there by accident; there was an ignorance of such arts in her honest angular diffidence. That I might be quite sure she was waiting for me she mentioned it at once, but telling me with it that Miss Bordereau wished to see me: she would take me into the room at that moment if I had time. If I had been late for a love-tryst I would have stayed for this, and I quickly signified that I should be delighted to wait on my benefactress. "She wants to talk with you — to know you," Miss Tina said, smiling as if she herself appreciated that idea; and she led me to the door of her aunt's apartment. I stopped her a moment before she had opened it, looking at her with some curiosity. I told her that this was a great satisfaction to me and a great honour; but all the same I should like to ask what had made Miss Bordereau so markedly and suddenly change. It had been only the other day that she would n't suffer me near her. Miss Tina was not embarrassed by my question; she had as many little unexpected serenities, plausibilities almost, as if she told fibs, but the odd part of them was that they had on the contrary their source in her truthfulness. "Oh my aunt varies," she answered; "it's so terribly dull — I suppose she's tired."

"But you told me she wanted more and more to be alone."

Poor Miss Tina coloured as if she found me too pushing. "Well, if you don't believe she wants to see you, I have n't invented it! I think people often are capricious when they're very old."

"That's perfectly true. I only wanted to be clear as to whether you 've repeated to her what I told you the other night."

"What you told me ?"

"About Jeffrey Aspern — that I'm looking for materials."

"If I had told her do you think she'd have sent for you ?"

"That's exactly what I want to know. If she wants to keep him to herself she might have sent for me to tell me so."

"She won't speak of him," said Miss Tina. Then as she opened the door she added in a lower tone : "I told her nothing."

The old woman was sitting in the same place in which I had seen her last, in the same position, with the same mystifying bandage over her eyes. Her welcome was to turn her almost invisible face to me and show me that while she sat silent she saw me clearly. I made no motion to shake hands with her; I now felt too well that this was out of place for ever. It had been sufficiently enjoined on me that she was too sacred for trivial modernisms — too venerable to touch. There was something so grim in her aspect — it was partly the accident of her green shade — as I stood there to be measured, that I ceased on the spot to doubt her suspecting me, though I did n't in the least myself suspect that Miss Tina had n't just spoken the truth. She had n't betrayed me, but the old woman's brooding instinct had served her; she had turned me over and over in the long still hours and had guessed. The worst of it was that she looked terribly like an old woman who at a pinch would, even like Sardanapalus, burn her treasure. Miss Tina pushed a chair forward, saying to me "This will be a good place for you to sit." As I took possession of it I asked after Miss Bordereau's health; expressed the hope that in spite of the very hot weather it was satisfactory. She answered that it was good enough — good enough; that it was a great thing to be alive.

"Oh as to that, it depends upon what you compare it with!" I returned with a laugh.

"I don't compare — I don't compare. If I did that I should have given everything up long ago."

I liked to take this for a subtle allusion to the rapture she had known in the society of Jeffrey Aspern — though it was true that such an allusion would have accorded ill with the wish I imputed to her to keep him buried in her soul. What it accorded with was my constant conviction that no human being had ever had a happier social gift than his, and what it seemed to convey was that nothing in the world was worth speaking of if one pretended to speak of that. But one did n't pretend! Miss Tina sat down beside her aunt, looking as if she had reason to believe some wonderful talk would come off between us.

"It's about the beautiful flowers," said the old lady; "you sent us so many — I ought to have thanked you for them before. But I don't write letters and I receive company but at long intervals."

She had n't thanked me while the flowers continued to come, but she departed from her custom so far as to send for me as soon as she began to fear they would n't come any more. I noted this; I remembered what an acquisitive propensity she had shown when it was a question of extracting gold from me, and I privately rejoiced at the happy thought I had had in suspending my tribute. She had missed it and was willing to make a concession to bring it back. At the first sign of this concession I could only go to meet her. "I'm afraid you have n't had many, of late, but they shall begin again immediately — to-morrow, to-night."

"Oh do send us some to-night!" Miss Tina cried as if it were a great affair.

"What else should you do with them? It is n't a manly taste to make a bower of your room," the old woman remarked.

"I don't make a bower of my room, but I'm exceedingly fond of growing flowers, of watching their ways. There's nothing unmanly in that; it has been the amusement of philosophers, of statesmen in retirement; even I think of great captains."

"I suppose you know you can sell them — those you don't use," Miss Bordereau went on. "I dare say they would n't give you much for them; still, you could make a bargain."

"Oh I've never in my life made a bargain, as you ought pretty well to have gathered. My gardener disposes of them and I ask no questions."

"I'd ask a few, I can promise you!" said Miss Bordereau; and it was so I first heard the strange sound of her laugh, which was as if the faint "walking" ghost of her old-time tone had suddenly cut a caper. I could n't get used to the idea that this vision of pecuniary profit was most what drew out the divine Juliana.

"Come into the garden yourself and pick them; come as often as you like; come every day. The flowers are all for you," I pursued, addressing Miss Tina and carrying off this veracious statement by treating it as an innocent joke. "I can't imagine why she does n't come down," I added for Miss Bordereau's benefit.

"You must make her come; you must come up and fetch her," the old woman said to my stupefaction. "That odd thing you've made in the corner will do very well for her to sit in."

The allusion to the most elaborate of my shady coverts, a sketchy "summer-house," was irreverent; it confirmed the impression I had already received that there was a flicker of impertinence in Miss Bordereau's talk, a vague echo of the boldness or the archness of her adventurous youth and which had somehow automatically outlived passions and faculties. None the less I asked: "Would n't it be possible for you to come down there yourself? Would n't it do you good to sit there in the shade and the sweet air?"

"Oh sir, when I move out of this it won't be to sit in the air, and I'm afraid that any that may be stirring around me won't be particularly sweet! It will be a very dark shade indeed. But that won't be just yet," Miss Bordereau continued cannily, as if to correct any hopes this free glance at the last receptacle of her mortality might lead me to entertain. "I've sat here many a day and have had enough of arbours in my time. But I'm not afraid to wait till I'm called."

Miss Tina had expected, as I felt, rare conversation, but perhaps she found it less gracious on her aunt's side — considering I had been sent for with a civil intention — than she had hoped. As to give the position a turn that would put our companion in a light more favourable she said to me: "Did n't I tell you the other night that she had sent me out? You see I can do what I like!"

"Do you pity her — do you teach her to pity herself?" Miss Bordereau demanded, before I had time to answer this appeal. "She has a much easier life than I had at her age."

"You must remember it has been quite open to me," I said, "to think you rather inhuman."

"Inhuman? That's what the poets used to call the women a hundred years ago. Don't try that; you won't do as well as they!" Juliana went on. "There's no more poetry in the world — that *I* know of at least. But I won't bandy words with you," she said, and I well remember the old-fashioned artificial sound she gave the speech. "You make me talk, talk, talk! It is n't good for me at all." I got up at this and told her I would take no more of her time; but she detained me to put a question. "Do you remember, the day I saw you about the rooms, that you offered us the use of your gondola?" And when I assented promptly, struck again with her disposition to make a "good thing" of my being there and wondering what she now had in her eye, she produced: "Why don't you take that girl out in it and show her the place?"

"Oh dear aunt, what do you want to do with me?" cried the "girl" with a piteous quaver. "I know all about the place!"

"Well then go with him and explain!" said Miss Bordereau, who gave an effect of cruelty to her implacable power of retort. This showed her as a sarcastic profane cynical old woman. "Have n't we heard that there have been all sorts of changes in all these years? You ought to see them, and at your age —I don't mean because you're so young — you ought to take the chances that come. You're old enough, my dear, and this gentleman won't hurt you. He'll show you the famous sunsets, if they still go on — do they go on? The sun set for me so long ago. But that's not a reason. Besides, I shall never miss you; you think you're too important. Take her to the Piazza; it used to be very pretty," Miss Bordereau continued, addressing herself to me. "What have they done with the funny old church? I hope it has n't tumbled down. Let her look at the shops; she may take some money, she may buy what she likes."

Poor Miss Tina had got up, discountenanced and helpless, and as we stood there before her aunt it would certainly have struck a spectator of the scene that our venerable friend was making rare sport of us. Miss Tina protested in a confusion of exclamations and murmurs; but I lost no time in saying that if she would do me the honour to accept the hospitality of my boat I would engage she really should n't be bored. Or if she did n't want so much of my company the boat itself, with the gondolier, was at her service; he was a capital oar and she might have every confidence. Miss Tina, without definitely answering this speech, looked away from me and out of the window, quite as if about to weep, and I remarked that once we had Miss Bordereau's approval we could easily come to an understanding. We would take an hour, whichever she liked, one of the very next days. As I made my obeisance to the old lady I asked her if she would kindly permit me to see her again.

For a moment she kept me ; then she said : "Is it very necessary to your happiness ?"

"It diverts me more than I can say."

"You 're wonderfully civil. Don't you know it almost kills *me* ?"

"How can I believe that when I see you more animated, more brilliant than when I came in ?"

"That's very true, aunt," said Miss Tina. "I think it does you good."

"Is n't it touching, the solicitude we each have that the other shall enjoy herself ?" sneered Miss Bordereau. "If you think me brilliant to-day you don't know what you 're talking about; you 've never seen an agreeable woman. What do you people know about good society ?" she cried; but before I could tell her, "Don't try to pay me a compliment ; I 've been spoiled," she went on. "My door's shut, but you may sometimes knock."

With this she dismissed me and I left the room. The latch closed behind me, but Miss Tina, contrary to my hope, had remained within. I passed slowly across the hall and before taking my way downstairs waited a little. My hope was answered; after a minute my conductress followed me. "That's a delightful idea about the Piazza," I said. "When will you go — to-night, to-morrow?"

She had been disconcerted, as I have mentioned, but I had already perceived, and I was to observe again, that when Miss Tina was embarrassed she did n't — as most women would have in like case — turn away, floundering and hedging, but came closer, as it were, with a deprecating, a clinging appeal to be spared, to be protected. Her attitude was a constant prayer for aid and explanation, and yet no woman in the world could have been less of a comedian. From the moment you were kind to her she depended on you absolutely; her self-consciousness dropped and she took the greatest intimacy, the innocent intimacy that was all she could conceive, for granted. She did n't know, she now declared, what possessed her aunt, who had changed so quickly, who had got some idea. I replied that she must catch the idea and let me have it: we would go and take an ice together at Florian's and she should report while we listened to the band.

"Oh it will take me a long time to be able to 'report'!" she said rather ruefully; and she could promise me this satisfaction neither for that night nor for the next. I was patient now, however, for I felt I had only to wait; and in fact at the end of the week, one lovely evening after dinner, she stepped into my gondola, to which in honour of the occasion I had attached a second oar.

We swept in the course of five minutes into the Grand Canal; whereupon she uttered a murmur of ecstasy as fresh as if she had been a tourist just arrived. She had forgotten the splendour of the great water-way on a clear summer evening, and how the sense of floating between marble palaces and reflected lights disposed the mind to freedom and ease. We floated long and far, and though my friend gave no high-pitched voice to her glee I was sure of her full surrender. She was more than pleased, she was transported; the whole thing was an immense liberation. The gondola moved with slow strokes, to give her time to enjoy it, and she listened to the plash of the oars, which grew louder and more musically liquid as we passed into narrow canals, as if it were a revelation of Venice. When I asked her how long it was since she had thus floated she answered: "Oh I don't know; a long time — not since my aunt began to be ill." This was not the only show of her extreme vagueness about the previous years and the line marking off the period of Miss Bordereau's eminence. I was not at liberty to keep her out long, but we took a considerable *giro* before going to the Piazza. I asked her no questions, holding off by design from her life at home and the things I wanted to know; I poured, rather, treasures of information about the objects before and around us into her ears, describing also Florence and Rome, discoursing on the charms and advantages of travel. She reclined, receptive, on the deep leather cushions, turned her eyes conscientiously to everything I noted and never mentioned to me till some time afterwards that she might be supposed to know Florence better than I, as she had lived there for years with her kins-woman. At last she said with the shy impatience of a child: "Are we not really going to the Piazza? That's what I want to see!" I immediately gave the order that we should go straight, after which we sat silent with the expectation of arrival. As some time still passed, however, she broke out of her own move-ment: "I've found out what's the matter with my aunt: she's afraid you'll go!"

I quite gasped. "What has put that into her head?"

"She has had an idea you've not been happy. That's why she's different now."

"You mean she wants to make me happier?"

"Well, she wants you not to go. She wants you to stay."

"I suppose you mean on account of the rent," I remarked candidly.

Miss Tina's candour but profited. "Yes, you know; so that I shall have more."

"How much does she want you to have?" I asked with all the gaiety I now felt. "She ought to fix the sum, so that I may stay till it's made up."

"Oh that would n't please me," said Miss Tina. "It would be unheard of, your taking that trouble."

"But suppose I should have my own reasons for staying in Venice?"

THE ASPERN PAPERS

"Then it would be better for you to stay in some other house."

"And what would your aunt say to that?"

"She would n't like it at all. But I should think you 'd do well to give up your reasons and go away altogether."

"Dear Miss Tina," I said, "it 's not so easy to give up my reasons!"

She made no immediate answer to this, but after a moment broke out afresh: "I think I know what your reasons are!"

"I dare say, because the other night I almost told you how I wished you 'd help me to make them good."

"I can't do that without being false to my aunt."

"What do you mean by being false to her?"

"Why she would never consent to what you want. She has been asked, she has been written to. It makes her fearfully angry."

"Then she *has* papers of value?" I precipitately cried.

"Oh she has everything!" sighed Miss Tina with a curious weariness, a sudden lapse into gloom.

These words caused all my pulses to throb, for I regarded them as precious evidence. I felt them too deeply to speak, and in the interval the gondola approached the Piazzetta. After we had disembarked I asked my companion if she would rather walk round the square or go and sit before the great café; to which she replied that she would do whichever I liked best — I must only remember again how little time she had. I assured her there was plenty to do both, and we made the circuit of the long arcades. Her spirits

revived at the sight of the bright shop-windows, and
she lingered and stopped, admiring or disapproving
of their contents, asking me what I thought of things,
theorising about prices. My attention wandered from
her; her words of a while before "Oh she has everything!" echoed so in my consciousness. We sat down
at last in the crowded circle at Florian's, finding an
unoccupied table among those that were ranged in the
square. It was a splendid night and all the world
out-of-doors; Miss Tina could n't have wished the
elements more auspicious for her return to society. I
saw she felt it all even more than she told, but her
impressions were well-nigh too many for her. She had
forgotten the attraction of the world and was learning
that she had for the best years of her life been rather
mercilessly cheated of it. This did n't make her
angry; but as she took in the charming scene her face
had, in spite of its smile of appreciation, the flush of a
wounded surprise. She did n't speak, sunk in the sense
of opportunities, for ever lost, that ought to have been
easy; and this gave me a chance to say to her: "Did
you mean a while ago that your aunt has a plan of
keeping me on by admitting me occasionally to her
presence?"

"She thinks it will make a difference with you if
you sometimes see her. She wants you so much to
stay that she's willing to make that concession."

"And what good does she consider I think it will
do me to see her?"

"I don't know; it must be interesting," said
Miss Tina simply. "You told her you found it so."

"So I did; but every one does n't think that."

"No, of course not, or more people would try."

"Well, if she's capable of making that reflexion she's capable also of making this further one," I went on: "that I must have a particular reason for not doing as others do, in spite of the interest she offers — for not leaving her alone." Miss Tina looked as if she failed to grasp this rather complicated proposition; so I continued: "If you've not told her what I said to you the other night may she not at least have guessed it?"

"I don't know — she's very suspicious."

"But she has n't been made so by indiscreet curiosity, by persecution?"

"No, no; it is n't that," said Miss Tina, turning on me a troubled face. "I don't know how to say it: it's on account of something — ages ago, before I was born — in her life."

"Something? What sort of thing?" — and I asked it as if I could have no idea.

"Oh she has never told me." And I was sure my friend spoke the truth.

Her extreme limpidity was almost provoking, and I felt for the moment that she would have been more satisfactory if she had been less ingenuous. "Do you suppose it's something to which Jeffrey Aspern's letters and papers — I mean the things in her possession — have reference?"

"I dare say it is!" my companion exclaimed as if this were a very happy suggestion. "I've never looked at any of those things."

"None of them? Then how do you know what they are?"

"I don't," said Miss Tina placidly. "I've never had them in my hands. But I've seen them when she has had them out."

"Does she have them out often?"

"Not now, but she used to. She's very fond of them."

"In spite of their being compromising?"

"Compromising?" Miss Tina repeated as if vague as to what that meant. I felt almost as one who corrupts the innocence of youth.

"I allude to their containing painful memories."

"Oh I don't think anything's painful.'

"You mean there's nothing to affect her reputation?"

An odder look even than usual came at this into the face of Miss Bordereau's niece — a confession, it seemed, of helplessness, an appeal to me to deal fairly, generously with her. I had brought her to the Piazza, placed her among charming influences, paid her an attention she appreciated, and now I appeared to show it all as a bribe — a bribe to make her turn in some way against her aunt. She was of a yielding nature and capable of doing almost anything to please a person markedly kind to her; but the greatest kindness of all would be not to presume too much on this. It was strange enough, as I afterwards thought, that she had not the least air of resenting my want of consideration for her aunt's character, which would have been in the worst possible taste if anything less vital — from my point of view — had been at stake. I don't think she really measured it. "Do you mean she ever did something bad?" she asked in a moment.

"Heaven forbid I should say so, and it's none of my business. Besides, if she did," I agreeably put it, "that was in other ages, in another world. But why should n't she destroy her papers?"

"Oh she loves them too much."

"Even now, when she may be near her end?"

"Perhaps when she's sure of that she will."

"Well, Miss Tina," I said, "that's just what I should like you to prevent."

"How can I prevent it?"

"Could n't you get them away from her?"

"And give them to you?"

This put the case, superficially, with sharp irony, but I was sure of her not intending that. "Oh I mean that you might let me see them and look them over. It is n't for myself, or that I should want them at any cost to any one else. It's simply that they would be of such immense interest to the public, such immeasurable importance as a contribution to Jeffrey Aspern's history."

She listened to me in her usual way, as if I abounded in matters she had never heard of, and I felt almost as base as the reporter of a newspaper who forces his way into a house of mourning. This was marked when she presently said: "There was a gentleman who some time ago wrote to her in very much those words. He also wanted her papers."

"And did she answer him?" I asked, rather ashamed of not having my friend's rectitude.

"Only when he had written two or three times. He made her very angry."

"And what did she say?"

"She said he was a devil," Miss Tina replied categorically.

"She used that expression in her letter?"

"Oh no; she said it to me. She made me write to him."

"And what did you say?"

"I told him there were no papers at all."

"Ah poor gentleman!" I groaned.

"I knew there were, but I wrote what she bade me."

"Of course you had to do that. But I hope I shan't pass for a devil."

"It will depend upon what you ask me to do for you," my companion smiled.

"Oh if there's a chance of *your* thinking so my affair 's in a bad way! I shan't ask you to steal for me, nor even to fib — for you *can't* fib, unless on paper. But the principal thing is this — to prevent her destroying the papers."

"Why I 've no control of her," said Miss Tina. "It 's she who controls me."

"But she does n't control her own arms and legs, does she? The way she would naturally destroy her letters would be to burn them. Now she can't burn them without fire, and she can't get fire unless you give it her."

"I 've always done everything she has asked," my poor friend pleaded. "Besides, there 's Olimpia."

I was on the point of saying that Olimpia was probably corruptible, but I thought it best not to sound that note. So I simply put it that this frail creature might perhaps be managed.

"Every one can be managed by my aunt," said

Miss Tina. And then she remembered that her holiday was over; she must go home.

I laid my hand on her arm, across the table, to stay her a moment. "What I want of you is a general promise to help me."

"Oh how *can* I, how *can* I?" she asked, wondering and troubled. She was half-surprised, half-frightened at my attaching that importance to her, at my calling on her for action.

"This is the main thing: to watch our friend carefully and warn me in time, before she commits that dreadful sacrilege."

"I can't watch her when she makes me go out."

"That's very true."

"And when you do too."

"Mercy on us — do you think she 'll have done anything to-night?"

"I don't know. She's very cunning."

"Are you trying to frighten me?" I asked.

I felt this question sufficiently answered when my companion murmured in a musing, almost envious way: "Oh but she loves them — she loves them!"

This reflexion, repeated with such emphasis, gave me great comfort; but to obtain more of that balm I said: "If she should n't intend to destroy the objects we speak of before her death she 'll probably have made some disposition by will."

"By will?"

"Has n't she made a will for your benefit?"

"Ah she has so little to leave. That's why she likes money," said Miss Tina.

"Might I ask, since we're really talking things over, what you and she live on?"

"On some money that comes from America, from a gentleman — I think a lawyer — in New York. He sends it every quarter. It is n't much!"

"And won't she have disposed of that?"

My companion hesitated — I saw she was blushing. "I believe it's mine," she said; and the look and tone which accompanied these words betrayed so the absence of the habit of thinking of herself that I almost thought her charming. The next instant she added: "But she had in an *avvocato* here once, ever so long ago. And some people came and signed something."

"They were probably witnesses. And you were n't asked to sign? Well then," I argued, rapidly and hopefully, "it's because you're the legatee. She must have left all her documents to you!"

"If she has it's with very strict conditions," Miss Tina responded, rising quickly, while the movement gave the words a small character of decision. They seemed to imply that the bequest would be accompanied with a proviso that the articles bequeathed should remain concealed from every inquisitive eye, and that I was very much mistaken if I thought her the person to depart from an injunction so absolute.

"Oh of course you'll have to abide by the terms," I said; and she uttered nothing to mitigate the rigour of this conclusion. None the less, later on, just before we disembarked at her own door after a return which had taken place almost in silence, she said to me abruptly: "I'll do what I can to help you." I was grateful for this — it was very well so far as it went; but it did n't keep me from remembering that night in a worried waking hour that I now had her word for it to re-enforce my own impression that the old woman was full of craft.

VII

THE fear of what this side of her character might have led her to do made me nervous for days afterwards. I waited for an intimation from Miss Tina; I almost read it as her duty to keep me informed, to let me know definitely whether or no Miss Bordereau had sacrificed her treasures. But as she gave no sign I lost patience and determined to put the case to the very touch of my own senses. I sent late one afternoon to ask if I might pay the ladies a visit, and my servant came back with surprising news. Miss Bordereau could be approached without the least difficulty; she had been moved out into the sala and was sitting by the window that overlooked the garden. I descended and found this picture correct; the old lady had been wheeled forth into the world and had a certain air, which came mainly perhaps from some brighter element in her dress, of being prepared again to have converse with it. It had not yet, however, begun to flock about her; she was perfectly alone and, though the door leading to her own quarters stood open, I had at first no glimpse of Miss Tina. The window at which she sat had the afternoon shade and, one of the shutters having been pushed back, she could see the pleasant garden, where the summer sun had by this time dried up too many of the plants — she could see the yellow light and the long shadows.

"Have you come to tell me you'll take the rooms

for six months more ?" she asked as I approached her, startling me by something coarse in her cupidity almost as much as if she had n't already given me a specimen of it. Juliana's desire to make our acquaintance lucrative had been, as I have sufficiently indicated, a false note in my image of the woman who had inspired a great poet with immortal lines; but I may say here definitely that I after all recognised large allowance to be made for her. It was I who had kindled the unholy flame; it was I who had put into her head that she had the means of making money. She appeared never to have thought of that; she had been living wastefully for years, in a house five times too big for her, on a footing that I could explain only by the presumption that, excessive as it was, the space she enjoyed cost her next to nothing and that, small as were her revenues, they left her, for Venice, an appreciable margin. I had descended on her one day and taught her to calculate, and my almost extravagant comedy on the subject of the garden had presented me irresistibly in the light of a victim. Like all persons who achieve the miracle of changing their point of view late in life, she had been intensely converted: she had seized my hint with a desperate tremulous clutch.

I invited myself to go and get one of the chairs that stood, at a distance, against the wall — she had given herself no concern as to whether I should sit or stand; and while I placed it near her I began gaily: "Oh dear madam, what an imagination you have, what an intellectual sweep! I'm a poor devil of a man of letters who lives from day to day. How can I take palaces

by the year? My existence is precarious. I don't
know whether six months hence I shall have bread to
put in my mouth. I've treated myself for once; it has
been an immense luxury. But when it comes to going
on —!"

"Are your rooms too dear? if they are you can
have more for the same money," Juliana responded.
"We can arrange, we can *combinare*, as they say
here."

"Well yes, since you ask me, they're too dear,
much too dear," I said. "Evidently you suppose me
richer than I am."

She looked at me as from the mouth of her cave.
"If you write books don't you sell them?"

"Do you mean don't people buy them? A little,
a very little — not so much as I could wish. Writing
books, unless one be a great genius — and even then!
— is the last road to fortune. I think there's no more
money to be made by good letters."

"Perhaps you don't choose nice subjects. What
do you write about?" Miss Bordereau implacably
pursued.

"About the books of other people. I'm a critic,
a commentator, an historian, in a small way." I
wondered what she was coming to.

"And what other people now?"

"Oh better ones than myself: the great writers
mainly — the great philosophers and poets of the
past; those who are dead and gone and can't, poor
darlings, speak for themselves."

"And what do you say about them?"

"I say they sometimes attached themselves to very

89

clever women!" I replied as for pleasantness. I had measured, as I thought, my risk, but as my words fell upon the air they were to strike me as imprudent. However, I had launched them and I was n't sorry, for perhaps after all the old woman would be willing to treat. It seemed tolerably obvious that she knew my secret: why therefore drag the process out? But she did n't take what I had said as a confession; she only asked:

"Do you think it's right to rake up the past?"

"I don't feel that I know what you mean by raking it up. How can we get at it unless we dig a little? The present has such a rough way of treading it down."

"Oh I like the past, but I don't like critics," my hostess declared with her hard complacency.

"Neither do I, but I like their discoveries."

"Are n't they mostly lies?"

"The lies are what they sometimes discover," I said, smiling at the quiet impertinence of this. "They often lay bare the truth."

"The truth is God's, it is n't man's: we had better leave it alone. Who can judge of it?—who can say?"

"We're terribly in the dark, I know," I admitted; "but if we give up trying what becomes of all the fine things? What becomes of the work I just mentioned, that of the great philosophers and poets? It's all vain words if there's nothing to measure it by."

"You talk as if you were a tailor," said Miss Bordereau whimsically; and then she added quickly and in a different manner: "This house is very fine; the proportions are magnificent. To-day I wanted to look at this part again. I made them bring me out here. When your man came just now to learn if I would see you I was on the point of sending for you to ask if you did n't mean to go on. I wanted to judge what I'm letting you have. This sala is very grand,". she pursued like an auctioneer, moving a little, as I guessed, her invisible eyes. "I don't believe you often have lived in such a house, eh?"

"I can't often afford to!" I said.

"Well then how much will you give me for six months?"

I was on the point of exclaiming — and the air of excruciation in my face would have denoted a moral fact — "Don't, Juliana; for *his* sake, don't!" But I controlled myself and asked less passionately: "Why should I remain so long as that?"

"I thought you liked it," said Miss Bordereau with her shrivelled dignity.

"So I thought I should."

For a moment she said nothing more, and I left my own words to suggest to her what they might. I half-expected her to say, coldly enough, that if I had been disappointed we need n't continue the discussion, and this in spite of the fact that I believed her now to have in her mind — however it had come there — what would have told her that my disappointment was natural. But to my extreme surprise she ended by observing: "If you don't think we've treated you well enough perhaps we can discover some way of treating you better." This speech was somehow so incongruous that it made me laugh again,

and I excused myself by saying that she talked as if
I were a sulky boy pouting in the corner and having
to be "brought round." I had n't a grain of com-
plaint to make; and could anything have exceeded
Miss Tina's graciousness in accompanying me a few
·nights before to the Piazza? At this the old woman
went on: "Well, you brought it on yourself!" And
then in a different tone: "She's a very fine girl." I
assented cordially to this proposition, and she expressed the hope that I did so not merely to be,
obliging, but that I really liked her. Meanwhile I
wondered still more what Miss Bordereau was coming to. "Except for me, to-day," she said, "she has n't
a relation in the world." Did she by describing her
niece as amiable and unencumbered wish to represent her as a *parti?*

It was perfectly true that I could n't afford to go
on with my rooms at a fancy price and that I had
already devoted to my undertaking almost all the
hard cash I had set apart for it. My patience and
my time were by no means exhausted, but I should
be able to draw upon them only on a more usual
Venetian basis. I was willing to pay the precious
personage with whom my pecuniary dealings were
such a discord twice as much as any other *padrona
di casa* would have asked, but I was n't willing to
pay her twenty times as much. I told her so plainly,
and my plainness appeared to have some success,
for she exclaimed: "Very good; you 've done what I
asked — you 've made an offer!"

"Yes, but not for half a year. Only by the month."

"Oh I must think of that then." She seemed disappointed that I would n't tie myself to a period, and I guessed that she wished both to secure me and to discourage me; to say severely: "Do you dream that you can get off with less than six months? Do you dream that even by the end of that time you 'll be appreciably nearer your victory?" What was most in my mind was that she had a fancy to play me the trick of making me engage myself when in fact she had sacrificed her treasure. There was a moment when my suspense on this point was so acute that I all but broke out with the question, and what kept it back was but an instinctive recoil — lest it should be a mistake — from the last violence of self-exposure. She was such a subtle old witch that one could never tell where one stood with her. You may imagine whether it cleared up the puzzle when, just after she had said she would think of my proposal and without any formal transition, she drew out of her pocket with an embarrassed hand a small object wrapped in crumpled white paper. She held it there a moment and then resumed: "Do you know much about curiosities?"

"About curiosities?"

"About antiquities, the old gimcracks that people pay so much for to-day. Do you know the kind of price they bring?"

I thought I saw what was coming, but I said ingenuously: "Do you want to buy something?"

"No, I want to sell. What would an amateur give me for that?" She unfolded the white paper and made a motion for me to take from her a small oval portrait. I possessed myself of it with fingers of which

I could only hope that they did n't betray the intensity of their clutch, and she added: "I would part with it only for a good price."

At the first glance I recognised Jeffrey Aspern, and was well aware that I flushed with the act. As she was watching me however I had the consistency to exclaim: "What a striking face! Do tell me who he is."

"He's an old friend of mine, a very distinguished man in his day. He gave it me himself, but I'm afraid to mention his name, lest you never should have heard of him, critic and historian as you are. I know the world goes fast and one generation forgets another. He was all the fashion when I was young."

She was perhaps amazed at my assurance, but I was surprised at hers; at her having the energy, in her state of health and at her time of life, to wish to sport with me to that tune simply for her private entertainment — the humour to test me and practise on me and befool me. This at least was the interpretation that I put upon her production of the relic, for I could n't believe she really desired to sell it or cared for any information I might give her. What she wished was to dangle it before my eyes and put a prohibitive price on it. "The face comes back to me, it torments me," I said, turning the object this way and that and looking at it very critically. It was a careful but not a supreme work of art, larger than the ordinary miniature and representing a young man with a remarkably handsome face, in a high-collared green coat and a buff waistcoat. I felt in the little work a virtue of likeness and judged it to have

been painted when the model was about twenty-five.
There are, as all the world knows, three other portraits of the poet in existence, but none of so early
a date as this elegant image. "I've never seen the
original, clearly a man of a past age, but I've seen
other reproductions of this face," I went on. "You
expressed doubt of this generation's having heard of
the gentleman, but he strikes me for all the world as
a celebrity. Now who is he? I can't put my finger
on him — I can't give him a label. Wasn't he a
writer? Surely he's a poet." I was determined that
it should be she, not I, who should first pronounce
Jeffrey Aspern's name.

My resolution was taken in ignorance of Miss
Bordereau's extremely resolute character, and her
lips never formed in my hearing the syllables that
meant so much for her. She neglected to answer my
question, but raised her hand to take back the picture, using a gesture which though impotent was
in a high degree peremptory. "It's only a person
who should know for himself that would give me my
price," she said with a certain dryness.

"Oh then you have a price?" I didn't restore
the charming thing; not from any vindictive purpose,
but because I instinctively clung to it. We looked at
each other hard while I retained it.

"I know the least I would take. What it occurred
to me to ask you about is the most I shall be able to
get."

She made a movement, drawing herself together
as if, in a spasm of dread at having lost her prize,
she had been impelled to the immense effort of rising

to snatch it from me. I instantly placed it in her hand again, saying as I did so: "I should like to have it myself, but with your ideas it would be quite beyond my mark."

She turned the small oval plate over in her lap, with its face down, and I heard her catch her breath as after a strain or an escape. This however did not prevent her saying in a moment: "You'd buy a likeness of a person you don't know by an artist who has no reputation?"

"The artist may have no reputation, but that thing's wonderfully well painted," I replied, to give myself a reason.

"It's lucky you thought of saying that, because the painter was my father."

"That makes the picture indeed precious!" I returned with gaiety; and I may add that a part of my cheer came from this proof I had been right in my theory of Miss Bordereau's origin. Aspern had of course met the young lady on his going to her father's studio as a sitter. I observed to Miss Bordereau that if she would entrust me with her property for twenty-four hours I should be happy to take advice on it; but she made no other reply than to slip it in silence into her pocket. This convinced me still more that she had no sincere intention of selling it during her lifetime, though she may have desired to satisfy herself as to the sum her niece, should she leave it to her, might expect eventually to obtain for it. "Well, at any rate, I hope you won't offer it without giving me notice," I said as she remained irresponsive. "Remember me as a possible purchaser."

"I should want your money first!" she returned with unexpected rudeness; and then, as if she bethought herself that I might well complain of such a tone and wished to turn the matter off, asked abruptly what I talked about with her niece when I went out with her that way of an evening.

"You speak as if we had set up the habit," I replied. "Certainly I should be very glad if it were to become our pleasant custom. But in that case I should feel a still greater scruple at betraying a lady's confidence."

"Her confidence? Has my niece confidence?"

"Here she is — she can tell you herself," I said; for Miss Tina now appeared on the threshold of the old woman's parlour. "Have you confidence, Miss Tina? Your aunt wants very much to know."

"Not in her, not in her!" the younger lady declared, shaking her head with a dolefulness that was neither jocular nor affected. "I don't know what to do with her; she has fits of horrid imprudence. She's so easily tired — and yet she has begun to roam, to drag herself about the house." And she looked down at her yoke-fellow of long years with a vacancy of wonder, as if all their contact and custom had n't made her perversities, on occasion, any more easy to follow.

"I know what I'm about. I'm not losing my mind. I dare say you'd like to think so," said Miss Bordereau with a crudity of cynicism.

"I don't suppose you came out here yourself. Miss Tina must have had to lend you a hand," I interposed for conciliation.

"Oh she insisted we should push her; and when she insists!" said Miss Tina, in the same tone of apprehension: as if there were no knowing what service she disapproved of her aunt might force her next to render.

"I've always got most things done I wanted, thank God! The people I've lived with have humoured me," the old woman continued, speaking out of the white ashes of her vanity.

I took it pleasantly up. "I suppose you mean they've obeyed you."

"Well, whatever it is — when they like one."

"It's just because I like you that I want to resist," said Miss Tina with a nervous laugh.

"Oh I suspect you'll bring Miss Bordereau upstairs next to pay me a visit," I went on; to which the old lady replied:

"Oh no; I can keep an eye on you from here!"

"You're very tired; you'll certainly be ill tonight!" cried Miss Tina.

"Nonsense, dear; I feel better at this moment than I've done for a month. To-morrow I shall come out again. I want to be where I can see this clever gentleman."

"Should n't you perhaps see me better in your sitting-room?" I asked.

"Don't you mean should n't you have a better chance at *me?*" she returned, fixing me a moment with her green shade.

"Ah I have n't that anywhere! I look at you but don't see you."

"You agitate her dreadfully — and that's not

good," said Miss Tina, giving me a reproachful deterrent headshake.

"I want to watch you — I want to watch you!" Miss Bordereau went on.

"Well then let us spend as much of our time together as possible — I don't care where. That will give you every facility."

"Oh I've seen you enough for to-day. I'm satisfied. Now I'll go home," Juliana said. Miss Tina laid her hands on the back of the wheeled chair and began to push, but I begged her to let me take her place. "Oh yes, you may move me this way — you shan't in any other!" the old woman cried as she felt herself propelled firmly and easily over the smooth hard floor. Before we reached the door of her own apartment she bade me stop, and she took a long last look up and down the noble sala. "Oh it's a prodigious house!" she murmured; after which I pushed her forward. When we had entered the parlour Miss Tina let me know she should now be able to manage, and at the same moment the little red-haired *donna* came to meet her mistress. Miss Tina's idea was evidently to get her aunt immediately back to bed. I confess that in spite of this urgency I was guilty of the indiscretion of lingering; it held me there to feel myself so close to the objects I coveted — which would be probably put away somewhere in the faded unsociable room. The place had indeed a bareness that suggested no hidden values; there were neither dusky nooks nor curtained corners, neither massive cabinets nor chests with iron bands. Moreover it was possible, it was perhaps even likely,

that the old lady had consigned her relics to her bedroom, to some battered box that was shoved under
the bed, to the drawer of some lame dressing-table,
where they would be in the range of vision by the dim
night-lamp. None the less I turned an eye on every
article of furniture, on every conceivable cover for a
hoard, and noticed that there were half a dozen things
with drawers, and in particular a tall old secretary
with brass ornaments of the style of the Empire — a
receptacle somewhat infirm but still capable of keeping rare secrets. I don't know why this article so
engaged me, small purpose as I had of breaking into
it; but I stared at it so hard that Miss Tina noticed
me and changed colour. Her doing this made me
think I was right and that, wherever they might have
been before, the Aspern papers at that moment lan-
guished behind the peevish little lock of the secretary.
It was hard to turn my attention from the dull mahogany front when I reflected that a plain panel
divided me from the goal of my hopes; but I gathered
up my slightly scattered prudence and with an effort
took leave of my hostess. To make the effort graceful
I said to her that I should certainly bring her an
opinion about the little picture.

"The little picture?" Miss Tina asked in surprise.

"What do *you* know about it, my dear?" the old
woman demanded. "You need n't mind. I've fixed
my price."

"And what may that be "

"A thousand pounds."

"Oh Lord!" cried poor Miss Tina irrepressibly.

"Is that what she talks to you about?" said Miss Bordereau.

"Imagine your aunt's wanting to know!" I had to separate from my younger friend with only those words, though I should have liked immensely to add: "For heaven's sake meet me to-night in the garden!"

VIII

As it turned out the precaution had not been needed,
for three hours later, just as I had finished my dinner,
Miss Tina appeared, unannounced, in the open
doorway of the room in which my simple repasts
were served. I remember well that I felt no surprise at seeing her; which is not a proof of my not
believing in her timidity. It was immense, but in
a case in which there was a particular reason for
boldness it never would have prevented her from
running up to my floor. I saw that she was now
quite full of a particular reason; it threw her forward
— made her seize me, as I rose to meet her, by the
arm.

"My aunt's very ill; I think she's dying!"

"Never in the world," I answered bitterly. "Don't
you be afraid!"

"Do go for a doctor — do, do! Olimpia's gone
for the one we always have, but she does n't come
back; I don't know what has happened to her. I
told her that if he was n't at home she was to follow
him where he had gone; but apparently she's following him all over Venice. I don't know what to do —
she looks so as if she were sinking."

"May I see her, may I judge?" I asked. "Of
course I shall be delighted to bring some one; but
had n't we better send my man instead, so that I may
stay with you?"

Miss Tina assented to this and I dispatched my
servant for the best doctor in the neighbourhood. I
hurried downstairs with her, and on the way she told
me that an hour after I quitted them in the afternoon
Miss Bordereau had had an attack of "oppression,"
a terrible difficulty in breathing. This had subsided,
but had left her so exhausted that she did n't come
up; she seemed all spent and gone. I repeated that she
was n't gone, that she would n't go yet; whereupon
Miss Tina gave me a sharper sidelong glance than she
had ever favoured me withal and said: "Really, what
do you mean? I suppose you don't accuse her of
making-believe!" I forget what reply I made to this,
but I fear that in my heart I thought the old woman
capable of any weird manœuvre. Miss Tina wanted
to know what I had done to her; her aunt had told
her I had made her so angry. I declared I had done
nothing whatever — I had been exceedingly careful;
to which my companion rejoined that our friend had
assured her she had had a scene with me — a scene
that had upset her. I answered with some resentment
that the scene had been of *her* making — that I
could n't think what she was angry with me for unless
for not seeing my way to give a thousand pounds for
the portrait of Jeffrey Aspern. "And did she show
you that? Oh gracious — oh deary me!" groaned
Miss Tina, who seemed to feel the situation pass out
of her control and the elements of her fate thicken
round her. I answered her I 'd give anything to possess it, yet that I had no thousand pounds; but I
stopped when we came to the door of Miss Bordereau's
room. I had an immense curiosity to pass it, but I

thought it my duty to represent to Miss Tina that if I made the invalid angry she ought perhaps to be spared the sight of me. "The sight of you? Do you think she can *see*?" my companion demanded almost with indignation. I did think so but forbore to say it, and I softly followed my conductress.

I remember that what I said to her as I stood for a moment beside the old woman's bed was: "Does she never show you her eyes then? Have you never seen them?" Miss Bordereau had been divested of her green shade, but — it was not my fortune to behold Juliana in her nightcap — the upper half of her face was covered by the fall of a piece of dingy lacelike muslin, a sort of extemporised hood which, wound round her head, descended to the end of her nose, leaving nothing visible but her white withered cheeks and puckered mouth, closed tightly and, as it were, consciously. Miss Tina gave me a glance of surprise, evidently not seeing a reason for my impatience. "You mean she always wears something? She does it to preserve them."

"Because they're so fine?"

"Oh to-day, to-day!" And Miss Tina shook her head speaking very low. "But they used to be magnificent!"

"Yes indeed, — we 've Aspern's word for that." And as I looked again at the old woman's wrappings I could imagine her not having wished to allow any supposition that the great poet had overdone it. But I did n't waste my time in considering Juliana, in whom the appearance of respiration was so slight as to suggest that no human attention could ever help her more. I turned my eyes once more all over the room, rummaging with them the closets, the chests of drawers, the tables. Miss Tina at once noted their direction and read, I think, what was in them; but she did n't answer it, turning away restlessly, anxiously, so that I felt rebuked, with reason, for an appetite well-nigh indecent in the presence of our dying companion. All the same I took another view, endeavouring to pick out mentally the receptacle to try first, for a person who should wish to put his hand on Miss Bordereau's papers directly after her death. The place was a dire confusion; it looked like the dressing-room of an old actress. There were clothes hanging over chairs, odd-looking shabby bundles here and there, and various pasteboard boxes piled together, battered, bulging and discoloured, which might have been fifty years old. Miss Tina after a moment noticed the direction of my eyes again, and, as if she guessed how I judged such appearances — forgetting I had no business to judge them at all — said, perhaps to defend herself from the imputation of complicity in the disorder:

"She likes it this way; we can't move things. There are old bandboxes she has had most of her life." Then she added, half-taking pity on my real thought: "Those things were *there*." And she pointed to a small low trunk which stood under a sofa that just allowed room for it. It struck me as a queer superannuated coffer, of painted wood, with elaborate handles and shrivelled straps and with the colour — it had last been endued with a coat of light green — much rubbed off. It evidently had travelled with

Juliana in the olden time — in the days of her adventures, which it had shared. It would have made a strange figure arriving at a modern hotel.

"*Were* there — they are n't now ?" I asked, startled by Miss Tina's implication.

She was going to answer, but at that moment the doctor came in — the doctor whom the little maid had been sent to fetch and whom she had at last overtaken. My servant, going on his own errand, had met her with her companion in tow, and in the sociable Venetian spirit, retracing his steps with them, had also come up to the threshold of the padrona's room, where I saw him peep over the doctor's shoulder. I motioned him away the more instantly that the sight of his prying face reminded me how little I myself had to do there — an admonition confirmed by the sharp way the little doctor eyed me, his air of taking me for a rival who had the field before him. He was a short fat brisk gentleman who wore the tall hat of his profession and seemed to look at everything but his patient. He kept me still in range, as if it struck him I too should be better for a dose, so that I bowed to him and left him with the women, going down to smoke a cigar in the garden. I was nervous; I could n't go further; I could n't leave the place. I don't know exactly what I thought might happen, but I felt it important to be there. I wandered about the alleys — the warm night had come on — smoking cigar after cigar and studying the light in Miss Bordereau's windows. They were open now, I could see; the situation was different. Sometimes the light moved, but not quickly; it did n't suggest the hurry of a crisis. Was

the old woman dying or was she already dead? Had
the doctor said that there was nothing to be done at
her tremendous age but to let her quietly pass away?
or had he simply announced with a look a little more
conventional that the end of the end had come? Were
the other two women just going and coming over the
offices that follow in such a case? It made me uneasy
not to be nearer, as if I thought the doctor himself
might carry away the papers with him. I bit my cigar
hard while it assailed me again that perhaps there
were now no papers to carry!

I wandered about an hour and more. I looked out
for Miss Tina at one of the windows, having a vague
idea that she might come there to give me some sign.
Would n't she see the red tip of my cigar in the dark
and feel sure I was hanging on to know what the
doctor had said? I'm afraid it's a proof of the grossness of my anxieties that I should have taken in some
degree for granted at such an hour, in the midst of the
greatest change that could fall on her, poor Miss
Tina's having also a free mind for them. My servant
came down and spoke to me; he knew nothing save
that the doctor had gone after a visit of half an hour.
If he had stayed half an hour then Miss Bordereau
was still alive: it could n't have taken so long to at-
test her decease. I sent the man out of the house;
there were moments when the sense of his curiosity
annoyed me, and this was one of them. *He* had been
watching my cigar-tip from an upper window, if Miss
Tina had n't; he could n't know what I was after and
I could n't tell him, though I suspected in him fantastic private theories about me which he thought fine

and which, had I more exactly known them, I should have thought offensive.

I went upstairs at last, but I mounted no higher than the sala. The door of Miss Bordereau's apartment was open, showing from the parlour the dimness of a poor candle. I went toward it with a light tread, and at the same moment Miss Tina appeared and stood looking at me as I approached. "She's better, she's better," she said even before I had asked. "The doctor has given her something; she woke up, came back to life while he was there. He says there's no immediate danger."

"No immediate danger? Surely he thinks her condition serious."

"Yes, because she had been excited. That affects her dreadfully."

"It will do so again then, because she works herself up. She did so this afternoon."

"Yes, she must n't come out any more," said Miss Tina with one of her lapses into a deeper detachment.

"What's the use of making such a remark as that," I permitted myself to ask, "if you begin to rattle her about again the first time she bids you?"

"I won't — I won't do it any more."

"You must learn to resist her," I went on.

"Oh yes, I shall; I shall do so better if you tell me it's right."

"You must n't do it for me — you must do it for yourself. It all comes back to you, if you're scared and upset."

"Well, I'm not upset now," said Miss Tina placidly enough. "She's very quiet."

"Is she conscious again — does she speak?"

"No, she does n't speak, but she takes my hand. She holds it fast."

"Yes," I returned, "I can see what force she still has by the way she grabbed that picture this afternoon. But if she holds you fast how comes it that you 're here?"

Miss Tina waited a little; though her face was in deep shadow — she had her back to the light in the parlour and I had put down my own candle far off, near the door of the sala — I thought I saw her smile ingenuously. "I came on purpose — I had heard your step."

"Why I came on tiptoe, as soundlessly as possible."

"Well, I had heard you," said Miss Tina.

"And is your aunt alone now?"

"Oh no — Olimpia sits there."

On my side I debated. "Shall we then pass in there?" And I nodded at the parlour; I wanted more and more to be on the spot.

"We can't talk there — she 'll hear us."

I was on the point of replying that in that case we 'd sit silent, but I felt too much this would n't do, there was something I desired so immensely to ask her. Thus I hinted we might walk a little in the sala, keeping more at the other end, where we should n't disturb our friend. Miss Tina assented unconditionally; the doctor was coming again, she said, and she would be there to meet him at the door. We strolled through the fine superfluous hall, where on the marble floor — particularly as at first we said nothing — our footsteps were more audible than I

had expected. When we reached the other end —
the wide window, inveterately closed, connecting
with the balcony that overhung the canal — I submitted that we had best remain there, as she would
see the doctor arrive the sooner. I opened the window
and we passed out on the balcony. The air of the
canal seemed even heavier, hotter than that of the
sala. The place was hushed and void; the quiet
neighbourhood had gone to sleep. A lamp, here and
there, over the narrow black water, glimmered in
double; the voice of a man going homeward singing,
his jacket on his shoulder and his hat on his ear,
came to us from a distance. This did n't prevent the
scene from being very *comme il faut,* as Miss Bordereau had called it the first time I saw her. Presently a gondola passed along the canal with its slow
rhythmical plash, and as we listened we watched it
in silence. It did n't stop, it did n't carry the doctor;
and after it had gone on I said to Miss Tina:

"And where are they now — the things that were
in the trunk?"

"In the trunk?"

"That green box you pointed out to me in her
room. You said her papers had been there; you
seemed to mean she had transferred them."

"Oh yes; they 're not in the trunk," said Miss
Tina.

"May I ask if you 've looked?"

"Yes, I 've looked — for you."

"How for me, dear Miss Tina? Do you mean
you 'd have given them to me if you had found them?"
— and I fairly trembled with the question.

She delayed to reply and I waited. Suddenly she broke out: "I don't know what I'd do — what I would n't!"

"Would you look again — somewhere else ?"

She had spoken with a strange unexpected emotion, and she went on in the same tone: "I can't — I can't — while she lies there. It is n't decent."

"No, it is n't decent," I replied gravely. "Let the poor lady rest in peace." And the words, on my lips, were not hypocritical, for I felt reprimanded and shamed.

Miss Tina added in a moment, as if she had guessed this and were sorry for me, but at the same time wished to explain that I did push her, or at least harp on the chord, too much: "I can't deceive her that way. I can't deceive her — perhaps on her deathbed."

"Heaven forbid I should ask you, though I've been guilty myself!"

"You've been guilty ?"

"I've sailed under false colours." I felt now I must make a clean breast of it, must tell her I had given her an invented name on account of my fear her aunt would have heard of me and so refuse to take me in. I explained this as well as that I had really been a party to the letter addressed them by John Cumnor months before.

She listened with great attention, almost in fact gaping for wonder, and when I had made my confession she said: "Then your real name — what is it ?" She repeated it over twice when I had told her, accompanying it with the exclamation "Gracious,

gracious!" Then she added: "I like your own best."

"So do I" — and I felt my laugh rueful. "Ouf! it's a relief to get rid of the other."

"So it was a regular plot — a kind of conspiracy?"

"Oh a conspiracy — we were only two," I replied, leaving out of course Mrs. Prest.

She considered; I thought she was perhaps going to pronounce us very base. But this was not her way, and she remarked after a moment, as in candid impartial contemplation: "How much you must want them!"

"Oh I do, passionately!" I grinned, I fear, to admit. And this chance made me go on, forgetting my compunction of a moment before. "How can she possibly have changed their place herself? How can she walk? How can she arrive at that sort of muscular exertion? How can she lift and carry things?"

"Oh when one wants and when one has so much will!" said Miss Tina as if she had thought over my question already herself and had simply had no choice but that answer — the idea that in the dead of night, or at some moment when the coast was clear, the old woman had been capable of a miraculous effort.

"Have you questioned Olimpia? Has n't she helped her — has n't she done it for her?" I asked; to which my friend replied promptly and positively that their servant had had nothing to do with the matter, though without admitting definitely that she had spoken to her. It was as if she were a little shy, a little ashamed now, of letting me see how much she had entered into my uneasiness and had me on her mind. Suddenly she said to me without any immediate relevance:

"I rather feel you a new person, you know, now that you've a new name."

"It isn't a new one; it's a very good old one, thank fortune!"

She looked at me a moment. "Well, I do like it better."

"Oh if you did n't I would almost go on with the other!"

"Would you really?"

I laughed again, but I returned for all answer: "Of course if she can rummage about that way she can perfectly have burnt them."

"You must wait — you must wait," Miss Tina mournfully moralised; and her tone ministered little to my patience, for it seemed after all to accept that wretched possibility. I would teach myself to wait, I declared nevertheless; because in the first place I could n't do otherwise and in the second I had her promise, given me the other night, that she would help me.

"Of course if the papers are gone that's no use," she said; not as if she wished to recede, but only to be conscientious.

"Naturally. But if you could only find out!" I groaned, quivering again.

"I thought you promised you'd wait."

"Oh you mean wait even for that?"

"For what then?"

113

"Ah nothing," I answered rather foolishly, being ashamed to tell her what had been implied in my acceptance of delay — the idea that she would perhaps do more for me than merely find out.

I know not if she guessed this; at all events she seemed to bethink herself of some propriety of showing me more rigour. "I did n't promise to deceive, did I? I don't think I did."

"It does n't much matter whether you did or not, for you could n't!"

Nothing is more possible than that she would n't have contested this even had n't she been diverted by our seeing the doctor's gondola shoot into the little canal and approach the house. I noted that he came as fast as if he believed our proprietress still in danger. We looked down at him while he disembarked and then went back into the sala to meet him. When he came up, however, I naturally left Miss Tina to go off with him alone, only asking her leave to come back later for news.

I went out of the house and walked far, as far as the Piazza, where my restlessness declined to quit me. I was unable to sit down; it was very late now though there were people still at the little tables in front of the cafés: I could but uneasily revolve, and I did so half a dozen times. The only comfort, none the less, was in my having told Miss Tina who I really was. At last I took my way home again, getting gradually and all but inextricably lost, as I did whenever I went out in Venice: so that it was considerably past midnight when I reached my door. The sala, upstairs, was as dark as usual and my lamp as I

crossed it found nothing satisfactory to show me. I
was disappointed, for I had notified Miss Tina that
I would come back for a report, and I thought she
might have left a light there as a sign. The door of
the ladies' apartment was closed; which seemed a
hint that my faltering friend had gone to bed in impatience of waiting for me. I stood in the middle of
the place, considering, hoping she would hear me and
perhaps peep out, saying to myself too that she would
never go to bed with her aunt in a state so critical;
she would sit up and watch — she would be in a chair,
in her dressing-gown. I went nearer the door; I
stopped there and listened. I heard nothing at all
and at last I tapped gently. No answer came and
after another minute I turned the handle. There
was no light in the room; this ought to have prevented my entrance, but it had no such effect. If I
have frankly stated the importunities, the indelica-
cies, of which my desire to possess myself of Jeffrey
Aspern's papers had made me capable I need n't
shrink, it seems to me, from confessing this last indiscretion. I regard it as the worst thing I did, yet
there were extenuating circumstances. I was deeply
though doubtless not disinterestedly anxious for
more news of Juliana, and Miss Tina had accepted
from me, as it were, a rendezvous which it might
have been a point of honour with me to keep. It may
be objected that her leaving the place dark was a
positive sign that she released me, and to this I can
only reply that I wished not to be released.

The door of Miss Bordereau's room was open and
I could see beyond it the faintness of a taper. There

was no sound — my footstep caused no one to stir.
I came further into the room; I lingered there lamp
in hand. I wanted to give Miss Tina a chance to come
to me if, as I could n't doubt, she were still with her
aunt. I made no noise to call her; I only waited to
see if she would n't notice my light. She did n't, and
I explained this — I found afterwārds I was right —
by the idea that she had fallen asleep. If she had
fallen asleep her aunt was not on her mind, and my
explanation ought to have led me to go out as I had
come. I must repeat again that it did n't, for I found
myself at the same moment given up to something
else. I had no definite purpose, no bad intention,
but felt myself held to the spot by an acute, though
absurd, sense of opportunity. Opportunity for what
I could n't have said, inasmuch as it was n't in my
mind that I might proceed to thievery. Even had
this tempted me I was confronted with the evident
fact that Miss Bordereau did n't leave her secretary,
her cupboard and the drawers of her tables gaping.
I had no keys, no tools and no ambition to smash her
furniture. None the less it came to me that I was
now, perhaps alone, unmolested, at the hour of freedom and safety, nearer to the source of my hopes
than I had ever been. I held up my lamp, let the
light play on the different objects as if it could tell
me something. Still there came no movement from
the other room. If Miss Tina was sleeping she was
sleeping sound. Was she doing so — generous creature — on purpose to leave me the field? Did she
know I was there and was she just keeping quiet to
see what I would do — what I *could* do? Yet might

I, when it came to that? She herself knew even better than I how little.

I stopped in front of the secretary, gaping at it vainly and no doubt grotesquely; for what had it to say to me after all? In the first place it was locked, and in the second it almost surely contained nothing in which I was interested. Ten to one the papers had been destroyed, and even if they had n't the keen old woman would n't have put them in such a place as that after removing them from the green trunk — would n't have transferred them, with the idea of their safety on her brain, from the better hiding-place to the worse. The secretary was more conspicuous, more exposed in a room in which she could no longer mount guard. It opened with a key, but there was a small brass handle, like a button, as well: I saw this as I played my lamp over it. I did something more, for the climax of my crisis; I caught a glimpse of the possibility that Miss Tina wished me really to understand. If she did n't so wish me, if she wished me to keep away, why had n't she locked the door of communication between the sitting-room and the sala? That would have been a definite sign that I was to leave them alone. If I did n't leave them alone she meant me to come for a purpose — a purpose now represented by the super-subtle inference that to oblige me she had unlocked the secretary. She had n't left the key, but the lid would probably move if I touched the button. This possibility pressed me hard and I bent very close to judge. I did n't propose to do anything, not even — not in the least — to let down the lid; I only wanted to test my theory, to see if the cover *would* move. I touched the button with my hand — a mere touch would tell me; and as I did so — it is embarrassing for me to relate it — I looked over my shoulder. It was a chance, an instinct, for I had really heard nothing. I almost let my luminary drop and certainly I stepped back, straightening myself up at what I saw. Juliana stood there in her night-dress, by the doorway of her room, watching me; her hands were raised, she had lifted the everlasting curtain that covered half her face, and for the first, the last, the only time I beheld her extraordinary eyes. They glared at me; they were like the sudden drench, for a caught burglar, of a flood of gaslight; they made me horribly ashamed. I never shall forget her strange little bent white tottering figure, with its lifted head, her attitude, her expression; neither shall I forget the tone in which as I turned, looking at her, she hissed out passionately, furiously:

"Ah you publishing scoundrel!"

I can't now say what I stammered to excuse myself, to explain; but I went toward her to tell her I meant no harm. She waved me off with her old hands, retreating before me in horror; and the next thing I knew she had fallen back with a quick spasm, as if death had descended on her, into Miss Tina's arms.

IX

I LEFT Venice the next morning, directly on learning
that my hostess had not succumbed, as I feared at
the moment, to the shock I had given her — the
shock I may also say she had given me. How in the
world could I have supposed her capable of getting
out of bed by herself? I failed to see Miss Tina before going; I only saw the *donna*, whom I entrusted
with a note for her younger mistress. In this note I
mentioned that I should be absent but a few days.
I went to Treviso, to Bassano, to Castelfranco; I
took walks and drives and looked at musty old
churches with ill-lighted pictures; I spent hours
seated smoking at the doors of cafés, where there were
flies and yellow curtains, on the shady side of sleepy
little squares. In spite of these pastimes, which were
mechanical and perfunctory, I scantly enjoyed my
travels: I had had to gulp down a bitter draught and
could n't get rid of the taste. It had been devilish
awkward, as the young men say, to be found by
Juliana in the dead of night examining the attach-
ment of her bureau; and it had not been less so to
have to believe for a good many hours after that it
was highly probable I had killed her. My humilia-
tion galled me, but I had to make the best of it,
had, in writing to Miss Tina, to minimise it, as well
as account for the posture in which I had been
discovered. As she gave me no word of answer I

could n't know what impression I made on her. It
rankled for me that I had been called a publishing
scoundrel, since certainly I did publish and no less
certainly had n't been very delicate. There was a
moment when I stood convinced that the only way
to purge my dishonour was to take myself straight
away on the instant; to sacrifice my hopes and relieve
the two poor women for ever of the oppression of my
intercourse. Then I reflected that I had better try
a short absence first, for I must already have had a
sense (unexpressed and dim) that in disappearing
completely it would n't be merely my own hopes I
should condemn to extinction. It would perhaps
answer if I kept dark long enough to give the elder
lady time to believe herself rid of me. That she would
wish to be rid of me after this — if I was n't rid of
her — was now not to be doubted: that midnight
monstrosity would have cured her of the disposition
to put up with my company for the sake of my dollars. I said to myself that after all I could n't abandon
Miss Tina, and I continued to say this even while I
noted that she quite ignored my earnest request —
I had given her two or three addresses, at little towns,
poste restante — for some sign of her actual state.
I would have made my servant write me news but
that he was unable to manage a pen. Could n't I
measure the scorn of Miss Tina's silence — little
disdainful as she had ever been? Really the soreness
pressed; yet if I had scruples about going back I had
others about not doing so, and I wanted to put myself on a better footing. The end of it was that I did
return to Venice on the twelfth day; and as my gon-

dola gently bumped against our palace steps a fine palpitation of suspense showed me the violence my absence had done me.

I had faced about so abruptly that I had n't even telegraphed to my servant. He was therefore not at the station to meet me, but he poked out his head from an upper window when I reached the house. "They have put her into earth, *quella vecchia*," he said to me in the lower hall while he shouldered my valise; and he grinned and almost winked as if he knew I should be pleased with his news.

"She's dead!" I cried, giving him a very different look.

"So it appears, since they've buried her."

"It's all over then? When was the funeral?"

"The other yesterday. But a funeral you could scarcely call it, signore: *roba da niente — un piccolo passeggio brutto* of two gondolas. Poveretta!" the man continued, referring apparently to Miss Tina. His conception of funerals was that they were mainly to amuse the living.

I wanted to know about Miss Tina, how she might be and generally where; but I asked him no more questions till we had got upstairs. Now that the fact had met me I took a bad view of it, especially of the idea that poor Miss Tina had had to manage by herself after the end. What did she know about arrangements, about the steps to take in such a case? Poveretta indeed! I could only hope the doctor had given her support and that she had n't been neglected by the old friends of whom she had told me, the little band of the faithful whose fidelity consisted in coming to the house once a year. I elicited from my servant that two old ladies and an old gentleman had in fact rallied round Miss Tina and had supported her — they had come for her in a gondola of their own — during the journey to the cemetery, the little red-walled island of tombs which lies to the north of the town and on the way to Murano. It appeared from these signs that the Misses Bordereau were Catholics, a discovery I had never made, as the old woman could n't go to church and her niece, so far as I per-ceived, either did n't, or went only to early mass in the parish before I was stirring. Certainly even the priests respected their seclusion; I had never caught the whisk of the curato's skirt. That evening, an hour later, I sent my servant down with five words on a card to ask if Miss Tina would see me a few moments. She was not in the house, where he had sought her, he told me when he came back, but in the garden walking about to refresh herself and picking the flowers quite as if they belonged to her. He had found her there and she would be happy to see me.

I went down and passed half an hour with poor Miss Tina. She had always had a look of musty mourning, as if she were wearing out old robes of sor-row that would n't come to an end; and in this par-ticular she made no different show. But she clearly had been crying, crying a great deal — simply, satis-fyingly, refreshingly, with a primitive retarded sense of solitude and violence. But she had none of the airs or graces of grief, and I was almost surprised to see her stand there in the first dusk with her hands full of admirable roses and smile at me with reddened eyes.

Her white face, in the frame of her mantilla, looked longer, leaner than usual. I had n't doubted her being irreconcileably disgusted with me, her considering I ought to have been on the spot to advise her, to help her; and, though I believed there was no rancour in her composition and no great conviction of the importance of her affairs, I had prepared myself for a change in her manner, for some air of injury and estrangement, which should say to my conscience: "Well, you 're a nice person to have professed things!" But historic truth compels me to declare that this poor lady's dull face ceased to be dull, almost ceased to be plain, as she turned it gladly to her late aunt's lodger. That touched him extremely and he thought it simplified his situation until he found it did n't. I was as kind to her that evening as I knew how to be, and I walked about the garden with her as long as seemed good. There was no explanation of any sort between us; I did n't ask her why she had n't answered my letter. Still less did I repeat what I had said to her in that communication; if she chose to let me suppose she had forgotten the position in which Miss Bordereau had surprised me and the effect of the discovery on the old woman, I was quite willing to take it that way: I was grateful to her for not treating me as if I had killed her aunt.

We strolled and strolled, though really not much passed between us save the recognition of her bereavement, conveyed in my manner and in the expression she had of depending on me now, since I let her see I still took an interest in her. Miss Tina's was no breast for the pride or the pretence of independence;

she did n't in the least suggest that she knew at present what would become of her. I forbore to press on
that question, however, for I certainly was not prepared to say that I would take charge of her. I was
cautious; not ignobly, I think, for I felt her knowledge
of life to be so small that in her unsophisticated vision
there would be no reason why — since I seemed to
pity her — I should n't somehow look after her. She
told me how her aunt had died, very peacefully at the
last, and how everything had been done afterwards by
the care of her good friends — fortunately, thanks to
me, she said, smiling, there was money in the house.
She repeated that when once the "nice" Italians
like you they are your friends for life, and when we
had gone into this she asked me about my *giro*, my
impressions, my adventures, the places I had seen. I
told her what I could, making it up partly, I'm
afraid, as in my disconcerted state I had taken little
in; and after she had heard me she exclaimed, quite
as if she had forgotten her aunt and her sorrow,
"Dear, dear, how much I should like to do such
things — to take an amusing little journey!" It came
over me for the moment that I ought to propose some
enterprise, say I would accompany her anywhere she
liked; and I remarked at any rate that a pleasant excursion — to give her a change — might be managed:
we would think of it, talk it over. I spoke never a
word of the Aspern documents, asked no question as
to what she had ascertained or what had otherwise
happened with regard to them before Juliana's death.
It was n't that I was n't on pins and needles to know,
but that I thought it more decent not to show greed

again so soon after the catastrophe. I hoped she herself would say something, but she never glanced that
way, and I thought this natural at the time. Later on,
however, that night, it occurred to me that her silence
was matter for suspicion; since if she had talked of my
movements, of anything so detached as the Giorgione
at Castelfranco, she might have alluded to what she
could easily remember was in my mind. It was not to
be supposed the emotion produced by her aunt's
death had blotted out the recollection that I was interested in that lady's relics, and I fidgeted afterwards as
it came to me that her reticence might very possibly
just mean that no relics survived. We separated in the
garden — it was she who said she must go in; now that
she was alone on the *piano nobile* I felt that (judged at
any rate by Venetian ideas) I was on rather a different
footing in regard to the invasion of it. As I shook
hands with her for good-night I asked if she had
some general plan, had thought over what she
had best do. "Oh yes, oh yes, but I have n't settled
anything yet," she replied quite cheerfully. Was her
cheerfulness explained by the impression that I would
settle for her?

I was glad the next morning that we had neglected
practical questions, as this gave me a pretext for
seeing her again immediately. There was a practical
enough question now to be touched on. I owed it to
her to let her know formally that of course I did n't
expect her to keep me on as a lodger, as also to show
some interest in her own tenure, what she might have
on her hands in the way of a lease. But I was not
destined, as befell, to converse with her for more than

an instant on either of these points. I sent her no message; I simply went down to the sala and walked to and fro there. I knew she would come out; she would promptly see me accessible. Somehow I preferred not to be shut up with her; gardens and big halls seemed better places to talk. It was a splendid morning, with something in the air that told of the waning of the long Venetian summer; a freshness from the sea that stirred the flowers in the garden and made a pleasant draught in the house, less shuttered and darkened now than when the old woman was alive. It was the beginning of autumn, of the end of the golden months. With this it was the end of my experiment — or would be in the course of half an hour, when I should really have learned that my dream had been reduced to ashes. After that there would be nothing left for me but to go to the station; for seriously — and as it struck me in the morning light — I could n't linger there to act as guardian to a piece of middle-aged female helplessness. If she had n't saved the papers wherein should I be indebted to her? I think I winced a little as I asked myself how much, if she *had* saved them, I should have to recognise and, as it were, reward such a courtesy. Might n't that service after all saddle me with a guardianship? If this idea did n't make me more uncomfortable as I walked up and down it was because I was convinced I had nothing to look to. If the old woman had n't destroyed everything before she pounced on me in the parlour she had done so the next day.

It took Miss Tina rather longer than I had expected to act on my calculation; but when at last she came

out she looked at me without surprise. I mentioned I
had been waiting for her and she asked why I had n't
let her know. I was glad a few hours later on that I
had checked myself before remarking that a friendly
intuition might have told her: it turned to comfort for
me that I had n't played even to that mild extent on
her sensibility. What I did say was virtually the truth
— that I was too nervous, since I expected her now to
settle my fate.

"Your fate?" said Miss Tina, giving me a queer
look; and as she spoke I noticed a rare change in her.
Yes, she was other than she had been the evening
before — less natural and less easy. She had been
crying the day before and was not crying now, yet she
struck me as less confident. It was as if something had
happened to her during the night, or at least as if she
had thought of something that troubled her — something in particular that affected her relations with me,
made them more embarrassing and more complicated. Had she simply begun to feel that her aunt's
not being there now altered my position?

"I mean about our papers. *Are* there any? You
must know now."

"Yes, there are a great many; more than I supposed." I was struck with the way her voice trembled
as she told me this.

"Do you mean you've got them in there — and
that I may see them?"

"I don't think you can see them," said Miss Tina
with an extraordinary expression of entreaty in her
eyes, as if the dearest hope she had in the world now
was that I would n't take them from her. But how

127

could she expect me to make such a sacrifice as that after all that had passed between us? What had I come back to Venice for but to see them, to take them? My joy at learning they were still in existence was such that if the poor woman had gone down on her knees to beseech me never to mention them again I would have treated the proceeding as a bad joke. "I've got them but I can't show them," she lamentably added.

"Not even to me? Ah Miss Tina!" I broke into a tone of infinite remonstrance and reproach.

She coloured and the tears came back to her eyes; I measured the anguish it cost her to take such a stand, which a dreadful sense of duty had imposed on her. It made me quite sick to find myself confronted with that particular obstacle; all the more that it seemed to me I had been distinctly encouraged to leave it out of account. I quite held Miss Tina to have assured me that if she had no greater hindrance than that —! "You don't mean to say you made her a deathbed promise? It was precisely against your doing anything of that sort that I thought I was safe. Oh I would rather she had burnt the papers outright than have to reckon with such a treachery as that."

"No, it isn't a promise," said Miss Tina.

"Pray what is it then?"

She hung fire, but finally said: "She tried to burn them, but I prevented it. She had hid them in her bed."

"In her bed —?"

"Between the mattresses. That's where she put

them when she took them out of the trunk. I can't understand how she did it, because Olimpia did n't help her. She tells me so and I believe her. My aunt only told her afterwards, so that she should n't undo the bed — anything but the sheets. So it was very badly made," added Miss Tina simply.

"I should think so! And how did she try to burn them?"

"She did n't try much; she was too weak those last days. But she told me — she charged me. Oh it was terrible! She could n't speak after that night. She could only make signs."

"And what did you do?"

"I took them away. I locked them up."

"In the secretary?"

"Yes, in the secretary," said Miss Tina, reddening again.

"Did you tell her you 'd burn them?"

"No, I did n't — on purpose."

"On purpose to gratify me?"

"Yes, only for that."

"And what good will you have done me if after all you won't show them?"

"Oh none. I know that — I know that," she dismally sounded.

"And did she believe you had destroyed them?"

"I don't know what she believed at the last. I could n't tell — she was too far gone."

"Then if there was no promise and no assurance I can't see what ties you."

"Oh she hated it so — she hated it so! She was so jealous. But here's the portrait — you may have that," the poor woman announced, taking the little picture, wrapped up in the same manner in which her aunt had wrapped it, out of her pocket.

"I may have it — do you mean you give it to me?" I gasped as it passed into my hand.

"Oh yes."

"But it's worth money — a large sum."

"Well!" said Miss Tina, still with her strange look.

I did n't know what to make of it, for it could scarcely mean that she wanted to bargain like her aunt. She spoke as for making me a present. "I can't take it from you as a gift," I said, "and yet I can't afford to pay you for it according to the idea Miss Bordereau had of its value. She rated it at a thousand pounds."

"Could n't we sell it?" my friend threw off.

"God forbid! I prefer the picture to the money."

"Well then keep it."

"You're very generous."

"So are you."

"I don't know why you should think so," I returned; and this was true enough, for the good creature appeared to have in her mind some rich reference that I did n't in the least seize.

"Well, you've made a great difference for me," she said.

I looked at Jeffrey Aspern's face in the little picture, partly in order not to look at that of my companion, which had begun to trouble me, even to frighten me a little — it had taken so very odd, so strained and unnatural a cast. I made no answer to this last declaration; I but privately consulted Jeffrey

Aspern's delightful eyes with my own — they were so young and brilliant and yet so wise and so deep: I asked him what on earth was the matter with Miss Tina. He seemed to smile at me with mild mockery; he might have been amused at my case. I had got into a pickle for him — as if he needed it! He was unsatisfactory for the only moment since I had known him. Nevertheless, now that I held the little picture in my hand I felt it would be a precious possession. "Is this a bribe to make me give up the papers?" I presently and all perversely asked. "Much as I value this, you know, if I were to be obliged to choose the papers are what I should prefer. Ah but ever so much!"

"How can you choose — how can you choose?" Miss Tina returned slowly and woefully.

"I see! Of course there's nothing to be said if you regard the interdiction that rests on you as quite insurmountable. In this case it must seem to you that to part with them would be an impiety of the worst kind, a simple sacrilege!"

She shook her head, only lost in the queerness of her case. "You'd understand if you had known her. I'm afraid," she quavered suddenly — "I'm afraid! She was terrible when she was angry."

"Yes, I saw something of that, that night. She was terrible. Then I saw her eyes. Lord, they were fine!"

"I see them — they stare at me in the dark!" said Miss Tina.

"You've grown nervous with all you've been through."

"Oh yes, very — very!"

"You must n't mind; that will pass away," I said

kindly. Then I added resignedly, for it really seemed to me that I must accept the situation: "Well, so it is, and it can't be helped. I must renounce." My friend, at this, with her eyes on me, gave a low soft moan, and I went on: "I only wish to goodness she had destroyed them: then there would be nothing more to say. And I can't understand why, with her ideas, she did n't."

"Oh she lived on them!" said Miss Tina.

"You can imagine whether that makes me want less to see them," I returned not quite so desperately. "But don't let me stand here as if I had it in my soul to tempt you to anything base. Naturally, you understand, I give up my rooms. I leave Venice immediately." And I took up my hat, which I had placed on a chair. We were still rather awkwardly on our feet in the middle of the sala. She had left the door of the apartments open behind her, but had not led me that way.

A strange spasm came into her face as she saw me take my hat. "Immediately — do you mean to-day?" The tone of the words was tragic — they were a cry of desolation.

"Oh no; not so long as I can be of the least service to you."

"Well, just a day or two more — just two or three days," she panted. Then controlling herself she added in another manner: "She wanted to say something to me — the last day — something very particular. But she could n't."

"Something very particular?"

"Something more about the papers."

"And did you guess — have you any idea?"

"No, I've tried to think — but I don't know. I've thought all kinds of things."

"As for instance?"

"Well, that if you were a relation it would be different."

I wondered. "If I were a relation —?"

"If you were n't a stranger. Then it would be the same for you as for me. Anything that's mine would be yours, and you could do what you like. I should n't be able to prevent you — and you'd have no responsibility."

She brought out this droll explanation with a nervous rush and as if speaking words got by heart. They gave me the impression of a subtlety which at first I failed to follow. But after a moment her face helped me to see further, and then the queerest of lights came to me. It was embarrassing, and I bent my head over Jeffrey Aspern's portrait. What an odd expression was in his face! "Get out of it as you can, my dear fellow!" I put the picture into the pocket of my coat and said to Miss Tina: "Yes, I'll sell it for you. I shan't get a thousand pounds by any means, but I shall get something good."

She looked at me through pitiful tears, but seemed to try to smile as she returned: "We can divide the money."

"No, no, it shall be all yours." Then I went on: "I think I know what your poor aunt wanted to say. She wanted to give directions that her papers should be buried with her."

Miss Tina appeared to weigh this suggestion; after

which she answered with striking decision, "Oh no, she would n't have thought that safe!"

"It seems to me nothing could be safer."

"She had an idea that when people want to publish they 're capable —!" And she paused, very red.

"Of violating a tomb? Mercy on us, what must she have thought of me!"

"She was n't just, she was n't generous!" my companion cried with sudden passion.

The light that had come into my mind a moment before spread further. "Ah don't say that, for we *are* a dreadful race." Then I pursued: "If she left a will, that may give you some idea."

"I 've found nothing of the sort — she destroyed it. She was very fond of me," Miss Tina added with an effect of extreme inconsequence. "She wanted me to be happy. And if any person should be kind to me — she wanted to speak of that."

I was almost awestricken by the astuteness with which the good lady found herself inspired, transparent astuteness as it was and stitching, as the phrase is, with white thread. "Depend upon it she did n't want to make any provision that would be agreeable to *me*."

"No, not to you, but quite to me. She knew I should like it if you could carry out your idea. Not because she cared for you, but because she did think of me," Miss Tina went on with her unexpected persuasive volubility. "You could see the things — you could use them." She stopped, seeing I grasped the sense of her conditional — stopped long enough for me to give some sign that I did n't give. She must have been conscious, however, that though my face showed the greatest embarrassment ever painted on a human countenance it was not set as a stone, it was also full of compassion. It was a comfort to me a long time afterwards to consider that she could n't have seen in me the smallest symptom of disrespect. "I don't know what to do; I'm too tormented, I'm too ashamed!" she continued with vehemence. Then turning away from me and burying her face in her hands she burst into a flood of tears. If she did n't know what to do it may be imagined whether I knew better. I stood there dumb, watching her while her sobs resounded in the great empty hall. In a moment she was up at me again with her streaming eyes. "I'd give you everything, and she'd understand, where she is — she'd forgive me!"

"Ah Miss Tina — ah Miss Tina," I stammered for all reply. I did n't know what to do, as I say, but at a venture I made a wild vague movement in consequence of which I found myself at the door. I remember standing there and saying "It would n't do, it would n't do!" — saying it pensively, awkwardly, grotesquely, while I looked away to the opposite end of the sala as at something very interesting. The next thing I remember is that I was downstairs and out of the house. My gondola was there and my gondolier, reclining on the cushions, sprang up as soon as he saw me. I jumped in and to his usual "*Dove commanda?*" replied, in a tone that made him stare: "Anywhere, anywhere; out into the lagoon!"

He rowed me away and I sat there prostrate,

groaning softly to myself, my hat pulled over my brow. What in the name of the preposterous did she mean if she did n't mean to offer me her hand? That was the price — that was the price! And did she think I wanted it, poor deluded infatuated extravagant lady? My gondolier, behind me, must have seen my ears red as I wondered, motionless there under the fluttering *tenda* with my hidden face, noticing nothing as we passed — wondered whether her delusion, her infatuation had been my own reckless work. Did she think I had made love to her even to get the papers? I had n't, I had n't; I repeated that over to myself for an hour, for two hours, till I was wearied if not convinced. I don't know where, on the lagoon, my gondolier took me; we floated aimlessly and with slow rare strokes. At last I became conscious that we were near the Lido, far up, on the right hand, as you turn your back to Venice, and I made him put me ashore. I wanted to walk, to move, to shed some of my bewilderment. I crossed the narrow strip and got to the sea-beach — I took my way toward Malamocco. But presently I flung myself down again on the warm sand, in the breeze, on the coarse dry grass. It took it out of me to think I had been so much at fault, that I had unwittingly but none the less deplorably trifled. But I had n't given her cause — distinctly I had n't. I had said to Mrs. Prest that I would make love to her; but it had been a joke without consequences and I had never said it to my victim. I had been as kind as possible because I really liked her; but since when had that become a crime where a woman of such an age and such an appearance was concerned? I am far from remembering clearly the succession of events and feelings during this long day of confusion, which I spent entirely in wandering about, without going home, until late at night: it only comes back to me that there were moments when I pacified my conscience and others when I lashed it into pain. I did n't laugh all day — that I do recollect; the case, however it might have struck others, seemed to me so little amusing. I should have been better employed perhaps in taking in the comic side of it. At any rate, whether I had given cause or not, there was no doubt whatever that I could n't pay the price. I could n't accept the proposal. I could n't, for a bundle of tattered papers, marry a ridiculous pathetic provincial old woman. It was a proof of how little she supposed the idea would come to me that she should have decided to suggest it herself in that practical argumentative heroic way — with the timidity, however, so much more striking than the boldness, that her reasons appeared to come first and her feelings afterward.

As the day went on I grew to wish I had never heard of Aspern's relics, and I cursed the extravagant curiosity that had put John Cumnor on the scent of them. We had more than enough material without them, and my predicament was the just punishment of that most fatal of human follies, our not having known when to stop. It was very well to say it was no predicament, that the way out was simple, that I had only to leave Venice by the first train in the morning, after addressing Miss Tina a

note which should be placed in her hand as soon as
I got clear of the house; for it was strong proof of my
quandary that when I tried to make up the note to
my taste in advance — I would put it on paper as
soon as I got home, before going to bed — I could n't
think of anything but "How can I thank you for
the rare confidence you've placed in me?" That
would never do; it sounded exactly as if an acceptance were to follow. Of course I might get off without writing at all, but that would be brutal, and my
idea was still to exclude brutal solutions. As my
confusion cooled I lost myself in wonder at the importance I had attached to Juliana's crumpled scraps;
the thought of them became odious to me and I was
as vexed with the old witch for the superstition that
had prevented her from destroying them as I was
with myself for having already spent more money
than I could afford in attempting to control their
fate. I forget what I did, where I went after leaving
the Lido and at what hour or with what recovery of
composure I made my way back to my boat. I only
know that in the afternoon, when the air was aglow
with the sunset, I was standing before the church of
Saints John and Paul and looking up at the small
square-jawed face of Bartolommeo Colleoni, the
terrible *condottiere* who sits so sturdily astride of his
huge bronze horse on the high pedestal on which
Venetian gratitude maintains him. The statue is
incomparable, the finest of all mounted figures, unless that of Marcus Aurelius, who rides benignant
before the Roman Capitol, be finer: but I was not
thinking of that; I only found myself staring at the

triumphant captain as if he had had an oracle on his lips. The western light shines into all his grimness at that hour and makes it wonderfully personal. But he continued to look far over my head, at the red immersion of another day — he had seen so many go down into the lagoon through the centuries — and if he were thinking of battles and stratagems they were of a different quality from any I had to tell him of. He could n't direct me what to do, gaze up at him as I might. Was it before this or after that I wandered about for an hour in the small canals, to the continued stupefaction of my gondolier, who had never seen me so restless and yet so void of a purpose and could extract from me no order but "Go any-where — everywhere — all over the place"? He reminded me that I had not lunched and expressed therefore respectfully the hope that I would dine earlier. He had had long periods of leisure during the day, when I had left the boat and rambled, so that I was not obliged to consider him, and I told him that till the morrow, for reasons, I should touch no meat. It was an effect of poor Miss Tina's proposal, not altogether auspicious, that I had quite lost my appetite. I don't know why it happened that on this occasion I was more than ever struck with that queer air of sociability, of cousinship and family life, which makes up half the expression of Venice. Without streets and vehicles, the uproar of wheels, the brutal-ity of horses, and with its little winding ways where people crowd together, where voices sound as in the corridors of a house, where the human step circulates as if it skirted the angles of furniture and shoes never wear out, the place has the character of an immense collective apartment, in which Piazza San Marco is the most ornamented corner and palaces and churches, for the rest, play the part of great divans of repose, tables of entertainment, expanses of decoration. And somehow the splendid common domicile, familiar domestic and resonant, also resembles a theatre with its actors clicking over bridges and, in straggling processions, tripping along fondamentas. As you sit in your gondola the footways that in certain parts edge the canals assume to the eye the importance of a stage, meeting it at the same angle, and the Venetian figures, moving to and fro against the battered scenery of their little houses of comedy, strike you as members of an endless dramatic troupe.

I went to bed that night very tired and without being able to compose an address to Miss Tina. Was this failure the reason why I became conscious the next morning as soon as I awoke of a determination to see the poor lady again the first moment she would receive me? That had something to do with it, but what had still more was the fact that during my sleep the oddest revulsion had taken place in my spirit. I found myself aware of this almost as soon as I opened my eyes: it made me jump out of my bed with the movement of a man who remembers that he has left the house-door ajar or a candle burning under a shelf. Was I still in time to save my goods? That question was in my heart; for what had now come to pass was that in the unconscious cerebration of sleep I had swung back to a passionate appreciation of Juliana's treasure. The pieces composing it were now more precious than ever and a positive ferocity had come into my need to acquire them. The condition Miss Tina had attached to that act no longer appeared an obstacle worth thinking of, and for an hour this morning my repentant imagination brushed it aside. It was absurd I should be able to invent nothing; absurd to renounce so easily and turn away helpless from the idea that the only way to become possessed was to unite myself to her for life. I might n't unite myself, yet I might still have what she had. I must add that by the time I sent down to ask if she would see me I had invented no alternative, though in fact I drew out my dressing in the interest of my wit. This failure was humiliating, yet what could the alternative be? Miss Tina sent back word I might come; and as I descended the stairs and crossed the sala to her door — this time she received me in her aunt's forlorn parlour — I hoped she would n't think my announcement was to be "favourable." She certainly would have understood my recoil of the day before.

As soon as I came into the room I saw that she had done so, but I also saw something which had not been in my forecast. Poor Miss Tina's sense of her failure had produced a rare alteration in her, but I had been too full of stratagems and spoils to think of that. Now I took it in; I can scarcely tell how it startled me. She stood in the middle of the room with a face of mildness bent upon me, and her look of forgiveness, of absolution, made her angelic. It beautified her; she was younger; she was not a ridiculous old woman. This trick of her expression, this magic of her spirit, transfigured her, and while I still noted it I heard a whisper somewhere in the depths of my conscience: "Why not, after all — why not?" It seemed to me I *could* pay the price. Still more distinctly however than the whisper I heard Miss Tina's own voice. I was so struck with the different effect she made on me that at first I was n't clearly aware of what she was saying; then I recognised she had bade me good-bye — she said something about hoping I should be very happy.

"Good-bye — good-bye?" I repeated with an inflexion interrogative and probably foolish.

I saw she did n't feel the interrogation, she only heard the words: she had strung herself up to accepting our separation and they fell upon her ear as a proof. "Are you going to-day?" she asked. "But it does n't matter, for whenever you go I shall not see you again. I don't want to." And she smiled strangely, with an infinite gentleness. She had never doubted my having left her the day before in horror. How *could* she, since I had n't come back before night to contradict, even as a simple form, even as an act of common humanity, such an idea? And now she had the force of soul — Miss Tina with force of soul was a new conception — to smile at me in her abjection.

"What shall you do — where shall you go?" I asked.

"Oh I don't know. I 've done the great thing. I 've destroyed the papers."

"Destroyed them?" I wailed.

"Yes; what was I to keep them for? I burnt them last night, one by one, in the kitchen."

"One by one?" I coldly echoed it.

"It took a long time — there were so many." The room seemed to go round me as she said this and a real darkness for a moment descended on my eyes. When it passed Miss Tina was there still, but the transfiguration was over and she had changed back to a plain dingy elderly person. It was in this character she spoke as she said "I can't stay with you longer, I can't"; and it was in this character she turned her back upon me, as I had turned mine upon her twenty-four hours before, and moved to the door of her room. Here she did what I had n't done when I quitted her — she paused long enough to give me one look. I have never forgotten it and I sometimes still suffer from it, though it was not resentful. No, there was no resentment, nothing hard or vindictive in poor Miss Tina; for when, later, I sent her, as the price of the portrait of Jeffrey Aspern, a larger sum of money than I had hoped to be able to gather for her, writing to her that I had sold the picture, she kept it with thanks; she never sent it back. I wrote her that I had sold the picture, but I admitted to Mrs. Prest at the time — I met this other friend in London that autumn — that it hangs above my writing-table. When I look at it I can scarcely bear my loss — I mean of the precious papers.

THE TURN OF THE SCREW

THE story had held us, round the fire, sufficiently breathless, but except the obvious remark that it was gruesome, as on Christmas Eve in an old house a strange tale should essentially be, I remember no comment uttered till somebody happened to note it as the only case he had met in which such a visitation had fallen on a child. The case, I may mention, was that of an apparition in just such an old house as had gathered us for the occasion — an appearance, of a dreadful kind, to a little boy sleeping in the room with his mother and waking her up in the terror of it; waking her not to dissipate his dread and soothe him to sleep again, but to encounter also herself, before she had succeeded in doing so, the same sight that had shocked him. It was this observation that drew from Douglas — not immediately, but later in the evening — a reply that had the interesting consequence to which I call attention. Some one else told a story not particularly effective, which I saw he was not following. This I took for a sign that he had himself something to produce and that we should only have to wait. We waited in fact till two nights later; but that same evening, before we scattered, he brought out what was in his mind.

"I quite agree — in regard to Griffin's ghost, or whatever it was — that its appearing first to the little boy, at so tender an age, adds a particular touch. But it's not the first occurrence of its charming kind that

147

I know to have been concerned with a child. If the child gives the effect another turn of the screw, what do you say to *two* children —?"

"We say of course," somebody exclaimed, "that two children give two turns! Also that we want to hear about them."

I can see Douglas there before the fire, to which he had got up to present his back, looking down at this converser with his hands in his pockets. "Nobody but me, till now, has ever heard. It's quite too horrible." This was naturally declared by several voices to give the thing the utmost price, and our friend, with quiet art, prepared his triumph by turning his eyes over the rest of us and going on: "It's beyond everything. Nothing at all that I know touches it."

"For sheer terror?" I remember asking.

He seemed to say it was n't so simple as that; to be really at a loss how to qualify it. He passed his hand over his eyes, made a little wincing grimace. "For dreadful — dreadfulness!"

"Oh how delicious!" cried one of the women.

He took no notice of her; he looked at me, but as if, instead of me, he saw what he spoke of. "For general uncanny ugliness and horror and pain."

"Well then," I said, "just sit right down and begin."

He turned round to the fire, gave a kick to a log, watched it an instant. Then as he faced us again: "I can't begin. I shall have to send to town." There was a unanimous groan at this, and much reproach; after which, in his preoccupied way, he explained.

"The story's written. It's in a locked drawer — it has not been out for years. I could write to my man and enclose the key; he could send down the packet as he finds it." It was to me in particular that he appeared to propound this — appeared almost to appeal for aid not to hesitate. He had broken a thickness of ice, the formation of many a winter; had had his reasons for a long silence. The others resented postponement, but it was just his scruples that charmed me. I adjured him to write by the first post and to agree with us for an early hearing; then I asked him if the experience in question had been his own. To this his answer was prompt. "Oh thank God, no!"

"And is the record yours? You took the thing down?"

"Nothing but the impression. I took that *here*" — he tapped his heart. "I've never lost it."

"Then your manuscript — ?"

"Is in old faded ink and in the most beautiful hand." He hung fire again. "A woman's. She has been dead these twenty years. She sent me the pages in question before she died." They were all listening now, and of course there was somebody to be arch, or at any rate to draw the inference. But if he put the inference by without a smile it was also without irritation. "She was a most charming person, but she was ten years older than I. She was my sister's governess," he quietly said. "She was the most agreeable woman I've ever known in her position; she'd have been worthy of any whatever. It was long ago, and this episode was long before. I was at Trinity, and I found her at home on my coming down the second sum-

mer I was much there that year — it was a beautiful
one; and we had, in her off-hours, some strolls and
talks in the garden — talks in which she struck me as
awfully clever and nice. Oh yes; don't grin: I liked
her extremely and am glad to this day to think she
liked me too. If she had n't she would n't have told
me. She had never told any one. It was n't simply
that she said so, but that I knew she had n't. I was
sure; I could see. You 'll easily judge why when you
hear."

"Because the thing had been such a scare ?"

He continued to fix me. "You 'll easily judge," he
repeated: "*you* will."

I fixed him too. "I see. She was in love."

He laughed for the first time. "You *are* acute.
Yes, she was in love. That is she *had* been. That
came out — she could n't tell her story without its
coming out. I saw it, and she saw I saw it; but neither
of us spoke of it. I remember the time and the place
— the corner of the lawn, the shade of the great
beeches and the long hot summer afternoon. It
was n't a scene for a shudder; but oh —!" He quitted
the fire and dropped back into his chair.

"You 'll receive the packet Thursday morning ?"
I said.

"Probably not till the second post."

"Well then; after dinner —"

"You 'll all meet me here ?" He looked us round
again. "Is n't anybody going ?" It was almost the
tone of hope.

"Everybody will stay!"

"*I* will — and *I* will!" cried the ladies whose departure had been fixed. Mrs. Griffin, however, expressed the need for a little more light. "Who was it she was in love with?"

"The story will tell," I took upon myself to reply.

"Oh I can't wait for the story!"

"The story *won't* tell," said Douglas; "not in any literal vulgar way."

"More's the pity then. That's the only way I ever understand."

"Won't *you* tell, Douglas?" somebody else enquired.

He sprang to his feet again. "Yes — to-morrow. Now I must go to bed. Good-night." And, quickly catching up a candlestick, he left us slightly bewildered. From our end of the great brown hall we heard his step on the stair; whereupon Mrs. Griffin spoke. "Well, if I don't know who she was in love with I know who *he* was."

"She was ten years older," said her husband.

"*Raison de plus* — at that age! But it's rather nice, his long reticence."

"Forty years!" Griffin put in.

"With this outbreak at last."

"The outbreak," I returned, "will make a tremendous occasion of Thursday night"; and every one so agreed with me that in the light of it we lost all attention for everything else. The last story, however incomplete and like the mere opening of a serial, had been told; we handshook and "candlestuck," as somebody said, and went to bed.

I knew the next day that a letter containing the key had, by the first post, gone off to his London apart-

ments; but in spite of — or perhaps just on account of
— the eventual diffusion of this knowledge we quite
let him alone till after dinner, till such an hour of the
evening in fact as might best accord with the kind of
emotion on which our hopes were fixed. Then he
became as communicative as we could desire, and
indeed gave us his best reason for being so. We had it
from him again before the fire in the hall, as we had
had our mild wonders of the previous night. It appeared that the narrative he had promised to read us
really required for a proper intelligence a few words of
prologue. Let me say here distinctly, to have done
with it, that this narrative, from an exact transcript of
my own made much later, is what I shall presently
give. Poor Douglas, before his death — when it was
in sight — committed to me the manuscript that
reached him on the third of these days and that, on
the same spot, with immense effect, he began to read
to our hushed little circle on the night of the fourth.
The departing ladies who had said they would stay
did n't, of course, thank heaven, stay: they departed,
in consequence of arrangements made, in a rage of
curiosity, as they professed, produced by the touches
with which he had already worked us up. But that
only made his little final auditory more compact and
select, kept it, round the hearth, subject to a common
thrill.

The first of these touches conveyed that the written
statement took up the tale at a point after it had, in a
manner, begun. The fact to be in possession of was
therefore that his old friend, the youngest of several
daughters of a poor country parson, had at the age of

twenty, on taking service for the first time in the schoolroom, come up to London, in trepidation, to answer in person an advertisement that had already placed her in brief correspondence with the advertiser. This person proved, on her presenting herself for judgement at a house in Harley Street that impressed her as vast and imposing — this prospective patron proved a gentleman, a bachelor in the prime of life, such a figure as had never risen, save in a dream or an old novel, before a fluttered anxious girl out of a Hampshire vicarage. One could easily fix his type; it never, happily, dies out. He was handsome and bold and pleasant, off-hand and gay and kind. He struck her, inevitably, as gallant and splendid, but what took her most of all and gave her the courage she afterwards showed was that he put the whole thing to her as a favour, an obligation he should gratefully incur. She figured him as rich, but as fearfully extravagant — saw him all in a glow of high fashion, of good looks, of expensive habits, of charming ways with women. He had for his town residence a big house filled with the spoils of travel and the trophies of the chase; but it was to his country home, an old family place in Essex, that he wished her immediately to proceed.

He had been left, by the death of his parents in India, guardian to a small nephew and a small niece, children of a younger, a military brother whom he had lost two years before. These children were, by the strangest of chances for a man in his position — a lone man without the right sort of experience or a grain of patience — very heavy on his hands. It had all been a great worry and, on his own part doubtless, a series of blunders, but he immensely pitied the poor chicks and had done all he could; had in particular sent them down to his other house, the proper place for them being of course the country, and kept them there from the first with the best people he could find to look after them, parting even with his own servants to wait on them and going down himself, whenever he might, to see how they were doing. The awkward thing was that they had practically no other relations and that his own affairs took up all his time. He had put them in possession of Bly, which was healthy and secure, and had placed at the head of their little establishment — but belowstairs only — an excellent woman, Mrs. Grose, whom he was sure his visitor would like and who had formerly been maid to his mother. She was now housekeeper and was also acting for the time as superintendent to the little girl, of whom, without children of her own, she was by good luck extremely fond. There were plenty of people to help, but of course the young lady who should go down as governess would be in supreme authority. She would also have, in holidays, to look after the small boy, who had been for a term at school — young as he was to be sent, but what else could be done ? — and who, as the holidays were about to begin, would be back from one day to the other. There had been for the two children at first a young lady whom they had had the misfortune to lose. She had done for them quite beautifully — she was a most respectable person — till her death, the great awkwardness of which had, precisely, left no

THE TURN OF THE SCREW

alternative but the school for little Miles. Mrs. Grose, since then, in the way of manners and things, had done as she could for Flora; and there were, further, a cook, a housemaid, a dairywoman, an old pony, an old groom and an old gardener, all likewise thoroughly respectable.

So far had Douglas presented his picture when some one put a question. "And what did the former governess die of? Of so much respectability?"

Our friend's answer was prompt. "That will come out. I don't anticipate."

"Pardon me — I thought that was just what you *are* doing."

"In her successor's place," I suggested, "I should have wished to learn if the office brought with it —"

"Necessary danger to life?" Douglas completed my thought. "She did wish to learn, and she did learn. You shall hear to-morrow what she learnt. Meanwhile of course the prospect struck her as slightly grim. She was young, untried, nervous: it was a vision of serious duties and little company, of really great loneliness. She hesitated — took a couple of days to consult and consider. But the salary offered much exceeded her modest measure, and on a second interview she faced the music, she engaged." And Douglas, with this, made a pause that, for the benefit of the company, moved me to throw in —

"The moral of which was of course the seduction exercised by the splendid young man. She succumbed to it."

He got up and, as he had done the night before, went to the fire, gave a stir to a log with his foot, then stood a moment with his back to us. "She saw him only twice."

"Yes, but that's just the beauty of her passion."

A little to my surprise, on this, Douglas turned round to me. "It *was* the beauty of it. There were others," he went on, "who had n't succumbed. He told her frankly all his difficulty — that for several applicants the conditions had been prohibitive. They were somehow simply afraid. It sounded dull — it sounded strange; and all the more so because of his main condition."

"Which was — ?"

"That she should never trouble him — but never, never: neither appeal nor complain nor write about anything; only meet all questions herself, receive all moneys from his solicitor, take the whole thing over and let him alone. She promised to do this, and she mentioned to me that when, for a moment, disburdened, delighted, he held her hand, thanking her for the sacrifice, she already felt rewarded."

"But was that all her reward?" one of the ladies asked.

"She never saw him again."

"Oh!" said the lady; which, as our friend immediately again left us, was the only other word of importance contributed to the subject till, the next night, by the corner of the hearth, in the best chair, he opened the faded red cover of a thin old-fashioned gilt-edged album. The whole thing took indeed more nights than one, but on the first occasion the same lady put another question. "What's your title?"

"I have n't one."

"Oh *I* have!" I said. But Douglas, without heeding me, had begun to read with a fine clearness that was like a rendering to the ear of the beauty of his author's hand.

I

I REMEMBER the whole beginning as a succession of flights and drops, a little see-saw of the right throbs and the wrong. After rising, in town, to meet his appeal I had at all events a couple of very bad days — found all my doubts bristle again, felt indeed sure I had made a mistake. In this state of mind I spent the long hours of bumping swinging coach that carried me to the stopping-place at which I was to be met by a vehicle from the house. This convenience, I was told, had been ordered, and I found, toward the close of the June afternoon, a commodious fly in waiting for me. Driving at that hour, on a lovely day, through a country the summer sweetness of which served as a friendly welcome, my fortitude revived and, as we turned into the avenue, took a flight that was probably but a proof of the point to which it had sunk. I suppose I had expected, or had dreaded, something so dreary that what greeted me was a good surprise. I remember as a thoroughly pleasant impression the broad clear front, its open windows and fresh curtains and the pair of maids looking out; I remember the lawn and the bright flowers and the crunch of my wheels on the gravel and the clustered tree-tops over which the rooks circled and cawed in the golden sky. The scene had a greatness that made it a different affair from my own scant home, and there immediately appeared at the door, with a little girl in her hand, a civil person who dropped me as decent a curtsey as if I had been the mistress or a distinguished visitor. I had received in Harley Street a narrower notion of the place, and that, as I recalled it, made me think the proprietor still more of a gentleman, suggested that what I was to enjoy might be a matter beyond his promise.

I had no drop again till the next day, for I was carried triumphantly through the following hours by my introduction to the younger of my pupils. The little girl who accompanied Mrs. Grose affected me on the spot as a creature too charming not to make it a great fortune to have to do with her. She was the most beautiful child I had ever seen, and I afterwards wondered why my employer had n't made more of a point to me of this. I slept little that night — I was too much excited; and this astonished me too, I recollect, remained with me, adding to my sense of the liberality with which I was treated. The large impressive room, one of the best in the house, the great state bed, as I almost felt it, the figured full draperies, the long glasses in which, for the first time, I could see myself from head to foot, all struck me — like the wonderful appeal of my small charge — as so many things thrown in. It was thrown in as well, from the first moment, that I should get on with Mrs. Grose in a relation over which, on my way, in the coach, I fear I had rather brooded. The one appearance indeed that in this early outlook might have made me shrink again was that of her being so inordinately glad to see me. I felt within half an hour

that she was so glad — stout simple plain clean
wholesome woman — as to be positively on her
guard against showing it too much. I wondered even
then a little why she should wish *not* to show it, and
that, with reflexion, with suspicion, might of course
have made me uneasy.

But it was a comfort that there could be no uneasiness in a connexion with anything so beatific as
the radiant image of my little girl, the vision of whose
angelic beauty had probably more than anything
else to do with the restlessness that, before morning,
made me several times rise and wander about my
room to take in the whole picture and prospect; to
watch from my open window the faint summer dawn,
to look at such stretches of the rest of the house as
I could catch, and to listen, while in the fading dusk
the first birds began to twitter, for the possible recurrence of a sound or two, less natural and not without
but within, that I had fancied I heard. There had
been a moment when I believed I recognised, faint
and far, the cry of a child; there had been another
when I found myself just consciously starting as at
the passage, before my door, of a light footstep. But
these fancies were not marked enough not to be
thrown off, and it is only in the light, or the gloom,
I should rather say, of other and subsequent matters
that they now come back to me. To watch, teach,
"form" little Flora would too evidently be the making of a happy and useful life. It had been agreed
between us downstairs that after this first occasion
I should have her as a matter of course at night, her
small white bed being already arranged, to that end,

in my room. What I had undertaken was the whole care of her, and she had remained just this last time with Mrs. Grose only as an effect of our consideration for my inevitable strangeness and her natural timidity. In spite of this timidity — which the child herself, in the oddest way in the world, had been perfectly frank and brave about, allowing it, without a sign of uncomfortable consciousness, with the deep sweet serenity indeed of one of Raphael's holy infants, to be discussed, to be imputed to her and to determine us — I felt quite sure she would presently like me. It was part of what I already liked Mrs. Grose herself for, the pleasure I could see her feel in my admiration and wonder as I sat at supper with four tall candles and with my pupil, in a high chair and a bib, brightly facing me between them over bread and milk. There were naturally things that in Flora's presence could pass between us only as prodigious and gratified looks, obscure and roundabout allusions.

"And the little boy — does he look like her? Is he too so very remarkable?"

One would n't, it was already conveyed between us, too grossly flatter a child. "Oh Miss, *most* remarkable. If you think well of this one!" — and she stood there with a plate in her hand, beaming at our companion, who looked from one of us to the other with placid heavenly eyes that contained nothing to check us.

"Yes; if I do — ?"

"You *will* be carried away by the little gentleman!"

"Well, that, I think, is what I came for — to be carried away. I'm afraid, however," I remember feeling the impulse to add, "I'm rather easily carried away. I was carried away in London!"

I can still see Mrs. Grose's broad face as she took this in. "In Harley Street?"

"In Harley Street."

"Well, Miss, you're not the first — and you won't be the last."

"Oh I've no pretensions," I could laugh, "to being the only one. My other pupil, at any rate, as I understand, comes back to-morrow?"

"Not to-morrow — Friday, Miss. He arrives, as you did, by the coach, under care of the guard, and is to be met by the same carriage."

I forthwith wanted to know if the proper as well as the pleasant and friendly thing would n't therefore be that on the arrival of the public conveyance I should await him with his little sister; a proposition to which Mrs. Grose assented so heartily that I somehow took her manner as a kind of comforting pledge — never falsified, thank heaven! — that we should on every question be quite at one. Oh she was glad I was there!

What I felt the next day was, I suppose, nothing that could be fairly called a reaction from the cheer of my arrival; it was probably at the most only a slight oppression produced by a fuller measure of the scale, as I walked round them, gazed up at them, took them in, of my new circumstances. They had, as it were, an extent and mass for which I had not been prepared and in the presence of which I found myself, freshly, a little scared not less than a little proud. Regular lessons, in this agitation, certainly suffered some wrong; I reflected that my first duty was, by the gentlest arts I could contrive, to win the child into the sense of knowing me. I spent the day with her out of doors; I arranged with her, to her great satisfaction, that it should be she, she only, who might show me the place. She showed it step by step and room by room and secret by secret, with droll delightful childish talk about it and with the result, in half an hour, of our becoming tremendous friends. Young as she was I was struck, throughout our little tour, with her confidence and courage, with the way, in empty chambers and dull corridors, on crooked staircases that made me pause and even on the summit of an old machicolated square tower that made me dizzy, her morning music, her disposition to tell me so many more things than she asked, rang out and led me on. I have not seen Bly since the day I left it, and I dare say that to my present older and more informed eyes it would show a very reduced importance. But as my little conductress, with her hair of gold and her frock of blue, danced before me round corners and pattered down passages, I had the view of a castle of romance inhabited by a rosy sprite, such a place as would somehow, for diversion of the young idea, take all colour out of story-books and fairy-tales. Was n't it just a story-book over which I had fallen a-doze and a-dream? No; it was a big ugly antique but convenient house, embodying a few features of a building still older, half-displaced and half-utilised, in which I had the fancy of our being almost as lost as a handful of passengers in a great drifting ship. Well, I was strangely at the helm!

II

THIS came home to me when, two days later, I drove
over with Flora to meet, as Mrs. Grose said, the little
gentleman; and all the more for an incident that, presenting itself the second evening, had deeply disconcerted me. The first day had been, on the whole, as I
have expressed, reassuring; but I was to see it wind
up to a change of note. The postbag that evening —
it came late — contained a letter for me which, however, in the hand of my employer, I found to be composed but of a few words enclosing another, addressed to himself, with a seal still unbroken. "This,
I recognise, is from the head-master, and the head-
master's an awful bore. Read him, please; deal with
him; but mind you don't report. Not a word. I'm
off!" I broke the seal with a great effort — so great
a one that I was a long time coming to it; took the
unopened missive at last up to my room and only
attacked it just before going to bed. I had better
have let it wait till morning, for it gave me a second
sleepless night. With no counsel to take, the next
day, I was full of distress; and it finally got so the
better of me that I determined to open myself at least
to Mrs. Grose.

"What does it mean? The child's dismissed his
school."

She gave me a look that I remarked at the moment;
then, visibly, with a quick blankness, seemed to try
to take it back. "But are n't they all —?"

"Sent home — yes. But only for the holidays. Miles may never go back at all."

Consciously, under my attention, she reddened. "They won't take him?"

"They absolutely decline."

At this she raised her eyes, which she had turned from me; I saw them fill with good tears. "What has he done?"

I cast about; then I judged best simply to hand her my document — which, however, had the effect of making her, without taking it, simply put her hands behind her. She shook her head sadly. "Such things are not for me, Miss."

My counsellor could n't read! I winced at my mistake, which I attenuated as I could, and opened the letter again to repeat it to her; then, faltering in the act and folding it up once more, I put it back in my pocket. "Is he really *bad?*"

The tears were still in her eyes. "Do the gentlemen say so?"

"They go into no particulars. They simply express their regret that it should be impossible to keep him. That can have but óne meaning." Mrs. Grose listened with dumb emotion; she forbore to ask me what this meaning might be; so that, presently, to put the thing with some coherence and with the mere aid of her presence to my own mind, I went on: "That he's an injury to the others."

At this, with one of the quick turns of simple folk, she suddenly flamed up. "Master Miles! — *him* an injury?"

There was such a flood of good faith in it that,

though I had not yet seen the child, my very fears made me jump to the absurdity of the idea. I found myself, to meet my friend the better, offering it, on the spot, sarcastically. "To his poor little innocent mates!"

"It's too dreadful," cried Mrs. Grose, "to say such cruel things! Why he's scarce ten years old."

"Yes, yes; it would be incredible."

She was evidently grateful for such a profession. "See him, Miss, first. *Then* believe it!" I felt forthwith a new impatience to see him; it was the beginning of a curiosity that, all the next hours, was to deepen almost to pain. Mrs. Grose was aware, I could judge, of what she had produced in me, and she followed it up with assurance. "You might as well believe it of the little lady. Bless her," she added the next moment — "*look* at her!"

I turned and saw that Flora, whom, ten minutes before, I had established in the schoolroom with a sheet of white paper, a pencil and a copy of nice "round O's," now presented herself to view at the open door. She expressed in her little way an extraordinary detachment from disagreeable duties, looking at me, however, with a great childish light that seemed to offer it as a mere result of the affection she had conceived for my person, which had rendered necessary that she should follow me. I needed nothing more than this to feel the full force of Mrs. Grose's comparison, and, catching my pupil in my arms, covered her with kisses in which there was a sob of atonement.

None the less, the rest of the day, I watched for

further occasion to approach my colleague, especially as, toward evening, I began to fancy she rather sought to avoid me. I overtook her, I remember, on the staircase; we went down together and at the bottom I detained her, holding her there with a hand on her arm. "I take what you said to me at noon as a declaration that *you've* never known him to be bad."

She threw back her head; she had clearly by this time, and very honestly, adopted an attitude. "Oh never known him — I don't pretend *that!*"

I was upset again. "Then you *have* known him — ?"

"Yes indeed, Miss, thank God!"

On reflexion I accepted this. "You mean that a boy who never is — ?"

"Is no boy for *me!*"

I held her tighter. "You like them with the spirit to be naughty?" Then, keeping pace with her answer, "So do I!" I eagerly brought out. "But not to the degree to contaminate —"

"To contaminate?" — my big word left her at a loss.

I explained it. "To corrupt."

She stared, taking my meaning in; but it produced in her an odd laugh. "Are you afraid he'll corrupt *you?*" She put the question with such a fine bold humour that with a laugh, a little silly doubtless, to match her own, I gave way for the time to the apprehension of ridicule.

But the next day, as the hour for my drive approached, I cropped up in another place. "What was the lady who was here before?"

"The last governess? She was also young and pretty — almost as young and almost as pretty, Miss, even as you."

"Ah then I hope her youth and her beauty helped her!" I recollect throwing off. "He seems to like us young and pretty!"

"Oh he *did*," Mrs. Grose assented: "it was the way he liked every one!" She had no sooner spoken indeed than she caught herself up. "I mean that's *his* way — the master's."

I was struck. "But of whom did you speak first?"

She looked blank, but she coloured. "Why of *him*."

"Of the master?"

"Of who else?"

There was so obviously no one else that the next moment I had lost my impression of her having accidentally said more than she meant; and I merely asked what I wanted to know. "Did *she* see anything in the boy — ?"

"That wasn't right? She never told me."

I had a scruple, but I overcame it. "Was she careful — particular?"

Mrs. Grose appeared to try to be conscientious. "About some things — yes."

"But not about all?"

Again she considered. "Well, Miss — she's gone. I won't tell tales."

"I quite understand your feeling," I hastened to reply; but I thought it after an instant not opposed to this concession to pursue: "Did she die here?"

"No — she went off."

I don't know what there was in this brevity of Mrs. Grose's that struck me as ambiguous. "Went off to die?" Mrs. Grose looked straight out of the window, but I felt that, hypothetically, I had a right to know what young persons engaged for Bly were expected to do. "She was taken ill, you mean, and went home?"

"She was not taken ill, so far as appeared, in this house. She left it, at the end of the year, to go home, as she said, for a short holiday, to which the time she had put in had certainly given her a right. We had then a young woman — a nursemaid who had stayed on and who was a good girl and clever; and *she* took the children altogether for the interval. But our young lady never came back, and at the very moment I was expecting her I heard from the master that she was dead."

I turned this over. "But of what?"

"He never told me! But please, Miss," said Mrs. Grose, "I must get to my work."

III

HER thus turning her back on me was fortunately not, for my just preoccupations, a snub that could check the growth of our mutual esteem. We met, after I had brought home little Miles, more intimately than ever on the ground of my stupefaction, my general emotion: so monstrous was I then ready to pronounce it that such a child as had now been revealed to me should be under an interdict. I was a little late on the scene of his arrival, and I felt, as he stood wistfully looking out for me before the door of the inn at which the coach had put him down, that I had seen him on the instant, without and within, in the great glow of freshness, the same positive fragrance of purity, in which I had from the first moment seen his little sister. He was incredibly beautiful, and Mrs. Grose had put her finger on it: everything but a sort of passion of tenderness for him was swept away by his presence. What I then and there took him to my heart for was something divine that I have never found to the same degree in any child — his indescribable little air of knowing nothing in the world but love. It would have been impossible to carry a bad name with a greater sweetness of innocence, and by the time I had got back to Bly with him I remained merely bewildered — so far, that is, as I was not outraged — by the sense of the horrible letter locked up in one of the drawers of my room. As soon as I could compass a private word with Mrs. Grose I declared to her that it was grotesque.

She promptly understood me. "You mean the cruel charge — ?"

"It does n't live an instant. My dear woman, *look* at him!"

She smiled at my pretension to have discovered his charm. "I assure you, Miss, I do nothing else! What will you say then ?" she immediately added.

"In answer to the letter?" I had made up my mind. "Nothing at all."

"And to his uncle ?"

I was incisive. "Nothing at all."

"And to the boy himself ?"

I was wonderful. "Nothing at all."

She gave with her apron a great wipe to her mouth. "Then I 'll stand by you. We 'll see it out."

"We 'll see it out!" I ardently echoed, giving her my hand to make it a vow.

She held me there a moment, then whisked up her apron again with her detached hand. "Would you mind, Miss, if I used the freedom —"

"To kiss me ? No!" I took the good creature in my arms and after we had embraced like sisters felt still more fortified and indignant.

This at all events was for the time: a time so full that as I recall the way it went it reminds me of all the art I now need to make it a little distinct. What I look back at with amazement is the situation I accepted. I had undertaken, with my companion, to see it out, and I was under a charm apparently that could smooth away the extent and the far and difficult connexions of such an effort. I was lifted aloft on a great wave of infatuation and pity. I found it simple, in my ignorance, my confusion and perhaps my conceit, to assume that I could deal with a boy whose education for the world was all on the point of beginning. I am unable even to remember at this day what proposal I framed for the end of his holidays and the resumption of his studies. Lessons with me indeed, that charming summer, we all had a theory that he was to have; but I now feel that for weeks the lessons must have been rather my own. I learnt something — at first certainly — that had not been one of the teachings of my small smothered life; learnt to be amused, and even amusing, and not to think for the morrow. It was the first time, in a manner, that I had known space and air and freedom, all the music of summer and all the mystery of nature. And then there was consideration — and consideration was sweet. Oh it was a trap — not designed but deep — to my imagination, to my delicacy, perhaps to my vanity; to whatever in me was most excitable. The best way to picture it all is to say that I was off my guard. They gave me so little trouble — they were of a gentleness so extraordinary. I used to speculate — but even this with a dim disconnectedness — as to how the rough future (for all futures are rough!) would handle them and might bruise them. They had the bloom of health and happiness; and yet, as if I had been in charge of a pair of little grandees, of princes of the blood, for whom everything, to be right, would have to be fenced about and ordered and arranged, the only form that in my fancy the after-years could take for them was that of a romantic, a really royal extension of the garden and the park. It may be of course above all that what suddenly broke into this gives the previous time a charm of stillness — that hush in which something gathers or crouches. The change was actually like the spring of a beast.

In the first weeks the days were long; they often, at their finest, gave me what I used to call my own hour, the hour when, for my pupils, tea-time and bed-time having come and gone, I had before my final retirement a small interval alone. Much as I liked my companions this hour was the thing in the day I liked most; and I liked it best of all when, as the light faded — or rather, I should say, the day lingered and the last calls of the last birds sounded, in a flushed sky, from the old trees — I could take a turn into the grounds and enjoy, almost with a sense of property that amused and flattered me, the beauty and dignity of the place. It was a pleasure at these moments to feel myself tranquil and justified; doubtless perhaps also to reflect that by my discretion, my quiet good sense and general high propriety, I was giving pleasure — if. he ever thought of it! — to the person to whose pressure I had yielded. What I was doing was what he had earnestly hoped and directly asked of me, and that I *could*, after all, do it proved even a greater joy than I had expected. I dare say I fancied myself in short a remarkable young woman and took comfort in the faith that this would more publicly appear. Well, I needed to be remarkable to offer a front to the remarkable things that presently gave their first sign.

It was plump, one afternoon, in the middle of my

very hour: the children were tucked away and I had
come out for my stroll. One of the thoughts that, as I
don't in the least shrink now from noting, used to be
with me in these wanderings was that it would be as
charming as a charming story suddenly to meet some
one. Some one would appear there at the turn of a
path and would stand before me and smile and ap-
prove. I did n't ask more than that — I only asked
that he should *know;* and the only way to be sure he
knew would be to see it, and the kind light of it, in his
handsome face. That was exactly present to me — by
which I mean the face was — when, on the first of
these occasions, at the end of a long June day, I
stopped short on emerging from one of the planta-
tions and coming into view of the house. What
arrested me on the spot — and with a shock much
greater than any vision had allowed for — was the
sense that my imagination had, in a flash, turned real.
He did stand there! — but high up, beyond the lawn
and at the very top of the tower to which, on that first
morning, little Flora had conducted me. This tower
was one of a pair — square incongruous crenellated
structures — that were distinguished, for some reason, though I could see little difference, as the new
and the old. They flanked opposite ends of the house
and were probably architectural absurdities, re-
deemed in a measure indeed by not being wholly dis-
engaged nor of a height too pretentious, dating, in
their gingerbread antiquity, from a romantic revival
that was already a respectable past. I admired them,
had fancies about them, for we could all profit in a
degree, especially when they loomed through the dusk,

by the grandeur of their actual battlements; yet it was not at such an elevation that the figure I had so often invoked seemed most in place.

It produced in me, this figure, in the clear twilight, I remember, two distinct gasps of emotion, which were, sharply, the shock of my first and that of my second surprise. My second was a violent perception of the mistake of my first: the man who met my eyes was not the person I had precipitately supposed. There came to me thus a bewilderment of vision of which, after these years, there is no living view that I can hope to give. An unknown man in a lonely place is a permitted object of fear to a young woman privately bred; and the figure that faced me was — a few more seconds assured me — as little any one else I knew as it was the image that had been in my mind. I had not seen it in Harley Street — I had not seen it anywhere. The place moreover, in the strangest way in the world, had on the instant and by the very fact of its appearance become a solitude. To me at least, making my statement here with a deliberation with which I have never made it, the whole feeling of the moment returns. It was as if, while I took in, what I did take in, all the rest of the scene had been stricken with death. I can hear again, as I write, the intense hush in which the sounds of evening dropped. The rooks stopped cawing in the golden sky and the friendly hour lost for the unspeakable minute all its voice. But there was no other change in nature, unless indeed it were a change that I saw with a stranger sharpness. The gold was still in the sky, the clearness in the air, and the man who looked at me over the battlements was as definite as a picture in a frame. That's how I thought, with extraordinary quickness, of each person he might have been and that he was n't. We were confronted across our distance quite long enough for me to ask myself with intensity who then he was and to feel, as an effect of my inability to say, a wonder that in a few seconds more became intense.

The great question, or one of these, is afterwards, I know, with regard to certain matters, the question of how long they have lasted. Well, this matter of mine, think what you will of it, lasted while I caught at a dozen possibilities, none of which made a difference for the better, that I could see, in there having been in the house — and for how long, above all? — a person of whom I was in ignorance. It lasted while I just bridled a little with the sense of how my office seemed to require that there should be no such ignorance and no such person. It lasted while this visitant, at all events — and there was a touch of the strange freedom, as I remember, in the sign of familiarity of his wearing no hat — seemed to fix me, from his position, with just the question, just the scrutiny through the fading light, that his own presence provoked. We were too far apart to call to each other, but there was a moment at which, at shorter range, some challenge between us, breaking the hush, would have been the right result of our straight mutual stare. He was in one of the angles, the one away from the house, very erect, as it struck me, and with both hands on the ledge. So I saw him as I see the letters I form on this page; then, exactly, after a minute, as if to add to the spectacle, he slowly changed his place — passed, looking at me hard all the while, to the opposite corner of the platform. Yes, it was intense to me that during this transit he never took his eyes from me, and I can see at this moment the way his hand, as he went, moved from one of the crenellations to the next. He stopped at the other corner, but less long, and even as he turned away still markedly fixed me. He turned away; that was all I knew.

IV

It was not that I did n't wait, on this occasion, for
more, since I was as deeply rooted as shaken. Was
there a "secret" at Bly — a mystery of Udolpho or an
insane, an unmentionable relative kept in unsuspected
confinement? I can't say how long I turned it over,
or how long, in a confusion of curiosity and dread, I
remained where I had had my collision; I only recall
that when I re-entered the house darkness had quite
closed in. Agitation, in the interval, certainly had held
me and driven me, for I must, in circling about the
place, have walked three miles; but I was to be later
on so much more overwhelmed that this mere dawn
of alarm was a comparatively human chill. The most
singular part of it in fact — singular as the rest had
been — was the part I became, in the hall, aware of
in meeting Mrs. Grose. This picture comes back to
me in the general train — the impression, as I received
it on my return, of the wide white panelled space,
bright in the lamplight and with its portraits and red
carpet, and of the good surprised look of my friend,
which immediately told me she had missed me. It
came to me straightway, under her contact, that, with
plain heartiness, mere relieved anxiety at my appearance, she knew nothing whatever that could bear upon
the incident I had there ready for her. I had not suspected in advance that her comfortable face would
pull me up, and I somehow measured the importance

of what I had seen by my thus finding myself hesitate to mention it. Scarce anything in the whole history seems to me so odd as this fact that my real beginning of fear was one, as I may say, with the instinct of sparing my companion. On the spot, accordingly, in the pleasant hall and with her eyes on me, I, for a reason that I could n't then have phrased, achieved an inward revolution — offered a vague pretext for my lateness and, with the plea of the beauty of the night and of the heavy dew and wet feet, went as soon as possible to my room.

Here it was another affair; here, for many days after, it was a queer affair enough. There were hours, from day to day — or at least there were moments, snatched even from clear duties — when I had to shut myself up to think. It was n't so much yet that I was more nervous than I could bear to be as that I was remarkably afraid of becoming so; for the truth I had now to turn over was simply and clearly the truth that I could arrive at no account whatever of the visitor with whom I had been so inexplicably and yet, as it seemed to me, so intimately concerned. It took me little time to see that I might easily sound, without forms of enquiry and without exciting remark, any domestic complication. The shock I had suffered must have sharpened all my senses; I felt sure, at the end of three days and as the result of mere closer attention, that I had not been practised upon by the servants nor made the object of any "game." Of whatever it was that I knew, nothing was known around me. There was but one sane inference: some one had taken a liberty rather monstrous. That was what, repeatedly,

I dipped into my room and locked the door to say to myself. We had been, collectively, subject to an intrusion; some unscrupulous traveller, curious in old houses, had made his way in unobserved, enjoyed the prospect from the best point of view and then stolen out as he came. If he had given me such a bold hard stare, that was but a part of his indiscretion. The good thing, after all, was that we should surely see no more of him.

This was not so good a thing, I admit, as not to leave me to judge that what, essentially, made nothing else much signify was simply my charming work. My charming work was just my life with Miles and Flora, and through nothing could I so like it as through feeling that to throw myself into it was to throw myself out of my trouble. The attraction of my small charges was a constant joy, leading me to wonder afresh at the vanity of my original fears, the distaste I had begun by entertaining for the probable grey prose of my office. There was to be no grey prose, it appeared, and no long grind; so how could work not be charming that presented itself as daily beauty? It was all the romance of the nursery and the poetry of the schoolroom. I don't mean by this of course that we studied only fiction and verse; I mean that I can express no otherwise the sort of interest my companions inspired. How can I describe that except by saying that instead of growing deadly used to them — and it's a marvel for a governess: I call the sisterhood to witness! — I made constant fresh discoveries. There was one direction, assuredly, in which these discoveries stopped: deep obscurity continued to cover the region of the

boy's conduct at school. It had been promptly given
me, I have noted, to face that mystery without a
pang. Perhaps even it would be nearer the truth to
say that — without a word — he himself had cleared
it up. He had made the whole charge absurd. My
conclusion bloomed there with the real rose-flush of
his innocence: he was only too fine and fair for the
little horrid unclean school-world, and he had paid a
price for it. I reflected acutely that the sense of such
individual differences, such superiorities of quality,
always, on the part of the majority — which could
include even stupid sordid head-masters — turns
infallibly to the vindictive.

Both the children had a gentleness — it was their
only fault, and it never made Miles a muff — that kept
them (how shall I express it?) almost impersonal and
certainly quite unpunishable. They were like those
cherubs of the anecdote who had — morally at any
rate — nothing to whack! I remember feeling with
Miles in especial as if he had had, as it were, nothing
to call even an infinitesimal history. We expect of a
small child scant enough "antecedents," but there
was in this beautiful little boy something extraordinarily sensitive, yet extraordinarily happy, that, more
than in any creature of his age I have seen, struck
me as beginning anew each day. He had never for a
second suffered. I took this as a direct disproof of his
having really been chastised. If he had been wicked
he would have "caught" it, and I should have caught
it by the rebound — I should have found the trace,
should have felt the wound and the dishonour. I could
reconstitute nothing at all, and he was therefore an

angel. He never spoke of his school, never mentioned a comrade or a master; and I, for my part, was quite too much disgusted to allude to them. Of course I was under the spell, and the wonderful part is that, even at the time, I perfectly knew I was. But I gave myself up to it; it was an antidote to any pain, and I had more pains than one. I was in receipt in these days of disturbing letters from home, where things were not going well. But with this joy of my children what things in the world mattered? That was the question I used to put to my scrappy retirements. I was dazzled by their loveliness.

There was a Sunday — to get on — when it rained with such force and for so many hours that there could be no procession to church; in consequence of which, as the day declined, I had arranged with Mrs. Grose that, should the evening show improvement, we would attend together the late service. The rain happily stopped, and I prepared for our walk, which, through the park and by the good road to the village, would be a matter of twenty minutes. Coming downstairs to meet my colleague in the hall, I remembered a pair of gloves that had required three stitches and that had received them — with a publicity perhaps not edifying — while I sat with the children at their tea, served on Sundays, by exception, in that cold clean temple of mahogany and brass, the "grown-up" dining-room. The gloves had been dropped there, and I turned in to recover them. The day was grey enough, but the afternoon light still lingered, and it enabled me, on crossing the threshold, not only to recognise, on a chair near the wide window, then closed, the articles I wanted, but to become aware of a person on the other side of the window and looking straight in. One step into the room had sufficed; my vision was instantaneous; it was all there. The person looking straight in was the person who had already appeared to me. He appeared thus again with I won't say greater distinctness, for that was impossible, but with a nearness that represented a forward stride in our intercourse and made me, as I met him, catch my breath and turn cold. He was the same — he was the same, and seen, this time, as he had been seen before, from the waist up, the window, though the dining-room was on the ground floor, not going down to the terrace on which he stood. His face was close to the glass, yet the effect of this better view was, strangely, just to'show me how intense the former had been. He remained but a few seconds — long enough to convince me he also saw and recognised; but it was as if I had been looking at him for years and had known him always. Something, however, happened this time that had not happened before; his stare into my face, through the glass and across the room, was as deep and hard as then, but it quitted me for a moment during which I could still watch it, see it fix successively several other things. On the spot there came to me the added shock of a certitude that it was not for me he had come. He had come for some one else.

The flash of this knowledge — for it was knowledge in the midst of dread — produced in me the most extraordinary effect, starting, as I stood there, a sudden vibration of duty and courage. I say courage because I was beyond all doubt already far gone. I bounded straight out of the door again, reached that of the house, got in an instant upon the drive and, passing along the terrace as fast as I could rush, turned a corner and came full in sight. But it was in sight of nothing now — my visitor had vanished. I stopped, almost dropped, with the real relief of this; but I took in the whole scene — I gave him time to reappear. I call it time, but how long was it ? I can't speak to the purpose to-day of the duration of these things. That kind of measure must have left me : they could n't have lasted as they actually appeared to me to last. The terrace and the whole place, the lawn and the garden beyond it, all I could see of the park, were empty with a great emptiness. There were shrubberies and big trees, but I remember the clear assurance I felt that none of them concealed him. He was there or was not there : not there if I did n't see him. I got hold of this; then, instinctively, instead of returning as I had come, went to the window. It was confusedly present to me that I ought to place myself where he had stood. I did so; I applied my face to the pane and looked, as he had looked, into the room. As if, at this moment, to show me exactly what his range had been, Mrs. Grose, as I had done for himself just before, came in from the hall. With this I had the full image of a repetition of what had already occurred. She saw me as I had seen my own visitant; she pulled up short as I had done; I gave her something of the shock that I had received. She turned white, and this made me ask myself if I had blanched as much. She stared, in short, and retreated just on *my* lines, and I knew she had then passed out and come round to me and that I should presently meet her. I remained where I was, and while I waited I thought of more things than one. But there's only one I take space to mention. I wondered why *she* should be scared.

V

OH she let me know as soon as, round the corner of the house, she loomed again into view. "What in the name of goodness is the matter — ?" She was now flushed and out of breath.

I said nothing till she came quite near. "With me?" I must have made a wonderful face. "Do I show it?"

"You're as white as a sheet. You look awful."

I considered; I could meet on this, without scruple, any degree of innocence. My need to respect the bloom of Mrs. Grose's had dropped, without a rustle, from my shoulders, and if I wavered for the instant it was not with what I kept back. I put out my hand to her and she took it; I held her hard a little, liking to feel her close to me. There was a kind of support in the shy heave of her surprise. "You came for me for church, of course, but I can't go."

"Has anything happened?"

"Yes. You must know now. Did I look very queer?"

"Through this window? Dreadful!"

"Well," I said, "I've been frightened." Mrs. Grose's eyes expressed plainly that *she* had no wish to be, yet also that she knew too well her place not to be ready to share with me any marked inconvenience. Oh it was quite settled that she *must* share! "Just what you saw from the dining-room a minute ago was the effect of that. What *I* saw — just before — was much worse."

Her hand tightened. "What was it?"

"An extraordinary man. Looking in."

"What extraordinary man?"

"I have n't the least idea."

Mrs. Grose gazed round us in vain. "Then where is he gone?"

"I know still less."

"Have you seen him before?"

"Yes — once. On the old tower."

She could only look at me harder. "Do you mean he's a stranger?"

"Oh very much!"

"Yet you did n't tell me?"

"No — for reasons. But now that you've guessed —"

Mrs. Grose's round eyes encountered this charge. "Ah I have n't guessed!" she said very simply. "How can I if *you* don't imagine?"

"I don't in the very least."

"You've seen him nowhere but on the tower?"

"And on this spot just now."

Mrs. Grose looked round again. "What was he doing on the tower?"

"Only standing there and looking down at me."

She thought a minute. "Was he a gentleman?"

I found I had no need to think. "No." She gazed in deeper wonder. "No."

"Then nobody about the place? Nobody from the village?"

"Nobody — nobody. I did n't tell you, but I made sure."

She breathed a vague relief: this was, oddly, so much to the good. It only went indeed a little way. "But if he is n't a gentleman —"

"What *is* he ? He 's a horror."

"A horror ?"

"He 's — God help me if I know *what* he is!"

Mrs. Grose looked round once more; she fixed her eyes on the duskier distance and then, pulling herself together, turned to me with full inconsequence. "It 's time we should be at church."

"Oh I 'm not fit for church!"

"Won't it do you good ?"

"It won't do *them* —!" I nodded at the house.

"The children ?"

"I can't leave them now."

"You 're afraid — ?"

I spoke boldly. "I 'm afraid of *him*."

Mrs. Grose's large face showed me, at this, for the first time, the far-away faint glimmer of a consciousness more acute : I somehow made out in it the delayed dawn of an idea I myself had not given her and that was as yet quite obscure to me. It comes back to me that I thought instantly of this as something I could get from her; and I felt it to be connected with the desire she presently showed to know more. "When was it — on the tower ?"

"About the middle of the month. At this same hour."

"Almost at dark," said Mrs. Grose.

"Oh no, not nearly. I saw him as I see you."

"Then how did he get in?"

"And how did he get out?" I laughed. "I had no opportunity to ask him! This evening, you see," I pursued, "he has not been able to get in."

"He only peeps?"

"I hope it will be confined to that!" She had now let go my hand; she turned away a little. I waited an instant; then I brought out: "Go to church. Goodbye. I must watch."

Slowly she faced me again. "Do you fear for them?"

We met in another long look. "Don't *you?*" Instead of answering she came nearer to the window and, for a minute, applied her face to the glass. "You see how he could see," I meanwhile went on.

She did n't move. "How long was he here?"

"Till I came out. I came to meet him."

Mrs. Grose at last turned round, and there was still more in her face. "*I* could n't have come out."

"Neither could I!" I laughed again. "But I did come. I've my duty."

"So have I mine," she replied; after which she added: "What's he like?"

"I've been dying to tell you. But he's like nobody."

"Nobody?" she echoed.

"He has no hat." Then seeing in her face that she already, in this, with a deeper dismay, found a touch of picture, I quickly added stroke to stroke. "He has red hair, very red, close-curling, and a pale face, long in shape, with straight good features and little rather queer whiskers that are as red as his hair. His eyebrows are somehow darker; they look particularly arched and as if they might move a good deal. His eyes are sharp, strange — awfully; but I only know clearly that they're rather small and very fixed. His mouth's wide, and his lips are thin, and except for his little whiskers he's quite clean-shaven. He gives me a sort of sense of looking like an actor."

"An actor!" It was impossible to resemble one less, at least, than Mrs. Grose at that moment.

"I've never seen one, but so I suppose them. He's tall, active, erect," I continued, "but never — no, never! — a gentleman."

My companion's face had blanched as I went on; her round eyes started and her mild mouth gaped. "A gentleman?" she gasped, confounded, stupefied: "a gentleman *he*?"

"You know him then?"

She visibly tried to hold herself. "But he *is* handsome?"

I saw the way to help her. "Remarkably!"

"And dressed — ?"

"In somebody's clothes. They're smart, but they're not his own."

She broke into a breathless affirmative groan. "They're the master's!"

I caught it up. "You *do* know him?"

She faltered but a second. "Quint!" she cried.

"Quint?"

"Peter Quint — his own man, his valet, when he was here!"

"When the master was?"

Gaping still, but meeting me, she pieced it all together. "He never wore his hat, but he did wear —

well, there were waistcoats missed! They were both here — last year. Then the master went, and Quint was alone."

I followed, but halting a little. "Alone?"

"Alone with *us*." Then as from a deeper depth, "In charge," she added.

"And what became of him?"

She hung fire so long that I was still more mystified. "He went too," she brought out at last.

"Went where?"

Her expression, at this, became extraordinary. "God knows where! He died."

"Died?" I almost shrieked.

She seemed fairly to square herself, plant herself more firmly to express the wonder of it. "Yes. Mr. Quint's dead."

VI

It took of course more than that particular passage
to place us together in presence of what we had now
to live with as we could, my dreadful liability to impressions of the order so vividly exemplified, and my
companion's knowledge henceforth — a knowledge
half consternation and half compassion — of that
liability. There had been this evening, after the
revelation that left me for an hour so prostrate —
there had been for either of us no attendance on any
service but a little service of tears and vows, of prayers
and promises, a climax to the series of mutual chal-
lenges and pledges that had straightway ensued on
our retreating together to the schoolroom and shutting ourselves up there to have everything out. The
result of our having everything out was simply to
reduce our situation to the last rigour of its elements.
She herself had seen nothing, not the shadow of a
shadow, and nobody in the house but the governess
was in the governess's plight; yet she accepted without directly impugning my sanity the truth as I gave
it to her, and ended by showing me on this ground
an awestricken tenderness, a deference to my more
than questionable privilege, of which the very breath
has remained with me as that of the sweetest of human charities.

What was settled between us accordingly that
night was that we thought we might bear things to-

193

gether; and I was not even sure that in spite of her exemption it was she who had the best of the burden. I knew at this hour, I think, as well as I knew later, what I was capable of meeting to shelter my pupils; but it took me some time to be wholly sure of what my honest comrade was prepared for to keep terms with so stiff an agreement. I was queer company enough — quite as queer as the company I received; but as I trace over what we went through I see how much common ground we must have found in the one idea that, by good fortune, *could* steady us. It was the idea, the second movement, that led me straight out, as I may say, of the inner chamber of my dread. I could take the air in the court, at least, and there Mrs. Grose could join me. Perfectly can I recall now the particular way strength came to me before we separated for the night. We had gone over and over every feature of what I had seen.

"He was looking for some one else, you say — some one who was not you?"

"He was looking for little Miles." A portentous clearness now possessed me. "*That's* whom he was looking for."

"But how do you know?"

"I know, I know, I know!" My exaltation grew. "And *you* know, my dear!"

She did n't deny this, but I required, I felt, not even so much telling as that. She took it up again in a moment. "What if *he* should see him?"

"Little Miles? That's what he wants!"

She looked immensely scared again. "The child?"

"Heaven forbid! The man. He wants to appear

to *them*." That he might was an awful conception, and yet somehow I could keep it at bay; which moreover, as we lingered there, was what I succeeded in practically proving. I had an absolute certainty that I should see again what I had already seen, but something within me said that by offering myself bravely as the sole subject of such experience, by accepting, by inviting, by surmounting it all, I should serve as an expiatory victim and guard the tranquillity of the rest of the household. The children in especial I should thus fence about and absolutely save. I recall one of the last things I said that night to Mrs. Grose.

"It does strike me that my pupils have never mentioned —!"

She looked at me hard as I musingly pulled up. "His having been here and the time they were with him?"

"The time they were with him, and his name, his presence, his history, in any way. They've never alluded to it."

"Oh the little lady does n't remember. She never heard or knew."

"The circumstances of his death?" I thought with some intensity. "Perhaps not. But Miles would remember — Miles would know."

"Ah don't try him!" broke from Mrs. Grose.

I returned her the look she had given me. "Don't be afraid." I continued to think. "It *is* rather odd."

"That he has never spoken of him?"

"Never by the least reference. And you tell me they were 'great friends.'"

"Oh it was n't *him!*" Mrs. Grose with emphasis

declared. "It was Quint's own fancy. To play with him, I mean — to spoil him." She paused a moment; then she added: "Quint was much too free."

This gave me, straight from my vision of his face — *such* a face! — a sudden sickness of disgust. "Too free with *my* boy?"

"Too free with every one!"

I forbore for the moment to analyse this description further than by the reflexion that a part of it applied to several of the members of the household, of the half-dozen maids and men who were still of our small colony. But there was everything, for our apprehension, in the lucky fact that no discomfortable legend, no perturbation of scullions, had ever, within any one's memory, attached to the kind old place. It had neither bad name nor ill fame, and Mrs. Grose, most apparently, only desired to cling to me and to quake in silence. I even put her, the very last thing of all, to the test. It was when, at midnight, she had her hand on the schoolroom door to take leave. "I *have* it from you then — for it's of great importance — that he was definitely and admittedly bad?"

"Oh not admittedly. *I* knew it—but the master did n't."

"And you never told him?"

"Well, he did n't like tale-bearing — he hated complaints. He was terribly short with anything of that kind, and if people were all right to *him* —"

"He would n't be bothered with more?" This squared well enough with my impression of him: he was not a trouble-loving gentleman, nor so very particular perhaps about some of the company he himself kept. All the same, I pressed my informant. "I promise you *I* would have told!"

She felt my discrimination. "I dare say I was wrong. But really I was afraid."

"Afraid of what?"

"Of things that man could do. Quint was so clever — he was so deep."

I took this in still more than I probably showed. "You were n't afraid of anything else? Not of his effect — ?"

"His effect?" she repeated with a face of anguish and waiting while I faltered.

"On innocent little precious lives. They were in your charge."

"No, they were n't in mine!" she roundly and distressfully returned. "The master believed in him and placed him here because he was supposed not to be quite in health and the country air so good for him. So he had everything to say. Yes" — she let me have it — "even about *them*."

"Them — that creature?" I had to smother a kind of howl. "And you could bear it?"

"No. I could n't — and I can't now!" And the poor woman burst into tears.

A rigid control, from the next day, was, as I have said, to follow them; yet how often and how passionately, for a week, we came back together to the subject! Much as we had discussed it that Sunday night, I was, in the immediate later hours in especial — for it may be imagined whether I slept — still haunted with the shadow of something she had not told me.

I myself had kept back nothing, but there was a word
Mrs. Grose had kept back. I was sure moreover by
morning that this was not from a failure of frankness,
but because on every side there were fears. It seems
to me indeed, in raking it all over, that by the time
the morrow's sun was high I had restlessly read into
the facts before us almost all the meaning they were
to receive from subsequent and more cruel occur-
rences. What they gave me above all was just the
sinister figure of the living man — the dead one
would keep a while! — and of the months he had
continuously passed at Bly, which, added up, made
a formidable stretch. The limit of this evil time had
arrived only when, on the dawn of a winter's morning,
Peter Quint was found, by a labourer going to early
work, stone dead on the road from the village: a
catastrophe explained — superficially at least — by
a visible wound to his head; such a wound as might
have been produced (and as, on the final evidence,
had been) by a fatal slip, in the dark and after leaving
the public-house, on the steepish icy slope, a wrong
path altogether, at the bottom of which he lay. The
icy slope, the turn mistaken at night and in liquor,
accounted for much — practically, in the end and
after the inquest and boundless chatter, for everything; but there had been matters in his life, strange
passages and perils, secret disorders, vices more than
suspected, that would have accounted for a good deal
more.

I scarce know how to put my story into words that
shall be a credible picture of my state of mind; but I
was in these days literally able to find a joy in the

extraordinary flight of heroism the occasion demanded of me. I now saw that I had been asked for a service admirable and difficult; and there would be a greatness in letting it be seen — oh in the right quarter! — that I could succeed where many another girl might have failed. It was an immense help to me — I confess I rather applaud myself as I look back! — that I saw my response so strongly and so simply. I was there to protect and defend the little creatures in the world the most bereaved and the most loveable, the appeal of whose helplessness had suddenly become only too explicit, a deep constant ache of one's own engaged affection. We were cut off, really, together; we were united in our danger. They had nothing but me, and I — well, I had *them*. It was in short a magnificent chance. This chance presented itself to me in an image richly material. I was a screen — I was to stand before them. The more I saw the less they would. I began to watch them in a stifled suspense, a disguised tension, that might well, had it continued too long, have turned to something like madness. What saved me, as I now see, was that it turned to another matter altogether. It did n't last as suspense — it was superseded by horrible proofs. Proofs, I say, yes — from the moment I really took hold.

This moment dated from an afternoon hour that I happened to spend in the grounds with the younger of my pupils alone. We had left Miles indoors, on the red cushion of a deep window-seat; he had wished to finish a book, and I had been glad to encourage a purpose so laudable in a young man whose only defect was a certain ingenuity of restlessness. His sister, on the contrary, had been alert to come out, and I strolled with her half an hour, seeking the shade, for the sun was still high and the day exceptionally warm. I was aware afresh with her, as we went, of how, like her brother, she contrived — it was the charming thing in both children — to let me alone without appearing to drop me and to accompany me without appearing to oppress. They were never importunate and yet never listless. My attention to them all really went to seeing them amuse themselves immensely without me: this was a spectacle they seemed actively to prepare and that employed me as an active admirer. I walked in a world of their invention — they had no occasion whatever to draw upon mine; so that my time was taken only with being for them some remarkable person or thing that the game of the moment required and that was merely, thanks to my superior, my exalted stamp, a happy and highly distinguished sinecure. I forget what I was on the present occasion; I only remember that I was something very important and very quiet and that Flora was playing very hard. We were on the edge of the lake, and, as we had lately begun geography, the lake was the Sea of Azof.

Suddenly, amid these elements, I became aware that on the other side of the Sea of Azof we had an interested spectator. The way this knowledge gathered in me was the strangest thing in the world — the strangest, that is, except the very much stranger in which it quickly merged itself. I had sat down with a piece of work — for I was something or other that could sit — on the old stone bench which overlooked the pond; and in this position I began to take in with certitude and yet without direct vision the presence, a good way off, of a third person. The old trees, the thick shrubbery, made a great and pleasant shade, but it was all suffused with the brightness of the hot still hour. There was no ambiguity in anything; none whatever at least in the conviction I from one moment to another found myself forming as to what I should see straight before me and across the lake as a consequence of raising my eyes. They were attached at this juncture to the stitching in which I was engaged, and I can feel once more the spasm of my effort not to move them till I should so have steadied myself as to be able to make up my mind what to do. There was an alien object in view — a figure whose right of presence I instantly and passionately questioned. I recollect counting over perfectly the possibilities, reminding myself that nothing was more natural for instance than the appearance of one of the men about the place, or even of a messenger, a postman or a tradesman's boy, from the village. That reminder had as little effect on my practical certitude as I was conscious — still even without looking — of its having upon the character and attitude of our visitor. Nothing was more natural than that these things should be the other things they absolutely were not.

Of the positive identity of the apparition I would assure myself as soon as the small clock of my courage should have ticked out the right second; meanwhile, with an effort that was already sharp enough, I transferred my eyes straight to little Flora, who, at the

moment, was about ten yards away. My heart had
stood still for an instant with the wonder and terror of
the question whether she too would see; and I held
my breath while I waited for what a cry from her,
what some sudden innocent sign either of interest or of
alarm, would tell me. I waited, but nothing came;
then in the first place — and there is something more
dire in this, I feel, than in anything I have to relate —
I was determined by a sense that within a minute all
spontaneous sounds from her had dropped; and in
the second by the circumstance that also within the
minute she had, in her play, turned her back to the
water. This was her attitude when I at last looked at
her — looked with the confirmed conviction that we
were still, together, under direct personal notice. She
had picked up a small flat piece of wood which happened to have in it a little hole that had evidently suggested to her the idea of sticking in another fragment
that might figure as a mast and make the thing a boat.
This second morsel, as I watched her, she was very
markedly and intently attempting to tighten in its
place. My apprehension of what she was doing sustained me so that after some seconds I felt I was ready
for more. Then I again shifted my eyes — I faced
what I had to face.

VII

I GOT hold of Mrs. Grose as soon after this as I could;
and I can give no intelligible account of how I fought
out the interval. Yet I still hear myself cry as I fairly
threw myself into her arms: "They *know* — it's too
monstrous: they know, they know!"

"And what on earth — ?" I felt her incredulity as
she held me.

"Why all that *we* know — and heaven knows what
more besides!" Then as she released me I made it
out to her, made it out perhaps only now with full
coherency even to myself. "Two hours ago, in the
garden" — I could scarce articulate — "Flora *saw!*"

Mrs. Grose took it as she might have taken a blow
in the stomach. "She has told you?" she panted.

"Not a word — that's the horror. She kept it to
herself! The child of eight, *that* child!" Unutterable
still for me was the stupefaction of it.

Mrs. Grose of course could only gape the wider.
"Then how do you know?"

"I was there — I saw with my eyes: saw she was
perfectly aware."

"Do you mean aware of *him?*"

"No — of *her.*" I was conscious as I spoke that I
looked prodigious things, for I got the slow reflexion
of them in my companion's face. "Another person —
this time; but a figure of quite as unmistakeable horror and evil: a woman in black, pale and dreadful —

with such an air also, and such a face! — on the other side of the lake. I was there with the child — quiet for the hour; and in the midst of it she came."

"Came how — from where?"

"From where they come from! She just appeared and stood there — but not so near."

"And without coming nearer?"

"Oh for the effect and the feeling she might have been as close as you!"

My friend, with an odd impulse, fell back a step. "Was she some one you've never seen?"

"Never. But some one the child has. Some one *you* have." Then to show how I had thought it all out: "My predecessor — the one who died."

"Miss Jessel?"

"Miss Jessel. You don't believe me?" I pressed.

She turned right and left in her distress. "How can you be sure?"

This drew from me, in the state of my nerves, a flash of impatience. "Then ask Flora — *she's* sure!" But I had no sooner spoken than I caught myself up. "No, for God's sake *don't!* She'll say she isn't — she'll lie!"

Mrs. Grose was not too bewildered instinctively to protest. "Ah how *can* you?"

"Because I'm clear. Flora doesn't want me to know."

"It's only then to spare you."

"No, no — there are depths, depths! The more I go over it the more I see in it, and the more I see in it the more I fear. I don't know what I *don't* see, what I *don't* fear!"

Mrs. Grose tried to keep up with me. "You mean you're afraid of seeing her again?"

"Oh no; that's nothing — now!" Then I explained. "It's of *not* seeing her."

But my companion only looked wan. "I don't understand."

"Why, it's that the child may keep it up — and that the child assuredly *will* — without my knowing it."

At the image of this possibility Mrs. Grose for a moment collapsed, yet presently to pull herself together again as from the positive force of the sense of what, should we yield an inch, there would really be to give way to. "Dear, dear — we must keep our heads! And after all, if she does n't mind it —!" She even tried a grim joke. "Perhaps she likes it!"

"Like *such* things — a scrap of an infant!"

"Is n't it just a proof of her blest innocence?" my friend bravely enquired.

She brought me, for the instant, almost round. "Oh we must clutch at *that* — we must cling to it! If it is n't a proof of what you say, it's a proof of — God knows what! For the woman's a horror of horrors."

Mrs. Grose, at this, fixed her eyes a minute on the ground; then at last raising them, "Tell me how you know," she said.

"Then you admit it's what she was?" I cried.

"Tell me how you know," my friend simply repeated.

"Know? By seeing her! By the way she looked."

"At you, do you mean — so wickedly?"

"Dear me, no — I could have borne that. She gave me never a glance. She only fixed the child."

Mrs. Grose tried to see it. "Fixed her?"

"Ah with such awful eyes!"

She stared at mine as if they might really have resembled them. "Do you mean of dislike?"

"God help us, no. Of something much worse."

"Worse than dislike?" — this left her indeed at a loss.

"With a determination — indescribable. With a kind of fury of intention."

I made her turn pale. "Intention?"

"To get hold of her." Mrs. Grose — her eyes just lingering on mine — gave a shudder and walked to the window; and while she stood there looking out I completed my statement. "*That's* what Flora knows."

After a little she turned round. "The person was in black, you say?"

"In mourning — rather poor, almost shabby. But — yes — with extraordinary beauty." I now recognised to what I had at last, stroke by stroke, brought the victim of my confidence, for she quite visibly weighed this. "Oh handsome — very, very," I insisted; "wonderfully handsome. But infamous."

She slowly came back to me. "Miss Jessel — *was* infamous." She once more took my hand in both her own, holding it as tight as if to fortify me against the increase of alarm I might draw from this disclosure. "They were both infamous," she finally said.

So for a little we faced it once more together; and I found absolutely a degree of help in seeing it now so straight. "I appreciate," I said, "the great decency of your not having hitherto spoken; but the time has certainly come to give me the whole thing." She appeared to assent to this, but still only in silence; seeing which I went on: "I must have it now. Of what did she die? Come, there was something between them."

"There was everything."

"In spite of the difference —?"

"Oh of their rank, their condition" — she brought it woefully out. "*She* was a lady."

I turned it over; I again saw. "Yes — she was a lady."

"And he so dreadfully below," said Mrs. Grose.

I felt that I doubtless need n't press too hard, in such company, on the place of a servant in the scale; but there was nothing to prevent an acceptance of my companion's own measure of my predecessor's abasement. There was a way to deal with that, and I dealt; the more readily for my full vision — on the evidence — of our employer's late clever good-looking "own" man; impudent, assured, spoiled, depraved. "The fellow was a hound."

Mrs. Grose considered as if it were perhaps a little a case for a sense of shades. "I've never seen one like him. He did what he wished."

"With *her?*"

"With them all."

It was as if now in my friend's own eyes Miss Jessel had again appeared. I seemed at any rate for an instant to trace their evocation of her as distinctly as I had seen her by the pond; and I brought out with decision: "It must have been also what *she* wished!"

Mrs. Grose's face signified that it had been indeed, but she said at the same time: "Poor woman — she paid for it!"

"Then you do know what she died of?" I asked.

"No — I know nothing. I wanted not to know; I was glad enough I did n't; and I thanked heaven she was well out of this!"

"Yet you had then your idea —"

"Of her real reason for leaving? Oh yes — as to that. She could n't have stayed. Fancy it here — for a governess! And afterwards I imagined — and I still imagine. And what I imagine is dreadful."

"Not so dreadful as what *I* do," I replied; on which I must have shown her — as I was indeed but too conscious — a front of miserable defeat. It brought out again all her compassion for me, and at the renewed touch of her kindness my power to resist broke down. I burst, as I had the other time made her burst, into tears; she took me to her motherly breast, where my lamentation overflowed. "I don't do it!" I sobbed in despair; "I don't save or shield them! It's far worse than I dreamed. They're lost!"

VIII

WHAT I had said to Mrs. Grose was true enough:
there were in the matter I had put before her depths
and possibilities that I lacked resolution to sound; so
that when we met once more in the wonder of it we
were of a common mind about the duty of resistance
to extravagant fancies. We were to keep our heads if
we should keep nothing else — difficult indeed as that
might be in the face of all that, in our prodigious experience, seemed least to be questioned. Late that
night, while the house slept, we had another talk in my
room; when she went all the way with me as to its
being beyond doubt that I had seen exactly what I had
seen. I found that to keep her thoroughly in the grip
of this I had only to ask her how, if I had "made it
up," I came to be able to give, of each of the persons
appearing to me, a picture disclosing, to the last de-
tail, their special marks — a portrait on the exhibition
of which she had instantly recognised and named
them. She wished, of course — small blame to her! —
to sink the whole subject; and I was quick to assure
her that my own interest in it had now violently taken
the form of a search for the way to escape from it. I
closed with her cordially on the article of the likeli-
hood that with recurrence — for recurrence we took
for granted — I should get used to my danger; distinctly professing that my personal exposure had suddenly become the least of my discomforts. It was my

new suspicion that was intolerable; and yet even to this complication the later hours of the day had brought a little ease.

On leaving her, after my first outbreak, I had of course returned to my pupils, associating the right remedy for my dismay with that sense of their charm which I had already recognised as a resource I could positively cultivate and which had never failed me yet. I had simply, in other words, plunged afresh into Flora's special society and there become aware — it was almost a luxury! — that she could put her little conscious hand straight upon the spot that ached. She had looked at me in sweet speculation and then had accused me to my face of having "cried." I had supposed the ugly signs of it brushed away; but I could literally — for the time at all events — rejoice, under this fathomless charity, that they had not entirely disappeared. To gaze into the depths of blue of the child's eyes and pronounce their loveliness a trick of premature cunning was to be guilty of a cynicism in preference to which I naturally preferred to abjure my judgement and, so far as might be, my agitation. I could n't abjure for merely wanting to, but I could repeat to Mrs. Grose — as I did there, over and over, in the small hours — that with our small friends' voices in the air, their pressure on one's heart and their fragrant faces against one's cheek, everything fell to the ground but their incapacity and their beauty. It was a pity that, somehow, to settle this once for all, I had equally to re-enumerate the signs of subtlety that, in the afternoon, by the lake, had made a miracle of my show of self-possession. It was a pity to be obliged to re-investigate the certitude of the moment itself and repeat how it had come to me as a revelation that the inconceivable communion I then surprised must have been for both parties a matter of habit. It was a pity I should have had to quaver out again the reasons for my not having, in my delusion, so much as questioned that the little girl saw our visitant even as I actually saw Mrs. Grose herself, and that she wanted, by just so much as she did thus see, to make me suppose she did n't, and at the same time, without showing anything, arrive at a guess as to whether I myself did! It was a pity I needed to recapitulate the portentous little activities by which she sought to divert my attention — the perceptible increase of movement, the greater intensity of play, the singing, the gabbling of nonsense and the invitation to romp.

Yet if I had not indulged, to prove there was nothing in it, in this review, I should have missed the two or three dim elements of comfort that still remained to me. I should n't for instance have been able to asseverate to my friend that I was certain — which was so much to the good — that *I* at least had not betrayed myself. I should n't have been prompted, by stress of need, by desperation of mind — I scarce know what to call it — to invoke such further aid to intelligence as might spring from pushing my colleague fairly to the wall. She had told me, bit by bit, under pressure, a great deal; but a small shifty spot on the wrong side of it all still sometimes brushed my brow like the wing of a bat; and I remember how on this occasion — for the sleeping house and the concentration alike of our danger and our watch seemed to help — I felt the importance of giving the last jerk to the curtain. "I don't believe anything so horrible," I recollect saying; "no, let us put it definitely, my dear, that I don't. But if I did, you know, there's a thing I should require now, just without sparing you the least bit more — oh not a scrap, come! — to get out of you. What was it you had in mind when, in our distress, before Miles came back, over the letter from his school, you said, under my insistence, that you did n't pretend for him he had n't literally *ever* been 'bad'? He has *not*, truly, 'ever,' in these weeks that I myself have lived with him and so closely watched him; he has been an imperturbable little prodigy of delightful loveable goodness. Therefore you might perfectly have made the claim for him if you had not, as it happened, seen an exception to take. What was your exception, and to what passage in your personal observation of him did you refer?"

It was a straight question enough, but levity was not our note, and in any case I had before the grey dawn admonished us to separate got my answer. What my friend had had in mind proved immensely to the purpose. It was neither more nor less than the particular fact that for a period of several months Quint and the boy had been perpetually together. It was indeed the very appropriate item of evidence of her having ventured to criticise the propriety, to hint at the incongruity, of so close an alliance, and even to go so far on the subject as a frank overture to Miss Jessel would take her. Miss Jessel had, with a very high manner about it, requested her to mind her business, and the good woman had on this directly approached little Miles. What she had said to him, since I pressed, was that *she* liked to see young gentlemen not forget their station.

I pressed again, of course, the closer for that. "You reminded him that Quint was only a base menial?"

"As you might say! And it was his answer, for one thing, that was bad."

"And for another thing?" I waited. "He repeated your words to Quint?"

"No, not that. It's just what he *would n't!*" she could still impress on me. "I was sure, at any rate," she added, "that he did n't. But he denied certain occasions."

"What occasions?"

"When they had been about together quite as if Quint were his tutor — and a very grand one — and Miss Jessel only for the little lady. When he had gone off with the fellow, I mean, and spent hours with him."

"He then prevaricated about it — he said he had n't?" Her assent was clear enough to cause me to add in a moment: "I see. He lied."

"Oh!" Mrs. Grose mumbled. This was a suggestion that it did n't matter; which indeed she backed up by a further remark. "You see, after all, Miss Jessel did n't mind. She did n't forbid him."

I considered. "Did he put that to you as a justification?"

At this she dropped again. "No, he never spoke of it."

"Never mentioned her in connexion with Quint?"

She saw, visibly flushing, where I was coming out. "Well, he did n't show anything. He denied," she repeated; "he denied."

Lord, how I pressed her now! "So that you could see he knew what was between the two wretches?"

"I don't know — I don't know!" the poor woman wailed.

"You do know, you dear thing," I replied; "only you have n't my dreadful boldness of mind, and you keep back, out of timidity and modesty and delicacy, even the impression that in the past, when you had, without my aid, to flounder about in silence, most of all made you miserable. But I shall get it out of you yet! There was something in the boy that suggested to you," I continued, "his covering and concealing their relation."

"Oh he could n't prevent —"

"Your learning the truth? I dare say! But, heavens," I fell, with vehemence, a-thinking, "what it shows that they must, to that extent, have succeeded in making of him!"

"Ah nothing that's not nice *now!*" Mrs. Grose lugubriously pleaded.

"I don't wonder you looked queer," I persisted, "when I mentioned to you the letter from his school!"

"I doubt if I looked as queer as you!" she retorted with homely force. "And if he was so bad then as that comes to, how is he such an angel now?"

"Yes indeed — and if he was a fiend at school! How, how, how? Well," I said in my torment, "you must put it to me again, though I shall not be able to tell you for some days. Only put it to me again!" I cried in a way that made my friend stare. "There are directions in which I must n't for the present let myself go." Meanwhile I returned to her first example — the one to which she had just previously referred — of the boy's happy capacity for an occasional slip. "If Quint — on your remonstrance at the time you speak of — was a base menial, one of the things Miles said to you, I find myself guessing, was that you were another." Again her admission was so adequate that I continued: "And you forgave him that?"

"Would n't *you?*"

"Oh yes!" And we exchanged there, in the stillness, a sound of the oddest amusement. Then I went on: "At all events, while he was with the man —"

"Miss Flora was with the woman. It suited them all!"

It suited me too, I felt, only too well; by which I mean that it suited exactly the particular deadly view I was in the very act of forbidding myself to entertain. But I so far succeeded in checking the expression of this view that I will throw, just here, no further light on it than may be offered by the mention of my final observation to Mrs. Grose. "His having lied and been impudent are, I confess, less engaging specimens than I had hoped to have from you of the outbreak in him of the little natural man. Still," I mused, "they must do, for they make me feel more than ever that I must watch."

It made me blush, the next minute, to see in my friend's face how much more unreservedly she had forgiven him than her anecdote struck me as pointing out to my own tenderness any way to do. This was marked when, at the schoolroom door, she quitted me. "Surely you don't accuse *him* —"

"Of carrying on an intercourse that he conceals from me? Ah remember that, until further evidence, I now accuse nobody." Then before shutting her out to go by another passage to her own place, "I must just wait," I wound up.

IX

I WAITED and waited, and the days took as they elapsed something from my consternation. A very few of them, in fact, passing, in constant sight of my pupils, without a fresh incident, sufficed to give to grievous fancies and even to odious memories a kind of brush of the sponge. I have spoken of the surrender to their extraordinary childish grace as a thing I could actively promote in myself, and it may be imagined if I neglected now to apply at this source for whatever balm it would yield. Stranger than I can express, certainly, was the effort to struggle against my new lights. It would doubtless have been a greater tension still, however, had it not been so frequently successful. I used to wonder how my little charges could help guessing that I thought strange things about them; and the circumstance that these things only made them more interesting was not by itself a direct aid to keeping them in the dark. I trembled lest they should see that they *were* so immensely more interesting. Putting things at the worst, at all events, as in meditation I so often did, any clouding of their innocence could only be — blameless and foredoomed as they were — a reason the more for taking risks. There were moments when I knew myself to catch them up by an irresistible impulse and press them to my heart. As soon as I had done so I used to wonder — "What will they think of that? Does'n't it betray too much?"

It would have been easy to get into a sad wild tangle about how much I might betray; but the real account, I feel, of the hours of peace I could still enjoy was that the immediate charm of my companions was a beguilement still effective even under the shadow of the possibility that it was studied. For if it occurred to me that I might occasionally excite suspicion by the little outbreaks of my sharper passion for them, so too I remember asking if I might n't see a queerness in the traceable increase of their own demonstrations.

They were at this period extravagantly and preternaturally fond of me; which, after all, I could reflect, was no more than a graceful response in children perpetually bowed down over and hugged. The homage of which they were so lavish succeeded in truth for my nerves quite as well as if I never appeared to myself, as I may say, literally to catch them at a purpose in it. They had never, I think, wanted to do so many things for their poor protectress; I mean — though they got their lessons better and better, which was naturally what would please her most — in the way of diverting, entertaining, surprising her; reading her passages, telling her stories, acting her charades, pouncing out at her, in disguises, as animals and historical characters, and above all astonishing her by the "pieces" they had secretly got by heart and could interminably recite. I should never get to the bottom — were I to let myself go even now — of the prodigious private commentary, all under still more private correction, with which I in these days overscored their full hours. They had shown me from the first a facility for everything, a general faculty which, taking a fresh start, achieved remarkable flights. They got their little tasks as if they loved them; they indulged, from the mere exuberance of the gift, in the most unimposed little miracles of memory. They not only popped out at me as tigers and as Romans, but as Shakespeareans, astronomers and navigators. This was so singularly the case that it had presumably much to do with the fact as to which, at the present day, I am at a loss for a different explanation: I allude to my unnatural composure on the subject of another school for Miles. What I remember is that I was content for the time not to open the question, and that contentment must have sprung from the sense of his perpetually striking show of cleverness. He was too clever for a bad governess, for a parson's daughter, to spoil; and the strangest if not the brightest thread in the pensive embroidery I just spoke of was the impressoin I might have got, if I had dared to work it out, that he was under some influence operating in his small intellectual life as a tremendous incitement.

If it was easy to reflect, however, that such a boy could postpone school, it was at least as marked that for such a boy to have been "kicked out" by a schoolmaster was a mystification without end. Let me add that in their company now — and I was careful almost never to be out of it — I could follow no scent very far. We lived in a cloud of music and affection and success and private theatricals. The musical sense in each of the children was of the quickest, but the elder in especial had a marvellous knack of catching and repeating. The schoolroom piano broke into all gruesome fancies; and when that failed there were confabulations in corners, with a sequel of one of them going out in the highest spirits in order to "come in" as something new. I had had brothers myself, and it was no revelation to me that little girls could be slavish idolaters of little boys. What surpassed everything was that there was a little boy in the world who could have for the inferior age, sex and intelligence so fine a consideration. They were extraordinarily at one, and to say that they never either quarrelled or complained is to make the note of praise coarse for their quality of sweetness. Sometimes perhaps indeed (when I dropped into coarseness) I came across traces of little understandings between them by which one of them should keep me occupied while the other slipped away. There is a naïf side, I suppose, in all diplomacy; but if my pupils practised upon me it was surely with the minimum of grossness. It was all in the other quarter that, after a lull, the grossness broke out.

I find that I really hang back; but I must take my horrid plunge. In going on with the record of what was hideous at Bly I not only challenge the most liberal faith — for which I little care; but (and this is another matter) I renew what I myself suffered, I again push my dreadful way through it to the end. There came suddenly an hour after which, as I look back, the business seems to me to have been all pure suffering; but I have at least reached the heart of it, and the straightest road out is doubtless to advance. One evening — with nothing to lead up or prepare it — I felt the cold touch of the impression that had breathed on me the night of my arrival and which, much lighter then as I have mentioned, I should probably have made little of in memory had my subsequent sojourn been less agitated. I had not gone to bed; I sat reading by a couple of candles. There was a roomful of old books at Bly — last-century fiction some of it, which, to the extent of a distinctly deprecated renown, but never to so much as that of a stray specimen, had reached the sequestered home and appealed to the unavowed curiosity of my youth. I remember that the book I had in my hand was Fielding's "Amelia"; also that I was wholly awake. I recall further both a general conviction that it was horribly late and a particular objection to looking at my watch. I figure finally that the white curtain draping, in the fashion of those days, the head of Flora's little bed, shrouded, as I had assured myself long before, the perfection of childish rest. I recollect in short that though I was deeply interested in my author I found myself, at the turn of a page and with his spell all scattered, looking straight up from him and hard at the door of my room. There was a moment during which I listened, reminded of the faint sense I had had, the first night, of there being something undefinably astir in the house, and noted the soft breath of the open casement just move the half-drawn blind. Then, with all the marks of a deliberation that must have seemed magnificent had there been any one to admire it, I laid down my book, rose to my feet and, taking a candle, went straight out of the room and, from the passage, on which my light made little impression, noiselessly closed and locked the door.

I can say now neither what determined nor what guided me, but I went straight along the lobby, holding my candle high, till I came within sight of the tall window that presided over the great turn of the staircase. At this point I precipitately found myself aware of three things. They were practically simultaneous, yet they had flashes of succession. My candle, under a bold flourish, went out, and I perceived, by the uncovered window, that the yielding dusk of earliest morning rendered it unnecessary. Without it, the next instant, I knew that there was a figure on the stair. I speak of sequences, but I required no lapse of seconds to stiffen myself for a third encounter with Quint. The apparition had reached the landing halfway up and was therefore on the spot nearest the window, where, at sight of me, it stopped short and fixed me exactly as it had fixed me from the tower and from the garden. He knew me as well as I knew him; and so, in the cold faint twilight, with a glimmer in the high glass and another on the polish of the oak stair below, we faced each other in our common intensity. He was absolutely, on this occasion, a living detestable dangerous presence. But that was not the wonder of wonders; I reserve this distinction for quite another circumstance: the circumstance that dread had unmistakeably quitted me and that there was nothing in me unable to meet and measure him.

I had plenty of anguish after that extraordinary moment, but I had, thank God, no terror. And he knew I had n't — I found myself at the end of an instant magnificently aware of this. I felt, in a fierce rigour of confidence, that if I stood my ground a minute I should cease — for the time at least — to have him to reckon with; and during the minute, accordingly, the thing was as human and hideous as a real interview : hideous just because it *was* human, as human as to have met alone, in the small hours, in a sleeping house, some enemy, some adventurer, some criminal. It was the dead silence of our long gaze at such close quarters that gave the whole horror, huge as it was, its only note of the unnatural. If I had met a murderer in such a place and at such an hour we still at least would have spoken. Something would have passed, in life, between us; if nothing had passed one of us would have moved. The moment was so prolonged that it would have taken but little more to make me doubt if even *I* were in life. I can't express what followed it save by saying that the silence itself — which was indeed in a manner an attestation of my strength — became the element into which I saw the figure disappear; in which I definitely saw it turn, as I might have seen the low wretch to which it had once belonged turn on receipt of an order, and pass, with my eyes on the villainous back that no hunch could have more disfigured, straight down the staircase and into the darkness in which the next bend was lost.

X

I REMAINED a while at the top of the stair, but with the effect presently of understanding that when my visitor had gone, he had gone; then I returned to my room. The foremost thing I saw there by the light of the candle I had left burning was that Flora's little bed was empty; and on this I caught my breath with all the terror that, five minutes before, I had been able to resist. I dashed at the place in which I had left her lying and over which — for the small silk counterpane and the sheets were disarranged — the white curtains had been deceivingly pulled forward; then my step, to my unutterable relief, produced an answering sound: I noticed an agitation of the window-blind, and the child, ducking down, emerged rosily from the other side of it. She stood there in so much of her candour and so little of her night-gown, with her pink bare feet and the golden glow of her curls. She looked intensely grave, and I had never had such a sense of losing an advantage acquired (the thrill of which had just been so prodigious) as on my consciousness that she addressed me with a reproach — "You naughty: where *have* you been?" Instead of challenging her own irregularity I found myself arraigned and explaining. She herself explained, for that matter, with the loveliest eagerest simplicity. She had known suddenly, as she lay there, that I was out of the room, and had jumped up to see what had become of me. I had dropped, with

the joy of her reappearance, back into my chair —
feeling then, and then only, a little faint; and she had
pattered straight over to me, thrown herself upon my
knee, given herself to be held with the flame of the
candle full in the wonderful little face that was still
flushed with sleep. I remember closing my eyes an instant, yieldingly, consciously, as before the excess of
something beautiful that shone out of the blue of her
own. "You were looking for me out of the window?"
I said. "You thought I might be walking in the
grounds?"

"Well, you know, I thought some one was" — she
never blanched as she smiled out that at me.

Oh how I looked at her now! "And did you see
any one?"

"Ah *no!*" she returned almost (with the full privilege of childish inconsequence) resentfully, though
with a long sweetness in her little drawl of the negative.

At that moment, in the state of my nerves, I absolutely believed she lied; and if I once more closed my
eyes it was before the dazzle of the three or four possible ways in which I might take this up. One of these
for a moment tempted me with such singular force
that, to resist it, I must have gripped my little girl
with a spasm that, wonderfully, she submitted to without a cry or a sign of fright. Why not break out at her
on the spot and have it all over? — give it to her
straight in her lovely little lighted face? "You see,
you see, you *know* that you do and that you already
quite suspect I believe it; therefore why not frankly
confess it to me, so that we may at least live with it

together and learn perhaps, in the strangeness of our fate, where we are and what it means ?" This solicitation dropped, alas, as it came: if I could immediately have succumbed to it I might have spared myself — well, you 'll see what. Instead of succumbing I sprang again to my feet, looked at her bed and took a helpless middle way. "Why did you pull the curtain over the place to make me think you were still there ?"

Flora luminously considered; after which, with her little divine smile: "Because I don't like to frighten you!"

"But if I had, by your idea, gone out — ?"

She absolutely declined to be puzzled; she turned her eyes to the flame of the candle as if the question were as irrelevant, or at any rate as impersonal, as Mrs. Marcet or nine-times-nine. "Oh but you know," she quite adequately answered, "that you might come back, you dear, and that you *have!*" And after a little, when she had got into bed, I had, a long time, by almost sitting on her for the retention of her hand, to show how I recognised the pertinence of my return.

You may imagine the general complexion, from that moment, of my nights. I repeatedly sat up till I did n't know when; I selected moments when my room-mate unmistakeably slept, and, stealing out, took noiseless turns in the passage. I even pushed as far as to where I had last met Quint. But I never met him there again, and I may as well say at once that I on no other occasion saw him in the house. I just missed, on the staircase, nevertheless, a different adventure. Looking down it from the top I once recognised the presence of a woman seated on one of

the lower steps with her back presented to me, her
body half-bowed and her head, in an attitude of woe,
in her hands. I had been there but an instant, however, when she vanished without looking round at me.
I knew, for all that, exactly what dreadful face she had
to show; and I wondered whether, if instead of being
above I had been below, I should have had the same
nerve for going up that I had lately shown Quint.
Well, there continued to be plenty of call for nerve.
On the eleventh night after my latest encounter with
that gentleman — they were all numbered now — I
had an alarm that perilously skirted it and that indeed, from the particular quality of its unexpectedness, proved quite my sharpest shock. It was precisely the first night during this series that, weary with
vigils, I had conceived I might again without laxity
lay myself down at my old hour. I slept immediately
and, as I afterwards knew, till about one o'clock; but
when I woke it was to sit straight up, as completely
roused as if a hand had shaken me. I had left a light
burning, but it was now out, and I felt an instant certainty that Flora had extinguished it. This brought
me to my feet and straight, in the darkness, to her
bed, which I found she had left. A glance at the window enlightened me further, and the striking of a
match completed the picture.

The child had again got up — this time blowing
out the taper, and had again, for some purpose of observation or response, squeezed in behind the blind
and was peering out into the night. That she now saw
— as she had not, I had satisfied myself, the previous
time — was proved to me by the fact that she was

disturbed neither by my re-illumination nor by the haste I made to get into slippers and into a wrap. Hidden, protected, absorbed, she evidently rested on the sill — the casement opened forward — and gave herself up. There was a great still moon to help her, and this fact had counted in my quick decision. She was face to face with the apparition we had met at the lake, and could now communicate with it as she had not then been able to do. What I, on my side, had to care for was, without disturbing her, to reach, from the corridor, some other window turned to the same quarter. I got to the door without her hearing me; I got out of it, closed it and listened, from the other side, for some sound from her. While I stood in the passage I had my eyes on her brother's door, which was but ten steps off and which, indescribably, pro-duced in me a renewal of the strange impulse that I lately spoke of as my temptation. What if I should go straight in and march to *his* window? — what if, by risking to his boyish bewilderment a revelation of my motive, I should throw across the rest of the mys-tery the long halter of my boldness?

This thought held me sufficiently to make me cross to his threshold and pause again. I preternaturally listened; I figured to myself what might portentously be; I wondered if his bed were also empty and he also secretly at watch. It was a deep soundless min-ute, at the end of which my impulse failed. He was quiet; he might be innocent; the risk was hideous; I turned away. There was a figure in the grounds — a figure prowling for a sight, the visitor with whom Flora was engaged; but it was n't the visitor most concerned with my boy. I hesitated afresh, but on other grounds and only a few seconds; then I had made my choice. There were empty rooms enough at Bly, and it was only a question of choosing the right one. The right one suddenly presented itself to me as the lower one — though high above the gardens — in the solid corner of the house that I have spoken of as the old tower. This was a large square chamber, arranged with some state as a bedroom, the extravagant size of which made it so inconvenient that it had not for years, though kept by Mrs. Grose in exemplary order, been occupied. I had often admired it and I knew my way about in it; I had only, after just faltering at the first chill gloom of its disuse, to pass across it and unbolt in all quietness one of the shutters. Achieving this transit I uncovered the glass without a sound and, applying my face to the pane, was able, the darkness without being much less than within, to see that I commanded the right direction. Then I saw something more. The moon made the night extraordinarily penetrable and showed me on the lawn a person, diminished by distance, who stood there motionless and as if fascinated, looking up to where I had appeared — looking, that is, not so much straight at me as at something that was apparently above me. There was clearly another person above me — there was a person on the tower; but the presence on the lawn was not in the least what I had conceived and had confidently hurried to meet. The presence on the lawn — I felt sick as I made it out — was poor little Miles himself.

XI

It was not till late next day that I spoke to Mrs. Grose; the rigour with which I kept my pupils in sight making it often difficult to meet her privately: the more as we each felt the importance of not provoking — on the part of the servants quite as much as on that of the children — any suspicion of a secret flurry or of a discussion of mysteries. I drew a great security in this particular from her mere smooth aspect. There was nothing in her fresh face to pass on to others the least of my horrible confidences. She believed me, I was sure, absolutely: if she had n't I don't know what would have become of me, for I could n't have borne the strain alone. But she was a magnificent monument to the blessing of a want of imagination, and if she could see in our little charges nothing but their beauty and amiability, their happiness and cleverness, she had no direct communication with the sources of my trouble. If they had been at all visibly blighted or battered she would doubtless have grown, on tracing it back, haggard enough to match them; as matters stood, however, I could feel her, when she surveyed them with her large white arms folded and the habit of serenity in all her look, thank the Lord's mercy that if they were ruined the pieces would still serve. Flights of fancy gave place, in her mind, to a steady fireside glow, and I had already begun to perceive how, with the development of the conviction that — as time went on without a public accident — our

230

young things could, after all, look out for themselves, she addressed her greatest solicitude to the sad case presented by their deputy-guardian. That, for myself, was a sound simplification: I could engage that, to the world, my face should tell no tales, but it would have been, in the conditions, an immense added worry to find myself anxious about hers.

At the hour I now speak of she had joined me, under pressure, on the terrace, where, with the lapse of the season, the afternoon sun was now agreeable; and we sat there together while before us and at a distance, yet within call if we wished, the children strolled to and fro in one of their most manageable moods. They moved slowly, in unison, below us, over the lawn, the boy, as they went, reading aloud from a story-book and passing his arm round his sister to keep her quite in touch. Mrs. Grose watched them with positive placidity; then I caught the suppressed intellectual creak with which she conscientiously turned to take from me a view of the back of the tapestry. I had made her a receptacle of lurid things, but there was an odd recognition of my superiority — my accomplishments and my function — in her patience under my pain. She offered her mind to my disclosures as, had I wished to mix a witch's broth and proposed it with assurance, she would have held out a large clean saucepan. This had become thoroughly her attitude by the time that, in my recital of the events of the night, I reached the point of what Miles had said to me when, after seeing him, at such a monstrous hour, almost on the very spot where he happened now to be, I had gone down to bring him in; choosing then, at the window, with a concentrated need of not alarming the house, rather that method than any noisier process. I had left her meanwhile in little doubt of my small hope of representing with success even to her actual sympathy my sense of the real splendour of the little inspiration with which, after I had got him into the house, the boy met my final articulate challenge. As soon as I appeared in the moonlight on the terrace he had come to me as straight as possible; on which I had taken his hand without a word and led him, through the dark spaces, up the staircase where Quint had so hungrily hovered for him, along the lobby where I had listened and trembled, and so to his forsaken room.

Not a sound, on the way, had passed between us, and I had wondered — oh *how* I had wondered! — if he were groping about in his dreadful little mind for something plausible and not too grotesque. It would tax his invention certainly, and I felt, this time, over his real embarrassment, a curious thrill of triumph. It was a sharp trap for any game hitherto successful. He could play no longer at perfect propriety, nor could he pretend to it; so how the deuce would he get out of the scrape? There beat in me indeed, with the passionate throb of this question, an equal dumb appeal as to how the deuce *I* should. I was confronted at last, as never yet, with all the risk attached even now to sounding my own horrid note. I remember in fact that as we pushed into his little chamber, where the bed had not been slept in at all and the window, uncovered to the moonlight, made the place so clear that there was no need of striking a match — I remember how I suddenly dropped, sank upon the edge of the bed from the force of the idea that he must know how he really, as they say, "had" me. He could do what he liked, with all his cleverness to help him, so long as I should continue to defer to the old tradition of the criminality of those caretakers of the young who minister to superstitions and fears. He "had" me indeed, and in a cleft stick; for who would ever absolve me, who would consent that I should go unhung, if, by the faintest tremor of an overture, I were the first to introduce into our perfect intercourse an element so dire? No, no: it was useless to attempt to convey to Mrs. Grose, just as it is scarcely less so to attempt to suggest here, how, during our short stiff brush there in the dark, he fairly shook me with admiration. I was of course thoroughly kind and merciful; never, never yet had I placed on his small shoulders hands of such tenderness as those with which, while I rested against the bed, I held him there well under fire. I had no alternative but, in form at least, to put it to him.

"You must tell me now — and all the truth. What did you go out for? What were you doing there?"

I can still see his wonderful smile, the whites of his beautiful eyes and the uncovering of his clear teeth, shine to me in the dusk. "If I tell you why, will you understand?" My heart, at this, leaped into my mouth. *Would* he tell me why? I found no sound on my lips to press it, and I was aware of answering only with a vague repeated grimacing nod. He was gentleness itself, and while I wagged my head at him he stood there more than ever a little fairy prince. It was his brightness indeed that gave me a respite. Would it be so great if he were really going to tell me? "Well," he said at last, "just exactly in order that you should do this."

"Do what?"

"Think me — for a change — *bad!*" I shall never forget the sweetness and gaiety with which he brought out the word, nor how, on top of it, he bent forward and kissed me. It was practically the end of everything. I met his kiss and I had to make, while I folded him for a minute in my arms, the most stupendous effort not to cry. He had given exactly the account of himself that permitted least my going behind it, and it was only with the effect of confirming my acceptance of it that, as I presently glanced about the room, I could say —

"Then you didn't undress at all?"

He fairly glittered in the gloom. "Not at all. I sat up and read."

"And when did you go down?"

"At midnight. When I'm bad I *am* bad!"

"I see, I see — it's charming. But how could you be sure I should know it?"

"Oh I arranged that with Flora." His answers rang out with a readiness! "She was to get up and look out."

"Which is what she did do." It was I who fell into the trap!

"So she disturbed you, and, to see what she was looking at, you also looked — you saw."

"While you," I concurred, "caught your death in the night air!"

He literally bloomed so from this exploit that I could afford radiantly to assent. "How otherwi should I have been bad enough?" he asked. The after another embrace, the incident and our intervie closed on my recognition of all the reserves of goo ness that, for his joke, he had been able to draw upo

XII

THE particular impression I had received proved in the morning light, I repeat, not quite successfully presentable to Mrs. Grose, though I re-enforced it with the mention of still another remark that he had made before we separated. "It all lies in half a dozen words," I said to her, "words that really settle the matter. 'Think, you know, what I *might* do!' He threw that off to show me how good he is. He knows down to the ground what he 'might do.' That's what he gave them a taste of at school."

"Lord, you do change!" cried my friend.

"I don't change — I simply make it out. The four, depend upon it, perpetually meet. If on either of these last nights you had been with either child you'd clearly have understood. The more I've watched and waited the more I've felt that if there were nothing else to make it sure it would be made so by the systematic silence of each. *Never*, by a slip of the tongue, have they so much as alluded to either of their old friends, any more than Miles has alluded to his expulsion. Oh yes, we may sit here and look at them, and they may show off to us there to their fill; but even while they pretend to be lost in their fairy-tale they're steeped in their vision of the dead restored to them. He's not reading to her," I declared; "they're talking of *them* — they're talking horrors! I go on, I know, as if I were crazy; and it's a wonder I'm not. What I've seen would have made *you* so; but it has only

236

made me more lucid, made me get hold of still other things."

My lucidity must have seemed awful, but the charming creatures who were victims of it, passing and repassing in their interlocked sweetness, gave my colleague something to hold on by; and I felt how tight she held as, without stirring in the breath of my passion, she covered them still with her eyes. "Of what other things have you got hold?"

"Why of the very things that have delighted, fascinated and yet, at bottom, as I now so strangely see, mystified and troubled me. Their more than earthly beauty, their absolutely unnatural goodness. It's a game," I went on; "it's a policy and a fraud!"

"On the part of little darlings — ?"

"As yet mere lovely babies? Yes, mad as that seems!" The very act of bringing it out really helped me to trace it — follow it all up and piece it all together. "They have n't been good — they've only been absent. It has been easy to live with them because they're simply leading a life of their own. They're not mine — they're not ours. They're his and they're hers!"

"Quint's and that woman's?"

"Quint's and that woman's. They want to get to them."

Oh how, at this, poor Mrs. Grose appeared to study them! "But for what?"

"For the love of all the evil that, in those dreadful days, the pair put into them. And to ply them with that evil still, to keep up the work of demons, is what brings the others back."

237

"Laws!" said my friend under her breath. The exclamation was homely, but it revealed a real acceptance of my further proof of what, in the bad time — for there had been a worse even than this! — must have occurred. There could have been no such justification for me as the plain assent of her experience to whatever depth of depravity I found credible in our brace of scoundrels. It was in obvious submission of memory that she brought out after a moment: "They *were* rascals! But what can they now do?" she pursued.

"Do?" I echoed so loud that Miles and Flora, as they passed at their distance, paused an instant in their walk and looked at us. "Don't they do enough?" I demanded in a lower tone, while the children, having smiled and nodded and kissed hands to us, resumed their exhibition. We were held by it a minute; then I answered: "They can destroy them!" At this my companion did turn, but the appeal she launched was a silent one, the effect of which was to make me more explicit. "They don't know as yet quite how — but they're trying hard. They're seen only across, as it were, and beyond — in strange places and on high places, the top of towers, the roof of houses, the outside of windows, the further edge of pools; but there's a deep design, on either side, to shorten the distance and overcome the obstacle: so the success of the tempters is only a question of time. They've only to keep to their suggestions of danger."

"For the children to come?"

"And perish in the attempt!" Mrs. Grose slowly

got up, and I scrupulously added: "Unless, of course, we can prevent!"

Standing there before me while I kept my seat she visibly turned things over. "Their uncle must do the preventing. He must take them away."

"And who's to make him?"

She had been scanning the distance, but she now dropped on me a foolish face. "You, Miss."

"By writing to him that his house is poisoned and his little nephew and niece mad?"

"But if they *are*, Miss?"

"And if I am myself, you mean? That's charming news to be sent him by a person enjoying his confidence and whose prime undertaking was to give him no worry."

Mrs. Grose considered, following the children again. "Yes, he do hate worry. That was the great reason —"

"Why those fiends took him in so long? No doubt, though his indifference must have been awful. As I'm not a fiend, at any rate, I should n't take him in."

My companion, after an instant and for all answer, sat down again and grasped my arm. "Make him at any rate come to you."

I stared. "To *me?*" I had a sudden fear of what she might do. "'Him'?"

"He ought to *be* here — he ought to help."

I quickly rose and I think I must have shown her a queerer face than ever yet. "You see me asking him for a visit?" No, with her eyes on my face she evidently could n't. Instead of it even — as a woman reads another — she could see what I myself saw: his

derision, his amusement, his contempt for the break-
down of my resignation at being left alone and for the
fine machinery I had set in motion to attract his attention to my slighted charms. She did n't know — no
one knew — how proud I had been to serve him and
to stick to our terms; yet she none the less took the
measure, I think, of the warning I now gave her. "If
you should so lose your head as to appeal to him for
me —"

She was really frightened. "Yes, Miss ?"

"I would leave, on the spot, both him and you."

XIII

IT was all very well to join them, but speaking to them
proved quite as much as ever an effort beyond my
strength — offered, in close quarters, difficulties as
insurmountable as before. This situation continued
a month, and with new aggravations and particular
notes, the note above all, sharper and sharper, of the
small ironic consciousness on the part of my pupils. It
was not, I am as sure to-day as I was sure then, my
mere infernal imagination: it was absolutely traceable
that they were aware of my predicament and that this
strange relation made, in a manner, for a long time,
the air in which we moved. I don't mean that they
had their tongues in their cheeks or did anything vulgar, for that was not one of their dangers: I do mean,
on the other hand, that the element of the unnamed
and untouched became, between us, greater than any
other, and that so much avoidance could n't have
been made successful without a great deal of tacit
arrangement. It was as if, at moments, we were perpetually coming into sight of subjects before which
we must stop short, turning suddenly out of alleys
that we perceived to be blind, closing with a little bang
that made us look at each other — for, like all bangs,
it was something louder than we had intended — the
doors we had indiscreetly opened. All roads lead to
Rome, and there were times when it might have
struck us that almost every branch of study or subject

of conversation skirted forbidden ground. Forbidden
ground was the question of the return of the dead in
general and of whatever, in especial, might survive,
for memory, of the friends little children had lost.
There were days when I could have sworn that one
of them had, with a small invisible nudge, said to the
other: "She thinks she'll do it this time — but she
won't!" To "do it" would have been to indulge for
instance — and for once in a way — in some direct
reference to the lady who had prepared them for my
discipline. They had a delightful endless appetite for
passages in my own history to which I had again and
again treated them; they were in possession of everything that had ever happened to me, had had, with
every circumstance, the story of my smallest adventures and of those of my brothers and sisters and of
the cat and the dog at home, as well as many particulars of the whimsical bent of my father, of the
furniture and arrangement of our house and of the
conversation of the old women of our village. There
were things enough, taking one with another, to chatter about, if one went very fast and knew by instinct
when to go round. They pulled with an art of their
own the strings of my invention and my memory; and
nothing else perhaps, when I thought of such occasions afterwards, gave me so the suspicion of being
watched from under cover. It was in any case over
my life, *my* past and *my* friends alone that we could
take anything like our ease; a state of affairs that led
them sometimes without the least pertinence to break
out into sociable reminders. I was invited — with no
visible connexion — to repeat afresh Goody Gosling's

celebrated *mot* or to confirm the details already sup-
plied as to the cleverness of the vicarage pony.

It was partly at such junctures as these and partly
at quite different ones that, with the turn my matters
had now taken, my predicament, as I have called it,
grew most sensible. The fact that the days passed for
me without another encounter ought, it would have
appeared, to have done something toward soothing
my nerves. Since the light brush, that second night
on the upper landing, of the presence of a woman at
the foot of the stair, I had seen nothing, whether in or
out of the house, that one had better not have seen.
There was many a corner round which I expected to
come upon Quint, and many a situation that, in a
merely sinister way, would have favoured the appearance of Miss Jessel. The summer had turned, the
summer had gone; the autumn had dropped upon
Bly and had blown out half our lights. The place,
with its grey sky and withered garlands, its bared
spaces and scattered dead leaves, was like a theatre
after the performance — all strewn with crumpled
playbills. There were exactly states of the air, conditions of sound and of stillness, unspeakable impressions of the *kind* of ministering moment, that brought
back to me, long enough to catch it, the feeling of the
medium in which, that June evening out of doors, I
had had my first sight of Quint, and in which too, at
those other instants, I had, after seeing him through
the window, looked for him in vain in the circle of
shrubbery. I recognised the signs, the portents — I
recognised the moment, the spot. But they remained
unaccompanied and empty, and I continued un-

molested; if unmolested one could call a young wo-man whose sensibility had, in the most extraordinary fashion, not declined but deepened. I had said in my talk with Mrs. Grose on that horrid scene of Flora's by the lake — and had perplexed her by so saying — that it would from that moment distress me much more to lose my power than to keep it. I had then expressed what was vividly in my mind: the truth that, whether the children really saw or not — since, that is, it was not yet definitely proved — I greatly preferred, as a safeguard, the fulness of my own ex-posure. I was ready to know the very worst that was to be known. What I had then had an ugly glimpse of was that my eyes might be sealed just while theirs were most opened. Well, my eyes *were* sealed, it ap-peared, at present — a consummation for which it seemed blasphemous not to thank God. There was, alas, a difficulty about that: I would have thanked him with all my soul had I not had in a proportionate measure this conviction of the secret of my pupils.

How can I retrace to-day the strange steps of my obsession? There were times of our being together when I would have been ready to swear that, liter-ally, in my presence, but with my direct sense of it closed, they had visitors who were known and were welcome. Then it was that, had I not been deterred by the very chance that such an injury might prove greater than the injury to be averted, my exaltation would have broken out. "They're here, they're here, you little wretches," I would have cried, "and you can't deny it now!" The little wretches denied it with all the added volume of their sociability and

their tenderness, just in the crystal depths of which
— like the flash of a fish in a stream — the mockery
of their advantage peeped up. The shock had in truth
sunk into me still deeper than I knew on the night
when, looking out either for Quint or for Miss Jessel
under the stars, I had seen there the boy over whose
rest I watched and who had immediately brought in
with him — had straightway there turned on me —
the lovely upward look with which, from the battlements above us, the hideous apparition of Quint had
played. If it was a question of a scare my discovery
on this occasion had scared me more than any other,
and it was essentially in the scared state that I drew
my actual conclusions. They harassed me so that
sometimes, at odd moments, I shut myself up audibly
to rehearse — it was at once a fantastic relief and a
renewed despair — the manner in which I might
come to the point. I approached it from one side and
the other while, in my room, I flung myself about, but
I always broke down in the monstrous utterance of
names. As they died away on my lips I said to myself
that I should indeed help them to represent something infamous if by pronouncing them I should violate as rare a little case of instinctive delicacy as any
schoolroom probably had ever known. When I said
to myself: "*They* have the manners to be silent, and
you, trusted as you are, the baseness to speak!" I felt
myself crimson and covered my face with my hands.
After these secret scenes I chattered more than ever,
going on volubly enough till one of our prodigious
palpable hushes occurred — I can call them nothing
else — the strange dizzy lift or swim (I try for terms!)

into a stillness, a pause of all life, that had nothing to
do with the more or less noise we at the moment
might be engaged in making and that I could hear
through any intensified mirth or quickened recitation
or louder strum of the piano. Then it was that the
others, the outsiders, were there. Though they were
not angels they "passed," as the French say, causing
me, while they stayed, to tremble with the fear of their
addressing to their younger victims some yet more
infernal message or more vivid image than they had
thought good enough for myself.

What it was least possible to get rid of was the cruel
idea that, whatever I had seen, Miles and Flora saw
more — things terrible and unguessable and that
sprang from dreadful passages of intercourse in the
past. Such things naturally left on the surface, for
the time, a chill that we vociferously denied we felt;
and we had all three, with repetition, got into such
splendid training that we went, each time, to mark
the close of the incident, almost automatically through
the very same movements. It was striking of the children at all events to kiss me inveterately with a wild
irrelevance and never to fail — one or the other — of
the precious question that had helped us through
many a peril. "When do you think he *will* come?
Don't you think we *ought* to write?" — there was
nothing like that enquiry, we found by experience,
for carrying off an awkwardness. "He" of course
was their uncle in Harley Street; and we lived in much
profusion of theory that he might at any moment
arrive to mingle in our circle. It was impossible to
have given less encouragement than he had admin-

istered to such a doctrine, but if we had not had the doctrine to fall back upon we should have deprived each other of some of our finest exhibitions. He never wrote to them — that may have been selfish, but it was a part of the flattery of his trust of myself; for the way in which a man pays his highest tribute to a woman is apt to be but by the more festal celebration of one of the sacred laws of his comfort. So I held that I carried out the spirit of the pledge given not to appeal to him when I let our young friends understand that their own letters were but charming literary exercises. They were too beautiful to be posted; I kept them myself; I have them all to this hour. This was a rule indeed which only added to the satiric effect of my being plied with the supposition that he might at any moment be among us. It was exactly as if our young friends knew how almost more awkward than anything else that might be for me. There appears to me moreover as I look back no note in all this more extraordinary than the mere fact that, in spite of my tension and of their triumph, I never lost patience with them. Adorable they must in truth have been, I now feel, since I did n't in these days hate them! Would exasperation, however, if relief had longer been postponed, finally have betrayed me? It little matters, for relief arrived. I call it relief though it was only the relief that a snap brings to a strain or the burst of a thunderstorm to a day of suffocation. It was at least change, and it came with a rush.

XIV

WALKING to church a certain Sunday morning, I had little Miles at my side and his sister, in advance of us and at Mrs. Grose's, well in sight. It was a crisp clear day, the first of its order for some time; the night had brought a touch of frost and the autumn air, bright and sharp, made the church-bells almost gay. It was an odd accident of thought that I should have happened at such a moment to be particularly and very gratefully struck with the obedience of my little charges. Why did they never resent my inexorable, my perpetual society? Something or other had brought nearer home to me that I had all but pinned the boy to my shawl, and that in the way our companions were marshalled before me I might have appeared to provide against some danger of rebellion. I was like a gaoler with an eye to possible surprises and escapes. But all this belonged — I mean their magnificent little surrender — just to the special array of the facts that were most abysmal. Turned out for Sunday by his uncle's tailor, who had had a free hand and a notion of pretty waistcoats and of his grand little air, Miles's whole title to independence, the rights of his sex and situation, were so stamped upon him that if he had suddenly struck for freedom I should have had nothing to say. I was by the strangest of chances wondering how I should meet him when the revolution unmistakeably occurred. I call it a revolution because I now see how, with the word he spoke, the curtain rose on the last act of my dreadful drama and the catastrophe was precipitated. "Look here, my dear, you know," he charmingly said, "when in the world, please, am I going back to school ?"

Transcribed here the speech sounds harmless enough, particularly as uttered in the sweet, high, casual pipe with which, at all interlocutors, but above all at his eternal governess, he threw off intonations as if he were tossing roses. There was something in them that always made one "catch," and I caught at any rate now so effectually that I stopped as short as if one of the trees of the park had fallen across the road. There was something new, on the spot, between us, and he was perfectly aware I recognised it, though to enable me to do so he had no need to look a whit less candid and charming than usual. I could feel in him how he already, from my at first finding nothing to reply, perceived the advantage he had gained. I was so slow to find anything that he had plenty of time, after a minute, to continue with his suggestive but inconclusive smile: "You know, my dear, that for a fellow to be with a lady *always* —!" His "my dear" was constantly on his lips for me, and nothing could have expressed more the exact shade of the sentiment with which I desired to inspire my pupils than its fond familiarity. It was so respectfully easy.

But oh how I felt that at present I must pick my own phrases! I remember that, to gain time, I tried to laugh, and I seemed to see in the beautiful face with which he watched me how ugly and queer I looked. "And always with the same lady?" I returned.

He neither blenched nor winked. The whole thing was virtually out between us. "Ah of course she's a jolly 'perfect' lady; but after all I'm a fellow, don't you see? who's — well, getting on."

I lingered there with him an instant ever so kindly. "Yes, you're getting on." Oh but I felt helpless!

I have kept to this day the heartbreaking little idea of how he seemed to know that and to play with it. "And you can't say I've not been awfully good, can you?"

I laid my hand on his shoulder, for though I felt how much better it would have been to walk on I was not yet quite able. "No, I can't say that, Miles."

"Except just that one night, you know —!"

"That one night?" I couldn't look as straight as he.

"Why when I went down — went out of the house."

"Oh yes. But I forget what you did it for."

"You forget?" — he spoke with the sweet extravagance of childish reproach. "Why it was just to show you I could!"

"Oh yes — you could."

"And I can again."

I felt I might perhaps after all succeed in keeping my wits about me. "Certainly. But you won't."

"No, not *that* again. It was nothing."

"It was nothing," I said. "But we must go on."

He resumed our walk with me, passing his hand into my arm. "Then when *am* I going back?"

I wore, in turning it over, my most responsible air. "Were you very happy at school?"

He just considered. "Oh I'm happy enough anywhere!"

"Well then," I quavered, "if you're just as happy here —!"

"Ah but that isn't everything! Of course *you* know a lot —"

"But you hint that you know almost as much?" I risked as he paused.

"Not half I want to!" Miles honestly professed. "But it isn't so much that."

"What is it then?"

"Well — I want to see more life."

"I see; I see." We had arrived within sight of the church and of various persons, including several of the household of Bly, on their way to it and clustered about the door to see us go in. I quickened our step; I wanted to get there before the question between us opened up much further; I reflected hungrily that he would have for more than an hour to be silent; and I thought with envy of the comparative dusk of the pew and of the almost spiritual help of the hassock on which I might bend my knees. I seemed literally to be running a race with some confusion to which he was about to reduce me, but I felt he had got in first when, before we had even entered the churchyard, he threw out —

"I want my own sort!"

It literally made me bound forward. "There aren't many of your own sort, Miles!" I laughed. "Unless perhaps dear little Flora!"

"You really compare me to a baby girl?"

This found me singularly weak. "Don't you then *love* our sweet Flora?"

"If I did n't — and you too; if I did n't —!" he repeated as if retreating for a jump, yet leaving his thought so unfinished that, after we had come into the gate, another stop, which he imposed on me by the pressure of his arm, had become inevitable. Mrs. Grose and Flora had passed into the church, the other worshippers had followed and we were, for the minute, alone among the old thick graves. We had paused, on the path from the gate, by a low oblong table-like tomb.

"Yes, if you did n't — ?"

He looked, while I waited, about at the graves. "Well, you know what!" But he did n't move, and he presently produced something that made me drop straight down on the stone slab as if suddenly to rest. "Does my uncle think what *you* think?"

I markedly rested. "How do you know what I think?"

"Ah well, of course I don't; for it strikes me you never tell me. But I mean does *he* know?"

"Know what, Miles?"

"Why the way I'm going on."

I recognised quickly enough that I could make, to this enquiry, no answer that would n't involve something of a sacrifice of my employer. Yet it struck me that we were all, at Bly, sufficiently sacrificed to make that venial. "I don't think your uncle much cares."

Miles, on this, stood looking at me. "Then don't you think he can be made to?"

"In what way?"

· "Why by his coming down."

"But who'll get him to come down?"

"*I* will!" the boy said with extraordinary brightness and emphasis. He gave me another look charged with that expression and then marched off alone into church.

XV

THE business was practically settled from the moment I never followed him. It was a pitiful surrender to agitation, but my being aware of this had somehow no power to restore me. I only sat there on my tomb and read into what our young friend had said to me the fulness of its meaning; by the time I had grasped the whole of which I had also embraced, for absence, the pretext that I was ashamed to offer my pupils and the rest of the congregation such an example of delay. What I said to myself above all was that Miles had got something out of me and that the gage of it for him would be just this awkward collapse. He had got out of me that there was something I was much afraid of, and that he should probably be able to make use of my fear to gain, for his own purpose, more freedom. My fear was of having to deal with the intolerable question of the grounds of his dismissal from school, since that was really but the question of the horrors gathered behind. That his uncle should arrive to treat with me of these things was a solution that, strictly speaking, I ought now to have desired to bring on; but I could so little face the ugliness and the pain of it that I simply procrastinated and lived from hand to mouth. The boy, to my deep discomposure, was immensely in the right, was in a position to say to me: "Either you clear up with my guardian the mystery of this interruption of my studies, or you cease to expect me to lead with you a life that's so unnatural for a boy." What was so unnatural for the particular boy I was concerned with was this sudden revelation of a consciousness and a plan.

That was what really overcame me, what prevented my going in. I walked round the church, hesitating, hovering; I reflected that I had already, with him, hurt myself beyond repair. Therefore I could patch up nothing and it was too extreme an effort to squeeze beside him into the pew: he would be so much more sure than ever to pass his arm into mine and make me sit there for an hour in close mute contact with his commentary on our talk. For the first minute since his arrival I wanted to get away from him. As I paused beneath the high east window and listened to the sounds of worship I was taken with an impulse that might master me, I felt, and completely, should I give it the least encouragement. I might easily put an end to my ordeal by getting away altogether. Here was my chance; there was no one to stop me; I could give the whole thing up — turn my back and bolt. It was only a question of hurrying again, for a few preparations, to the house which the attendance at church of so many of the servants would practically have left unoccupied. No one, in short, could blame me if I should just drive desperately off. What was it to get away if I should get away only till dinner? That would be in a couple of hours, at the end of which — I had the acute prevision — my little pupils would play at innocent wonder about my non-appearance in their train.

"What *did* you do, you naughty bad thing? Why in the world, to worry us so — and take our thoughts off too, don't you know? — did you desert us at the very door?" I could n't meet such questions nor, as they asked them, their false little lovely eyes; yet it was all so exactly what I should have to meet that, as the prospect grew sharp to me, I at last let myself go.

I got, so far as the immediate moment was concerned, away; I came straight out of the churchyard and, thinking hard, retraced my steps through the park. It seemed to me that by the time I reached the house I had made up my mind to cynical flight. The Sunday stillness both of the approaches and of the interior, in which I met no one, fairly stirred me with a sense of opportunity. Were I to get off quickly this way I should get off without a scene, without a word. My quickness would have to be remarkable, however, and the question of a conveyance was the great one to settle. Tormented, in the hall, with difficulties and obstacles, I remember sinking down at the foot of the staircase — suddenly collapsing there on the lowest step and then, with a revulsion, recalling that it was exactly where, more than a month before, in the darkness of night and just so bowed with evil things, I had seen the spectre of the most horrible of women. At this I was able to straighten myself; I went the rest of the way up; I made, in my turmoil, for the schoolroom, where there were objects belonging to me that I should have to take. But I opened the door to find again, in a flash, my eyes unsealed. In the presence of what I saw I reeled straight back upon resistance.

Seated at my own table in the clear noonday light I saw a person whom, without my previous experience, I should have taken at the first blush for some housemaid who might have stayed at home to look after the place and who, availing herself of rare relief from observation and of the schoolroom table and my pens, ink and paper, had applied herself to the considerable effort of a letter to her sweetheart. There was an effort in the way that, while her arms rested on the table, her hands, with evident weariness, supported her head; but at the moment I took this in I had already become aware that, in spite of my entrance, her attitude strangely persisted. Then it was — with the very act of its announcing itself — that her identity flared up in a change of posture. She rose, not as if she had heard me, but with an indescribable grand melancholy of indifference and detachment, and, within a dozen feet of me, stood there as my vile predecessor. Dishonoured and tragic, she was all before me; but even as I fixed and, for memory, secured it, the awful image passed away. Dark as midnight in her black dress, her haggard beauty and her unutterable woe, she had looked at me long enough to appear to say that her right to sit at my table was as good as mine to sit at hers. While these instants lasted indeed I had the extraordinary chill of a feeling that it was I who was the intruder. It was as a wild protest against it that, actually addressing her — "You terrible miserable woman!" — I heard myself break into a sound that, by the open door, rang through the long passage and the empty house. She looked at me as if she heard me, but I had recovered myself and cleared the air. There was nothing in the room the next minute but the sunshine and the sense that I must stay.

XVI

I HAD so perfectly expected the return of the others to be marked by a demonstration that I was freshly upset at having to find them merely dumb and discreet about my desertion. Instead of gaily denouncing and caressing me they made no allusion to my having failed them, and I was left, for the time, on perceiving that she too said nothing, to study Mrs. Grose's odd face. I did this to such purpose that I made sure they had in some way bribed her to silence; a silence that, however, I would engage to break down on the first private opportunity. This opportunity came before tea: I secured five minutes with her in the housekeeper's room, where, in the twilight, amid a smell of lately-baked bread, but with the place all swept and garnished, I found her sitting in pained placidity before the fire. So I see her still, so I see her best: facing the flame from her straight chair in the dusky shining room, a large clean picture of the "put away" — of drawers closed and locked and rest without a remedy.

"Oh yes, they asked me to say nothing; and to please them — so long as they were there — of course I promised. But what had happened to you?"

"I only went with you for the walk," I said. "I had then to come back to meet a friend."

She showed her surprise. "A friend — *you?*"

"Oh yes, I've a couple!" I laughed. "But did the children give you a reason?"

"For not alluding to your leaving us? Yes; they said you'd like it better. *Do* you like it better?"

My face had made her rueful. "No, I like it worse!" But after an instant I added: "Did they say why I should like it better?"

"No; Master Miles only said 'We must do nothing but what she likes!'"

"I wish indeed he would! And what did Flora say?"

"Miss Flora was too sweet. She said 'Oh of course, of course!' — and I said the same."

I thought a moment. "You were too sweet too — I can hear you all. But none the less, between Miles and me, it's now all out."

"All out?" My companion stared. "But what, Miss?"

"Everything. It does n't matter. I've made up my mind. I came home, my dear," I went on, "for a talk with Miss Jessel."

I had by this time formed the habit of having Mrs. Grose literally well in hand in advance of my sounding that note; so that even now, as she bravely blinked under the signal of my word, I could keep her comparatively firm. "A talk! Do you mean she spoke?"

"It came to that. I found her, on my return, in the schoolroom."

"And what did she say?" I can hear the good woman still, and the candour of her stupefaction.

"That she suffers the torments —!"

It was this, of a truth, that made her, as she filled out my picture, gape. "Do you mean," she faltered " — of the lost?"

"Of the lost. Of the damned. And that's why, to share them —" I faltered myself with the horror of it.

But my companion, with less imagination, kept me up. "To share them — ?"

"She wants Flora." Mrs. Grose might, as I gave it to her, fairly have fallen away from me had I not been prepared. I still held her there, to show I was. "As I've told you, however, it does n't matter."

"Because you've made up your mind? But to what?"

"To everything."

"And what do you call 'everything'?"

"Why to sending for their uncle."

"Oh Miss, in pity do," my friend broke out.

"Ah but I will, I *will!* I see it's the only way. What's 'out,' as I told you, with Miles is that if he thinks I'm afraid to — and has ideas of what he gains by that — he shall see he's mistaken. Yes, yes; his uncle shall have it here from me on the spot (and before the boy himself if necessary) that if I'm to be reproached with having done nothing again about more school —"

"Yes, Miss —" my companion pressed me.

"Well, there's that awful reason."

There were now clearly so many of these for my poor colleague that she was excusable for being vague. "But — a — which?"

"Why the letter from his old place."

"You'll show it to the master?"

"I ought to have done so on the instant."

"Oh no!" said Mrs. Grose with decision.

"I'll put it before him," I went on inexorably, "that I can't undertake to work the question on behalf of a child who has been expelled —"

"For we've never in the least known what!" Mrs. Grose declared.

"For wickedness. For what else — when he's so clever and beautiful and perfect? Is he stupid? Is he untidy? Is he infirm? Is he ill-natured? He's exquisite — so it can be only *that;* and that would open up the whole thing. After all," I said, "it's their uncle's fault. If he left here such people —!"

"He did n't really in the least know them. The fault's mine." She had turned quite pale.

"Well, you shan't suffer," I answered.

"The children shan't!" she emphatically returned.

I was silent a while; we looked at each other. "Then what am I to tell him?"

"You need n't tell him anything. *I'll* tell him."

I measured this. "Do you mean you'll write —?" Remembering she could n't, I caught myself up. "How do you communicate?"

"I tell the bailiff. *He* writes."

"And should you like him to write our story?"

My question had a sarcastic force that I had not fully intended, and it made her after a moment inconsequently break down. The tears were again in her eyes. "Ah Miss, *you* write!"

"Well — to-night," I at last returned; and on this we separated.

XVII

I WENT so far, in the evening, as to make a beginning. The weather had changed back, a great wind was abroad, and beneath the lamp, in my room, with Flora at peace beside me, I sat for a long time before a blank sheet of paper and listened to the lash of the rain and the batter of the gusts. Finally I went out, taking a candle; I crossed the passage and listened a minute at Miles's door. What, under my endless obsession, I had been impelled to listen for was some betrayal of his not being at rest, and I presently caught one, but not in the form I had expected. His voice tinkled out. "I say, you there — come in." It was gaiety in the gloom!

I went in with my light and found him in bed, very wide awake but very much at his ease. "Well, what are *you* up to?" he asked with a grace of sociability in which it occurred to me that Mrs. Grose, had she been present, might have looked in vain for proof that anything was "out."

I stood over him with my candle. "How did you know I was there?"

"Why of course I heard you. Did you fancy you made no noise? You're like a troop of cavalry!" he beautifully laughed.

"Then you were n't asleep?"

"Not much! I lie awake and think."

I had put my candle, designedly, a short way off,

and then, as he held out his friendly old hand to me, had sat down on the edge of his bed. "What is it," I asked, "that you think of?"

"What in the world, my dear, but *you*?"

"Ah the pride I take in your appreciation does n't insist on that! I had so far rather you slept."

"Well, I think also, you know, of this queer business of ours."

I marked the coolness of his firm little hand. "Of what queer business, Miles?"

"Why the way you bring me up. And all the rest!"

I fairly held my breath a minute, and even from my glimmering taper there was light enough to show how he smiled up at me from his pillow. "What do you mean by all the rest?"

"Oh you know, you know!"

I could say nothing for a minute, though I felt as I held his hand and our eyes continued to meet that my silence had all the air of admitting his charge and that nothing in the whole world of reality was perhaps at that moment so fabulous as our actual relation. "Certainly you shall go back to school," I said, "if it be that that troubles you. But not to the old place — we must find another, a better. How could I know it did trouble you, this question, when you never told me so, never spoke of it at all?" His clear listening face, framed in its smooth whiteness, made him for the minute as appealing as some wistful patient in a children's hospital; and I would have given, as the resemblance came to me, all I possessed on earth really to be the nurse or the sister of charity who might have helped to cure him. Well, even as it was I perhaps might help! "Do you know you've never said a word to me about your school — I mean the old one; never mentioned it in any way?"

He seemed to wonder; he smiled with the same loveliness. But he clearly gained time; he waited, he called for guidance. "Have n't I?" It was n't for *me* to help him — it was for the thing I had met!

Something in his tone and the expression of his face, as I got this from him, set my heart aching with such a pang as it had never yet known; so unutterably touching was it to see his little brain puzzled and his little resources taxed to play, under the spell laid on him, a part of innocence and consistency. "No, never — from the hour you came back. You've never mentioned to me one of your masters, one of your comrades, nor the least little thing that ever happened to you at school. Never, little Miles — no never — have you given me an inkling of anything that *may* have happened there. Therefore you can fancy how much I'm in the dark. Until you came out, that way, this morning, you had since the first hour I saw you scarce even made a reference to anything in your previous life. You seemed so perfectly to accept the present." It was extraordinary how my absolute conviction of his secret precocity — or whatever I might call the poison of an influence that I dared but half-phrase — made him, in spite of the faint breath of his inward trouble, appear as accessible as an older person, forced me to treat him as an intelligent equal. "I thought you wanted to go on as you are."

It struck me that at this he just faintly coloured. He gave, at any rate, like a convalescent slightly fatigued, a languid shake of his head. "I don't — I don't. I want to get away."

"You're tired of Bly ?"

"Oh no, I like Bly."

"Well then — ?"

"Oh *you* know what a boy wants!"

I felt I did n't know so well as Miles, and I took temporary refuge. "You want to go to your uncle ?"

Again, at this, with his sweet ironic face, he made a movement on the pillow. "Ah you can't get off with that!"

I was silent a little, and it was I now, I think, who changed colour. "My dear, I don't want to get off!"

"You can't even if you do. You can't, you can't!" — he lay beautifully staring. "My uncle must come down and you must completely settle things."

"If we do," I returned with some spirit, "you may be sure it will be to take you quite away."

"Well, don't you understand that that's exactly what I'm working for ? You'll have to *tell* him — about the way you 've let it all drop : you 'll have to tell him a tremendous lot!"

The exultation with which he uttered this helped me somehow for the instant to meet him rather more. "And how much will *you*, Miles, have to tell him ? There are things he 'll ask you!"

He turned it over. "Very likely. But what things ?"

"The things you 've never told me. To make up his mind what to do with you. He can't send you back —"

"I don't want to go back!" he broke in. "I want a new field."

He said it with admirable serenity, with positive unimpeachable gaiety; and doubtless it was that very note that most evoked for me the poignancy, the unnatural childish tragedy, of his probable reappearance at the end of three months with all this bravado and still more dishonour. It overwhelmed me now that I should never be able to bear that, and it made me let myself go. I threw myself upon him and in the tenderness of my pity I embraced him. "Dear little Miles, dear little Miles —!"

My face was close to his, and he let me kiss him, simply taking it with indulgent good humour. "Well, old lady?"

"Is there nothing — nothing at all that you want to tell me?"

He turned off a little, facing round toward the wall and holding up his hand to look at as one had seen sick children look. "I've told you — I told you this morning."

Oh I was sorry for him! "That you just want me not to worry you?"

He looked round at me now as if in recognition of my understanding him; then ever so gently, "To let me alone," he replied.

There was even a strange little dignity in it, something that made me release him, yet, when I had slowly risen, linger beside him. God knows *I* never wished to harass him, but I felt that merely, at this, to turn my back on him was to abandon or, to put it more truly, lose him. "I've just begun a letter to your uncle," I said.

"Well then, finish it!"

I waited a minute. "What happened before?"

He gazed up at me again. "Before what?"

"Before you came back. And before you went away."

For some time he was silent, but he continued to meet my eyes. "What happened?"

It made me, the sound of the words, in which it seemed to me I caught for the very first time a small faint quaver of consenting consciousness — it made me drop on my knees beside the bed and seize once more the chance of possessing him. "Dear little Miles, dear little Miles, if you *knew* how I want to help you! It's only that, it's nothing but that, and I'd rather die than give you a pain or do you a wrong — I'd rather die than hurt a hair of you. Dear little Miles" — oh I brought it out now even if I *should* go too far — "I just want you to help me to save you!" But I knew in a moment after this that I had gone too far. The answer to my appeal was instantaneous, but it came in the form of an extraordinary blast and chill, a gust of frozen air and a shake of the room as great as if, in the wild wind, the casement had crashed in. The boy gave a loud high shriek which, lost in the rest of the shock of sound, might have seemed, indistinctly, though I was so close to him, a note either of jubilation or of terror. I jumped to my feet again and was conscious of darkness. So for a moment we remained, while I stared about me and saw the drawn curtains unstirred and the window still tight. "Why the candle's out!" I then cried.

"It was I who blew it, dear!" said Miles.

XVIII

THE next day, after lessons, Mrs. Grose found a moment to say to me quietly: "Have you written, Miss?"

"Yes — I've written." But I did n't add — for the hour — that my letter, sealed and directed, was still in my pocket. There would be time enough to send it before the messenger should go to the village. Meanwhile there had been on the part of my pupils no more brilliant, more exemplary morning. It was exactly as if they had both had at heart to gloss over any recent little friction. They performed the dizziest feats of arithmetic, soaring quite out of *my* feeble range, and perpetrated, in higher spirits than ever, geographical and historical jokes. It was conspicuous of course in Miles in particular that he appeared to wish to show how easily he could let me down. This child, to my memory, really lives in a setting of beauty and misery that no words can translate; there was a distinction all his own in every impulse he revealed; never was a small natural creature, to the uninformed eye all frankness and freedom, a more ingenious, a more extraordinary little gentleman. I had perpetually to guard against the wonder of contemplation into which my initiated view betrayed me; to check the irrelevant gaze and discouraged sigh in which I constantly both attacked and renounced the enigma of what such a little gentleman could have done that deserved a penalty. Say that, by the dark prodigy I knew, the imagination of all evil *had* been opened up to him : all the justice within me ached for the proof that it could ever have flowered into an act.

He had never at any rate been such a little gentleman as when, after our early dinner on this dreadful day, he came round to me and asked if I should n't like him for half an hour to play to me. David playing to Saul could never have shown a finer sense of the occasion. It was literally a charming exhibition of tact, of magnanimity, and quite tantamount to his saying outright: "The true knights we love to read about never push an advantage too far. I know what you mean now: you mean that — to be let alone yourself and not followed up — you 'll cease to worry and spy upon me, won't keep me so close to you, will let me go and come. Well, I 'come,' you see — but I don't go! There 'll be plenty of time for that. I do really delight in your society and I only want to show you that I contended for a principle." It may be imagined whether I resisted this appeal or failed to accompany him again, hand in hand, to the schoolroom. He sat down at the old piano and played as he had never played; and if there are those who think he had better have been kicking a football I can only say that I wholly agree with them. For at the end of a time that under his influence I had quite ceased to measure I started up with a strange sense of having literally slept at my post. It was after luncheon, and by the schoolroom fire, and yet I had n't really in the least slept; I had only done something much worse — I had forgotten. Where all this time was Flora? When I

269

put the question to Miles he played on a minute before answering, and then could only say: "Why, my dear, how do *I* know?" — breaking moreover into a happy laugh which immediately after, as if it were a vocal accompaniment, he prolonged into incoherent extravagant song.

I went straight to my room, but his sister was not there; then, before going downstairs, I looked into several others. As she was nowhere about she would surely be with Mrs. Grose, whom in the comfort of that theory I accordingly proceeded in quest of. I found her where I had found her the evening before, but she met my quick challenge with blank scared ignorance. She had only supposed that, after the repast, I had carried off both the children; as to which she was quite in her right, for it was the very first time I had allowed the little girl out of my sight without some special provision. Of course now indeed she might be with the maids, so that the immediate thing was to look for her without an air of alarm. This we promptly arranged between us; but when, ten minutes later and in pursuance of our arrangement, we met in the hall, it was only to report on either side that after guarded enquiries we had altogether failed to trace her. For a minute there, apart from observation, we exchanged mute alarms, and I could feel with what high interest my friend returned me all those I had from the first given her.

"She'll be above," she presently said — "in one of the rooms you have n't searched."

"No; she's at a distance." I had made up my mind. "She has gone out."

Mrs. Grose stared. "Without a hat?"

I naturally also looked volumes. "Isn't that woman always without one?"

"She's with *her*?"

"She's with *her!*" I declared. "We must find them."

My hand was on my friend's arm, but she failed for the moment, confronted with such an account of the matter, to respond to my pressure. She communed, on the contrary, where she stood, with her uneasiness. "And where's Master Miles?"

"Oh *he's* with Quint. They'll be in the schoolroom."

"Lord, Miss!" My view, I was myself aware — and therefore I suppose my tone — had never yet reached so calm an assurance.

"The trick's played," I went on; "they've successfully worked their plan. He found the most divine little way to keep me quiet while she went off."

"'Divine'?" Mrs. Grose bewilderedly echoed.

"Infernal then!" I almost cheerfully rejoined. "He has provided for himself as well. But come!"

She had helplessly gloomed at the upper regions. "You leave him — ?"

"So long with Quint? Yes — I don't mind that now."

She always ended at these moments by getting possession of my hand, and in this manner she could at present still stay me. But after gasping an instant at my sudden resignation, "Because of your letter?" she eagerly brought out.

I quickly, by way of answer, felt for my letter, drew

it forth, held it up, and then, freeing myself, went and laid it on the great hall-table. "Luke will take it," I said as I came back. I reached the house-door and opened it; I was already on the steps.

My companion still demurred: the storm of the night and the early morning had dropped, but the afternoon was damp and grey. I came down to the drive while she stood in the doorway. "You go with nothing on?"

"What do I care when the child has nothing? I can't wait to dress," I cried, "and if you must do so I leave you. Try meanwhile yourself upstairs."

"With *them?*" Oh on this the poor woman promptly joined me!

XIX

WE went straight to the lake, as it was called at Bly, and I dare say rightly called, though it may have been a sheet of water less remarkable than my untravelled eyes supposed it. My acquaintance with sheets of water was small, and the pool of Bly, at all events on the few occasions of my consenting, under the protection of my pupils, to affront its surface in the old flat-bottomed boat moored there for our use, had impressed me both with its extent and its agitation. The usual place of embarkation was half a mile from the house, but I had an intimate conviction that, wherever Flora might be, she was not near home. She had not given me the slip for any small adventure, and, since the day of the very great one that I had shared with her by the pond, I had been aware, in our walks, of the quarter to which she most inclined. This was why I had now given to Mrs. Grose's steps so marked a direction — a direction making her, when she perceived it, oppose a resistance that showed me she was freshly mystified. "You're going to the water, Miss? — you think she's *in* — ?"

"She may be, though the depth is, I believe, nowhere very great. But what I judge most likely is that she's on the spot from which, the other day, we saw together what I told you."

"When she pretended not to see — ?"

"With that astounding self-possession! I've always been sure she wanted to go back alone. And now her brother has managed it for her."

Mrs. Grose still stood where she had stopped. "You suppose they really *talk* of them?"

I could meet this with an assurance! "They say things that, if we heard them, would simply appal us."

"And if she *is* there —?"

"Yes?"

"Then Miss Jessel is?"

"Beyond a doubt. You shall see."

"Oh thank you!" my friend cried, planted so firm that, taking it in, I went straight on without her. By the time I reached the pool, however, she was close behind me, and I knew that, whatever, to her apprehension, might befall me, the exposure of sticking to me struck her as her least danger. She exhaled a moan of relief as we at last came in sight of the greater part of the water without a sight of the child. There was no trace of Flora on that nearer side of the bank where my observation of her had been most startling, and none on the opposite edge, where, save for a margin of some twenty yards, a thick copse came down to the pond. This expanse, oblong in shape, was so narrow compared to its length that, with its ends out of view, it might have been taken for a scant river. We looked at the empty stretch, and then I felt the suggestion in my friend's eyes. I knew what she meant and I replied with a negative headshake.

"No, no; wait! She has taken the boat."

My companion stared at the vacant mooring-place and then again across the lake. "Then where is it?"

"Our not seeing it is the strongest of proofs. She has used it to go over, and then has managed to hide it."

"All alone — that child?"

"She's not alone, and at such times she's not a child: she's an old, old woman." I scanned all the visible shore while Mrs. Grose took again, into the queer element I offered her, one of her plunges of submission; then I pointed out that the boat might perfectly be in a small refuge formed by one of the recesses of the pool, an indentation masked, for the hither side, by a projection of the bank and by a clump of trees growing close to the water.

"But if the boat's there, where on earth's *she?*" my colleague anxiously asked.

"That's exactly what we must learn." And I started to walk further.

"By going all the way round?"

"Certainly, far as it is. It will take us but ten minutes, yet it's far enough to have made the child prefer not to walk. She went straight over."

"Laws!" cried my friend again: the chain of my logic was ever too strong for her. It dragged her at my heels even now, and when we had got halfway round — a devious tiresome process, on ground much broken and by a path choked with overgrowth — I paused to give her breath. I sustained her with a grateful arm, assuring her that she might hugely help me; and this started us afresh, so that in the course of but few minutes more we reached a point from which we found the boat to be where I had supposed it. It had been intentionally left as much as possible out of sight and was tied to one of the stakes of a fence that came, just there, down to the brink and that had been an assistance to disembarking. I recognised, as I looked at the pair of short thick oars, quite safely drawn up, the prodigious character of the feat for a little girl; but I had by this time lived too long among wonders and had panted to too many livelier measures. There was a gate in the fence, through which we passed, and that brought us after a trifling interval more into the open. Then "There she is!" we both exclaimed at once.

Flora, a short way off, stood before us on the grass and smiled as if her performance had now become complete. The next thing she did, however, was to stoop straight down and pluck — quite as if it were all she was there for — a big ugly spray of withered fern. I at once felt sure she had just come out of the copse. She waited for us, not herself taking a step, and I was conscious of the rare solemnity with which we presently approached her. She smiled and smiled, and we met; but it was all done in a silence by this time flagrantly ominous. Mrs. Grose was the first to break the spell: she threw herself on her knees and, drawing the child to her breast, clasped in a long embrace the little tender yielding body. While this dumb convulsion lasted I could only watch it — which I did the more intently when I saw Flora's face peep at me over our companion's shoulder. It was serious now — the flicker had left it; but it strengthened the pang with which I at that moment envied Mrs. Grose the simplicity of *her* relation. Still, all this while, nothing more passed between us save that Flora had let her foolish fern again drop to the ground. What she and I had

virtually said to each other was that pretexts were useless now. When Mrs. Grose finally got up she kept
the child's hand, so that the two were still before me;
and the singular reticence of our communion was even
more marked in the frank look she addressed me.
"I'll be hanged," it said, "if *I'll* speak!"

It was Flora who, gazing all over me in candid
wonder, was the first. She was struck with our bare-
headed aspect. "Why where are your things?"

"Where yours are, my dear!" I promptly returned.

She had already got back her gaiety and appeared
to take this as an answer quite sufficient. "And
where's Miles?" she went on.

There was something in the small valour of it that
quite finished me: these three words from her were in
a flash like the glitter of a drawn blade the jostle of
the cup that my hand for weeks and weeks had held
high and full to the brim and that now, even before
speaking, I felt overflow in a deluge. "I'll tell you if
you'll tell *me* —" I heard myself say, then heard the
tremor in which it broke.

"Well, what?"

Mrs. Grose's suspense blazed at me, but it was too
late now, and I brought the thing out handsomely.
"Where, my pet, is Miss Jessel?"

XX

Just as in the churchyard with Miles, the whole thing was upon us. Much as I had made of the fact that this name had never once, between us, been sounded, the quick smitten glare with which the child's face now received it fairly likened my breach of the silence to the smash of a pane of glass. It added to the interposing cry, as if to stay the blow, that Mrs. Grose at the same instant uttered over my violence — the shriek of a creature scared, or rather wounded, which, in turn, within a few seconds, was completed by a gasp of my own. I seized my colleague's arm. "She's there, she's there!"

Miss Jessel stood before us on the opposite bank exactly as she had stood the other time, and I remember, strangely, as the first feeling now produced in me, my thrill of joy at having brought on a proof. She was there, so I was justified; she was there, so I was neither cruel nor mad. She was there for poor scared Mrs. Grose, but she was there most for Flora; and no moment of my monstrous time was perhaps so extraordinary as that in which I consciously threw out to her — with the sense that, pale and ravenous demon as she was, she would catch and understand it — an inarticulate message of gratitude. She rose erect on the spot my friend and I had lately quitted, and there was n't in all the long reach of her desire an inch of her evil that fell short. This first vividness of vision and emotion were things of a few seconds, during which Mrs. Grose's dazed blink across to where I pointed struck me as showing that she too at last saw, just as it carried my own eyes precipitately to the child. The revelation then of the manner in which Flora was affected startled me in truth far more than it would have done to find her also merely agitated, for direct dismay was of course not what I had expected. Prepared and on her guard as our pursuit had actually made her, she would repress every betrayal; and I was therefore at once shaken by my first glimpse of the particular one for which I had not allowed. To see her, without a convulsion of her small pink face, not even feign to glance in the direction of the prodigy I announced, but only, instead of that, turn at *me* an expression of hard still gravity, an expression absolutely new and unprecedented and that appeared to read and accuse and judge me — this was a stroke that somehow converted the little girl herself into a figure portentous. I gaped at her coolness even though my certitude of her thoroughly seeing was never greater than at that instant, and then, in the immediate need to defend myself, I called her passionately to witness. "She's there, you little unhappy thing — there, there, *there*, and you know it as well as you know me!" I had said shortly before to Mrs. Grose that she was not at these times a child, but an old, old woman, and my description of her could n't have been more strikingly confirmed than in the way in which, for all notice of this, she simply showed me, without an expressional concession or admission, a countenance of deeper and deeper, of indeed suddenly quite fixed reprobation. I was by this time — if I can put the whole thing at all together — more appalled at what I may properly call her manner than at anything else, though it was quite simultaneously that I became aware of having Mrs. Grose also, and very formidably, to reckon with. My elder companion, the next moment, at any rate, blotted out everything but her own flushed face and her loud shocked protest, a burst of high disapproval. "What a dreadful turn, to be sure, Miss! Where on earth do you see anything?"

I could only grasp her more quickly yet, for even while she spoke the hideous plain presence stood undimmed and undaunted. It had already lasted a minute, and it lasted while I continued, seizing my colleague, quite thrusting her at it and presenting her to it, to insist with my pointing hand. "You don't see her exactly as *we* see? — you mean to say you don't now — *now*? She's as big as a blazing fire! Only look, dearest woman, *look* —!" She looked, just as I did, and gave me, with her deep groan of negation, repulsion, compassion — the mixture with her pity of her relief at her exemption — a sense, touching to me even then, that she would have backed me up if she had been able. I might well have needed that, for with this hard blow of the proof that her eyes were hopelessly sealed I felt my own situation horribly crumble, I felt — I *saw* — my livid predecessor press, from her position, on my defeat, and I took the measure, more than all, of what I should have from this instant to deal with in the astounding little attitude of Flora. Into this attitude Mrs. Grose immediately and violently entered, breaking, even while there pierced through my sense of ruin a prodigious private triumph, into breathless reassurance.

"She is n't there, little lady, and nobody 's there — and you never see nothing, my sweet! How can poor Miss Jessel — when poor Miss Jessel's dead and buried?" *We* know, don't we, love?" — and she appealed, blundering in, to the child. "It's all a mere mistake and a worry and a joke — and we'll go home as fast as we can!"

Our companion, on this, had responded with a strange quick primness of propriety, and they were again, with Mrs. Grose on her feet, united, as it were, in shocked opposition to me. Flora continued to fix me with her small mask of disaffection, and even at that minute I prayed God to forgive me for seeming to see that, as she stood there holding tight to our friend's dress, her incomparable childish beauty had suddenly failed, had quite vanished. I've said it already — she was literally, she was hideously hard; she had turned common and almost ugly. "I don't know what you mean. I see nobody. I see nothing. I never *have*. I think you're cruel. I don't like you!" Then, after this deliverance, which might have been that of a vulgarly pert little girl in the street, she hugged Mrs. Grose more closely and buried in her skirts the dreadful little face. In this position she launched an almost furious wail. "Take me away, take me away — oh take me away from *her*!"

"From *me*?" I panted.

"From you — from you!" she cried.

Even Mrs. Grose looked across at me dismayed; while I had nothing to do but communicate again with

the figure that, on the opposite bank, without a movement, as rigidly still as if catching, beyond the interval, our voices, was as vividly there for my disaster as
it was not there for my service. The wretched child
had spoken exactly as if she had got from some outside source each of her stabbing little words, and I
could therefore, in the full despair of all I had to accept, but sadly shake my head at her. "If I had ever
doubted all my doubt would at present have gone.
I've been living with the miserable truth, and now it
has only too much closed round me. Of course I've
lost you: I've interfered, and you've seen, under *her*
dictation" — with which I faced, over the pool again,
our infernal witness — "the easy and perfect way to
meet it. I've done my best, but I've lost you. Good-
bye." For Mrs. Grose I had an imperative, an almost
frantic "Go, go!" before which, in infinite distress,
but mutely possessed of the little girl and clearly convinced, in spite of her blindness, that something awful
had occurred and some collapse engulfed us, she
retreated, by the way we had come, as fast as she
could move.

Of what first happened when I was left alone I had
no subsequent memory. I only knew that at the end
of, I suppose, a quarter of an hour, an odorous damp-
ness and roughness, chilling and piercing my trouble,
had made me understand that I must have thrown
myself, on my face, to the ground and given way to a
wildness of grief. I must have lain there long and
cried and wailed, for when I raised my head the day
was almost done. I got up and looked a moment,
through the twilight, at the grey pool and its blank

haunted edge, and then I took, back to the house, my
dreary and difficult course. When I reached the gate
in the fence the boat, to my surprise, was gone, so that
I had a fresh reflexion to make on Flora's extraordinary command of the situation. She passed that night,
by the most tacit and, I should add, were not the word
so grotesque a false note, the happiest of arrangements, with Mrs. Grose. I saw neither of them on my
return, but on the other hand I saw, as by an ambiguous compensation, a great deal of Miles. I saw — I
can use no other phrase — so much of him that it
fairly measured more than it had ever measured. No
evening I had passed at Bly was to have had the portentous quality of this one; in spite of which — and in
spite also of the deeper depths of consternation that
had opened beneath my feet — there was literally, in
the ebbing actual, an extraordinarily sweet sadness.
On reaching the house I had never so much as looked
for the boy; I had simply gone straight to my room to
change what I was wearing and to take in, at a glance,
much material testimony to Flora's rupture. Her
little belongings had all been removed. When later,
by the schoolroom fire, I was served with tea by the
usual maid, I indulged, on the article of my other
pupil, in no enquiry whatever. He had his freedom
now — he might have it to the end! Well, he did have
it; and it consisted — in part at least — of his coming
in at about eight o'clock and sitting down with me in
silence. On the removal of the tea-things I had blown
out the candles and drawn my chair closer: I was conscious of a mortal coldness and felt as if I should never
again be warm. So when he appeared I was sitting in

the glow with my thoughts. He paused a moment by
the door as if to look at me; then — as if to share them
— came to the other side of the hearth and sank into
a chair. We sat there in absolute stillness; yet he
wanted, I felt, to be with me.

XXI

BEFORE a new day, in my room, had fully broken, my
eyes opened to Mrs. Grose, who had come to my bedside with worse news. Flora was so markedly feverish
that an illness was perhaps at hand; she had passed a
night of extreme unrest, a night agitated above all by
fears that had for their subject not in the least her
former but wholly her present governess. It was not
against the possible re-entrance of Miss Jessel on the
scene that she protested — it was conspicuously and
passionately against mine. I was at once on my feet,
and with an immense deal to ask; the more that my
friend had discernibly now girded her loins to meet
me afresh. This I felt as soon as I had put to her the
question of her sense of the child's sincerity as against
my own. "She persists in denying to you that she saw,
or has ever seen, anything?"

My visitor's trouble truly was great. "Ah Miss, it
isn't a matter on which I can push her! Yet it isn't
either, I must say, as if I much needed to. It has made
her, every inch of her, quite old."

"Oh I see her perfectly from here. She resents,
for all the world like some high little personage, the
imputation on her truthfulness and, as it were, her
respectability. 'Miss Jessel indeed — *she!*' Ah she's
'respectable,' the chit! The impression she gave me
there yesterday was, I assure you, the very strangest
of all: it was quite beyond any of the others. I *did* put
my foot in it! She'll never speak to me again."

Hideous and obscure as it all was, it held Mrs. Grose briefly silent; then she granted my point with a frankness which, I made sure, had more behind it. "I think indeed, Miss, she never will. She do have a grand manner about it!"

"And that manner" — I summed it up — "is practically what's the matter with her now."

Oh that manner, I could see in my visitor's face, and not a little else besides! "She asks me every three minutes if I think you're coming in."

"I see — I see." I too, on my side, had so much more than worked it out. "Has she said to you since yesterday — except to repudiate her familiarity with anything so dreadful — a single other word about Miss Jessel?"

"Not one, Miss. And of course, you know," my friend added, "I took it from her by the lake that just then and there at least there *was* nobody."

"Rather! And naturally you take it from her still."

"I don't contradict her. What else can I do?"

"Nothing in the world! You've the cleverest little person to deal with. They've made them — their two friends, I mean — still cleverer even than nature did; for it was wondrous material to play on! Flora has now her grievance, and she'll work it to the end."

"Yes, Miss; but to *what* end?"

"Why that of dealing with me to her uncle. She'll make me out to him the lowest creature —!"

I winced at the fair show of the scene in Mrs. Grose's face; she looked for a minute as if she sharply saw them together. "And him who thinks so well of you!"

"He has an odd way — it comes over me now,"
I laughed, "— of proving it! But that does n't matter. What Flora wants of course is to get rid of
me."

My companion bravely concurred. "Never again
to so much as look at you."

"So that what you 've come to me now for," I asked,
"is to speed me on my way?" Before she had time to
reply, however, I had her in check. "I 've a better
idea — the result of my reflexions. My going *would*
seem the right thing, and on Sunday I was terribly
near it. Yet that won't do. It 's *you* who must go.
You must take Flora."

My visitor, at this, did speculate. "But where in
the world — ?"

"Away from here. Away from *them*. Away, even
most of all, now, from me. Straight to her uncle."

"Only to tell on you — ?"

"No, not 'only'! To leave me, in addition, with
my remedy."

She was still vague. "And what *is* your remedy?"

"Your loyalty, to begin with. And then Miles's."

She looked at me hard. "Do you think he — ?"

"Won't, if he has the chance, turn on me? Yes,
I venture still to think it. At all events I want to try.
Get off with his sister as soon as possible and leave me
with him alone." I was amazed, myself, at the spirit I
had still in reserve, and therefore perhaps a trifle the
more disconcerted at the way in which, in spite of this
fine example of it, she hesitated. "There 's one thing,
of course," I went on: "they must n't, before she goes,
see each other for three seconds." Then it came over

me that, in spite of Flora's presumable sequestration from the instant of her return from the pool, it might already be too late. "Do you mean," I anxiously asked, "that they *have* met?"

At this she quite flushed. "Ah, Miss, I'm not such a fool as that! If I've been obliged to leave her three or four times, it has been each time with one of the maids, and at present, though she's alone, she's locked in safe. And yet — and yet!" There were too many things.

"And yet what?"

"Well, are you so sure of the little gentleman?"

"I'm not sure of anything but *you*. But I have, since last evening, a new hope. I think he wants to give me an opening. I do believe that — poor little exquisite wretch! — he wants to speak. Last evening, in the firelight and the silence, he sat with me for two hours as if it were just coming."

Mrs. Grose looked hard through the window at the grey gathering day. "And did it come?"

"No, though I waited and waited I confess it did n't, and it was without a breach of the silence, or so much as a faint allusion to his sister's condition and absence, that we at last kissed for good-night. All the same," I continued, "I can't, if her uncle sees her, consent to his seeing her brother without my having given the boy — and most of all because things have got so bad — a little more time."

My friend appeared on this ground more reluctant than I could quite understand. "What do you mean by more time?"

"Well, a day or two — really to bring it out. He'll

then be on *my* side — of which you see the importance. If nothing comes I shall only fail, and you at
the worst have helped me by doing on your arrival
in town whatever you may have found possible." So
I put it before her, but she continued for a little so
lost in other reasons that I came again to her aid.
"Unless indeed," I wound up, "you really want *not*
to go."

I could see it, in her face, at last clear itself: she
put out her hand to me as a pledge. "I'll go — I'll
go. I'll go this morning."

I wanted to be very just. "If you *should* wish still
to wait I'd engage she should n't see me."

"No, no: it's the place itself. She must leave it."
She held me a moment with heavy eyes, then brought
out the rest. "Your idea's the right one. I myself,
Miss —"

"Well ?"

"I can't stay."

The look she gave me with it made me jump at
possibilities. "You mean that, since yesterday, you
have seen —?"

She shook her head with dignity. "I've *heard* —!"

"Heard ?"

"From that child — horrors! There!" she sighed
with tragic relief. "On my honour, Miss, she says
things —!" But at this evocation she broke down;
she dropped with a sudden cry upon my sofa and,
as I had seen her do before, gave way to all the
anguish of it.

It was quite in another manner that I for my part
let myself go. "Oh thank God!"

She sprang up again at this, drying her eyes with a groan. "'Thank God'?"

"It so justifies me!"

"It does that, Miss!"

I could n't have desired more emphasis, but I just waited. "She's so horrible?"

I saw my colleague scarce knew how to put it. "Really shocking."

"And about me?"

"About you, Miss — since you must have it. It's beyond everything, for a young lady; and I can't think wherever she must have picked up —"

"The appalling language she applies to me? I can then!" I broke in with a laugh that was doubtless significant enough.

It only in truth left my friend still more grave. "Well, perhaps I ought to also — since I've heard some of it before! Yet I can't bear it," the poor woman went on while with the same movement she glanced, on my dressing-table, at the face of my watch. "But I must go back."

I kept her, however. "Ah if you can't bear it —!"

"How can I stop with her, you mean? Why just for that: to get her away. Far from this," she pursued, "far from them —"

"She may be different? she may be free?" I seized her almost with joy. "Then in spite of yesterday you believe —"

"In such doings?" Her simple description of them required, in the light of her expression, to be carried no further, and she gave me the whole thing as she had never done. "I believe."

Yes, it was a joy, and we were still shoulder to shoulder: if I might continue sure of that I should care but little what else happened. My support in the presence of disaster would be the same as it had been in my early need of confidence, and if my friend would answer for my honesty I would answer for all the rest. On the point of taking leave of her, none the less, I was to some extent embarrassed. "There's one thing of course — it occurs to me — to remember. My letter giving the alarm will have reached town before you."

I now felt still more how she had been beating about the bush and how weary at last it had made her. "Your letter won't have got there. Your letter never went."

"What then became of it?"

"Goodness knows! Master Miles —"

"Do you mean *he* took it?" I gasped.

She hung fire, but she overcame her reluctance. "I mean that I saw yesterday, when I came back with Miss Flora, that it wasn't where you had put it. Later in the evening I had the chance to question Luke, and he declared that he had neither noticed nor touched it." We could only exchange, on this, one of our deeper mutual soundings, and it was Mrs. Grose who first brought up the plumb with an almost elate "You see!"

"Yes, I see that if Miles took it instead he probably will have read it and destroyed it."

"And don't you see anything else?"

I faced her a moment with a sad smile. "It strikes me that by this time your eyes are open even wider than mine."

They proved to be so indeed, but she could still almost blush to show it. "I make out now what he must have done at school." And she gave, in her simple sharpness, an almost droll disillusioned nod. "He stole!"

I turned it over — I tried to be more judicial. "Well — perhaps."

She looked as if she found me unexpectedly calm. "He stole *letters!*"

She could n't know my reasons for a calmness after all pretty shallow; so I showed them off as I might. "I hope then it was to more purpose than in this case! The note, at all events, that I put on the table yesterday," I pursued, "will have given him so scant an advantage — for it contained only the bare demand for an interview — that he 's already much ashamed of having gone so far for so little, and that what he had on his mind last evening was precisely the need of confession." I seemed to myself for the instant to have mastered it, to see it all. "Leave us, leave us" — I was already, at the door, hurrying her off. "I 'll get it out of him. He 'll meet me. He 'll confess. If he confesses he 's saved. And if he 's saved —"

"Then *you* are?" The dear woman kissed me on this, and I took her farewell. "I 'll save you without him!" she cried as she went.

XXII

YET it was when she had got off — and I missed her on the spot — that the great pinch really came. If I had counted on what it would give me to find myself alone with Miles I quickly recognised that it would give me at least a measure. No hour of my stay in fact was so assailed with apprehensions as that of my coming down to learn that the carriage containing Mrs. Grose and my younger pupil had already rolled out of the gates. Now I *was*, I said to myself, face to face with the elements, and for much of the rest of the day, while I fought my weakness, I could consider that I had been supremely rash. It was a tighter place still than I had yet turned round in; all the more that, for the first time, I could see in the aspect of others a confused reflexion of the crisis. What had happened naturally caused them all to stare; there was too little of the explained, throw out whatever we might, in the suddenness of my colleague's act. The maids and the men looked blank; the effect of which on my nerves was an aggravation until I saw the necessity of making it a positive aid. It was in short by just clutching the helm that I avoided total wreck; and I dare say that, to bear up at all, I became that morning very grand and very dry. I welcomed the consciousness that I was charged with much to do, and I caused it to be known as well that, left thus to myself, I was quite remarkably firm. I wandered with that manner, for the next hour or two, all over the place and looked, I have no doubt, as if I were ready for any onset. So, for the benefit of whom it might concern, I paraded with a sick heart.

The person it appeared least to concern proved to be, till dinner, little Miles himself. My perambulations had given me meanwhile no glimpse of him, but they had tended to make more public the change taking place in our relation as a consequence of his having at the piano, the day before, kept me, in Flora's interest, so beguiled and befooled. The stamp of publicity had of course been fully given by her confinement and departure, and the change itself was now ushered in by our non-observance of the regular custom of the schoolroom. He had already disappeared when, on my way down, I pushed open his door, and I learned below that he had breakfasted — in the presence of a couple of the maids — with Mrs. Grose and his sister. He had then gone out, as he said, for a stroll; than which nothing, I reflected, could better have expressed his frank view of the abrupt transformation of my office. What he would now permit this office to consist of was yet to be settled: there was at the least a queer relief — I mean for myself in especial — in the renouncement of one pretension. If so much had sprung to the surface I scarce put it too strongly in saying that what had perhaps sprung highest was the absurdity of our prolonging the fiction that I had anything more to teach him. It sufficiently stuck out that, by tacit little tricks in which even more than myself he carried out the care for my dignity, I had had to appeal to him to let me off straining to meet him on the ground of his true capacity. He had at any rate his freedom now; I was never to touch it again: as I had amply shown, moreover, when, on his joining me in the schoolroom the previous night, I uttered, in reference to the interval just concluded, neither challenge nor hint. I had too much, from this moment, my other ideas. Yet when he at last arrived the difficulty of applying them, the accumulations of my problem, were brought straight home to me by the beautiful little presence on which what had occurred had as yet, for the eye, dropped neither stain nor shadow.

To mark, for the house, the high state I cultivated I decreed that my meals with the boy should be served, as we called it, downstairs; so that I had been awaiting him in the ponderous pomp of the room outside the window of which I had had from Mrs. Grose, that first scared Sunday, my flash of something it would scarce have done to call light. Here at present I felt afresh — for I had felt it again and again — how my equilibrium depended on the success of my rigid will, the will to shut my eyes as tight as possible to the truth that what I had to deal with was, revoltingly, against nature. I could only get on at all by taking "nature" into my confidence and my account, by treating my monstrous ordeal as a push in a direction unusual, of course, and unpleasant, but demanding after all, for a fair front, only another turn of the screw of ordinary human virtue. No attempt, none the less, could well require more tact than just this attempt to supply, one's self, *all* the nature. How could I put even a little of that article into a suppression of reference to what had occurred ? How on the other hand could I make a reference without a new plunge into the hideous obscure ? Well, a sort of answer, after a time, had come to me, and it was so far confirmed as that I was met, incontestably, by the quickened vision of what was rare in my little companion. It was indeed as if he had found even now — as he had so often found at lessons — still some other delicate way to ease me off. Was n't there light in the fact which, as we shared our solitude, broke out with a specious glitter it had never yet quite worn ? — the fact that (opportunity aiding, precious opportunity which had now come) it would be preposterous, with a child so endowed, to forego the help one might wrest from absolute intelligence ? What had his intelligence been given him for but to save him ? Might n't one, to reach his mind, risk the stretch of a stiff arm across his character ? It was as if, when we were face to face in the dining-room, he had literally shown me the way. The roast mutton was on the table and I had dispensed with attendance. Miles, before he sat down, stood a moment with his hands in his pockets and looked at the joint, on which he seemed on the point of passing some humorous judgement. But what he presently produced was: "I say, my dear, is she really very awfully ill ?"

"Little Flora ? Not so bad but that she 'll presently be better. London will set her up. Bly had ceased to agree with her. Come here and take your mutton."

He alertly obeyed me, carried the plate carefully to his seat and, when he was established, went on. "Did Bly disagree with her so terribly all at once ?"

"Not so suddenly as you might think. One had seen it coming on."

"Then why did n't you get her off before?"

"Before what?" ·

"Before she became too ill to travel."

I found myself prompt. "She's *not* too ill to travel; she only might have become so if she had stayed. This was just the moment to seize. The journey will dissipate the influence" — oh I was grand! — "and carry it off."

"I see, I see" — Miles, for that matter, was grand too. He settled to his repast with the charming little "table manner" that, from the day of his arrival, had relieved me of all grossness of admonition. Whatever he had been expelled from school for, it was n't for ugly feeding. He was irreproachable, as always, to-day; but was unmistakeably more conscious. He was discernibly trying to take for granted more things than he found, without assistance, quite easy; and he dropped into peaceful silence while he felt his situation. Our meal was of the briefest — mine a vain pretence, and I had the things immediately removed. While this was done Miles stood again with his hands in his little pockets and his back to me — stood and looked out of the wide window through which, that other day, I had seen what pulled me up. We continued silent while the maid was with us — as silent, it whimsically occurred to me, as some young couple who, on their wedding-journey, at the inn, feel shy in the presence of the waiter. He turned round only when the waiter had left us. "Well — so we're alone!"

XXIII

"Oh more or less." I imagine my smile was pale.
"Not absolutely. We should n't like that!" I went on.

"No — I suppose we should n't. Of course we've
the others."

"We've the others — we've indeed the others," I
concurred.

"Yet even though we have them," he returned, still
with his hands in his pockets and planted there in
front of me, "they don't much count, do they?"

I made the best of it, but I felt wan. "It depends
on what you call 'much'!"

"Yes" — with all accommodation — "everything
depends!" On this, however, he faced to the window
again and presently reached it with his vague restless
cogitating step. He remained there a while with his
forehead against the glass, in contemplation of the
stupid shrubs I knew and the dull things of November.
I had always my hypocrisy of "work," behind which
I now gained the sofa. Steadying myself with it there
as I had repeatedly done at those moments of torment
that I have described as the moments of my knowing
the children to be given to something from which I
was barred, I sufficiently obeyed my habit of being
prepared for the worst. But an extraordinary impression dropped on me as I extracted a meaning from the
boy's embarrassed back — none other than the impression that I was not barred now. This inference
grew in a few minutes to sharp intensity and seemed

bound up with the direct perception that it was positively *he* who was. The frames and squares of the great window were a kind of image, for him, of a kind of failure. I felt that I saw him, in any case, shut in or shut out. He was admirable but not comfortable: I took it in with a throb of hope. Was n't he looking through the haunted pane for something he could n't see? — and was n't it the first time in the whole business that he had known such a lapse? The first, the very first: I found it a splendid portent. It made him anxious, though he watched himself; he had been anxious all day and, even while in his usual sweet little manner he sat at table, had needed all his small strange genius to give it a gloss. When he at last turned round to meet me it was almost as if this genius had succumbed. "Well, I think I'm glad Bly agrees with *me!*"

"You'd certainly seem to have seen, these twenty-four hours, a good deal more of it than for some time before. I hope," I went on bravely, "that you've been enjoying yourself."

"Oh yes, I've been ever so far; all round about — miles and miles away. I've never been so free."

He had really a manner of his own, and I could only try to keep up with him. "Well, do you like it?"

He stood there smiling; then at last he put into two words — "Do *you?*" — more discrimination than I had ever heard two words contain. Before I had time to deal with that, however, he continued as if with the sense that this was an impertinence to be softened. "Nothing could be more charming than the way you take it, for of course if we're alone together now it's you that are alone most. But I hope," he threw in, "you don't particularly mind!"

"Having to do with you?" I asked. "My dear child, how can I help minding? Though I've renounced all claim to your company — you're so beyond me — I at least greatly enjoy it. What else should I stay on for?"

He looked at me more directly, and the expression of his face, graver now, struck me as the most beautiful I had ever found in it. "You stay on just for *that?*"

"Certainly. I stay on as your friend and from the tremendous interest I take in you till something can be done for you that may be more worth your while. That need n't surprise you." My voice trembled so that I felt it impossible to suppress the shake. "Don't you remember how I told you, when I came and sat on your bed the night of the storm, that there was nothing in the world I would n't do for you?"

"Yes, yes!" He, on his side, more and more visibly nervous, had a tone to master; but he was so much more successful than I that, laughing out through his gravity, he could pretend we were pleasantly jesting. "Only that, I think, was to get me to do something for you!"

"It was partly to get you to do something," I conceded. "But, you know, you did n't do it."

"Oh yes," he said with the brightest superficial eagerness, "you wanted me to tell you something."

"That's it. Out, straight out. What you have on your mind, you know."

"Ah then is *that* what you've stayed over for?"

300

He spoke with a gaiety through which I could still catch the finest little quiver of resentful passion; but I can't begin to express the effect upon me of an implication of surrender even so faint. It was as if what I had yearned for had come at last only to astonish me. "Well, yes — I may as well make a clean breast of it. It was precisely for that."

He waited so long that I supposed it for the purpose of repudiating the assumption on which my action had been founded; but what he finally said was: "Do you mean now — here?"

"There couldn't be a better place or time." He looked round him uneasily, and I had the rare — oh the queer! — impression of the very first symptom I had seen in him of the approach of immediate fear. It was as if he were suddenly afraid of me — which struck me indeed as perhaps the best thing to make him. Yet in the very pang of the effort I felt it vain to try sternness, and I heard myself the next instant so gentle as to be almost grotesque. "You want so to go out again?"

"Awfully!" He smiled at me heroically, and the touching little bravery of it was enhanced by his actually flushing with pain. He had picked up his hat, which he had brought in, and stood twirling it in a way that gave me, even as I was just nearly reaching port, a perverse horror of what I was doing. To do it in *any* way was an act of violence, for what did it consist of but the obtrusion of the idea of grossness and guilt on a small helpless creature who had been for me a revelation of the possibilities of beautiful intercourse? Wasn't it base to create for a being so exquisite a mere alien awkwardness? I suppose I now read into our situation a clearness it could n't have had at the time, for I seem to see our poor eyes already lighted with some spark of a prevision of the anguish that was to come. So we circled about with terrors and scruples, fighters not daring to close. But it was for each other we feared! That kept us a little longer suspended and unbruised. "I 'll tell you everything," Miles said — "I mean I 'll tell you anything you like. You 'll stay on with me, and we shall both be all right, and I *will* tell you — I *will*. But not now."

"Why not now?"

My insistence turned him from me and kept him once more at his window in a silence during which, between us, you might have heard a pin drop. Then he was before me again with the air of a person for whom, outside, some one who had frankly to be reckoned with was waiting. "I have to see Luke."

I had not yet reduced him to quite so vulgar a lie, and I felt proportionately ashamed. But, horrible as it was, his lies made up my truth. I achieved thoughtfully a few loops of my knitting. "Well then go to Luke, and I 'll wait for what you promise. Only in return for that satisfy, before you leave me, one very much smaller request."

He looked as if he felt he had succeeded enough to be able still a little to bargain. "Very much smaller — ?"

"Yes, a mere fraction of the whole. Tell me" — oh my work preoccupied me, and I was off-hand! — "if, yesterday afternoon, from the table in the hall, you took, you know, my letter."

XXIV

My grasp of how he received this suffered for a minute from something that I can describe only as a fierce split of my attention — a stroke that at first, as I sprang straight up, reduced me to the mere blind movement of getting hold of him, drawing him close and, while I just fell for support against the nearest piece of furniture, instinctively keeping him with his back to the window. The appearance was full upon us that I had already had to deal with here: Peter Quint had come into view like a sentinel before a prison. The next thing I saw was that, from outside, he had reached the window, and then I knew that, close to the glass and glaring in through it, he offered once more to the room his white face of damnation. It represents but grossly what took place within me at the sight to say that on the second my decision was made; yet I believe that no woman so overwhelmed ever in so short a time recovered her command of the *act*. It came to me in the very horror of the immediate presence that the act would be, seeing and facing what I saw and faced, to keep the boy himself unaware. The inspiration — I can call it by no other name — was that I felt how voluntarily, how transcendently, I *might*. It was like fighting with a demon for a human soul, and when I had fairly so appraised it I saw how the human soul — held out, in the tremor of my hands, at arms' length — had a perfect dew of sweat on a lovely childish forehead. The face that was close to mine was as white as the face against the glass, and out of it presently came a sound, not low nor weak, but as if from much further away, that I drank like a waft of fragrance.

— "Yes — I took it."

At this, with a moan of joy, I enfolded, I drew him close; and while I held him to my breast, where I could feel in the sudden fever of his little body the tremendous pulse of his little heart, I kept my eyes on the thing at the window and saw it move and shift its posture. I have likened it to a sentinel, but its slow wheel, for a moment, was rather the prowl of a baffled beast. My present quickened courage, however, was such that, not too much to let it through, I had to shade, as it were, my flame. Meanwhile the glare of the face was again at the window, the scoundrel fixed as if to watch and wait. It was the very confidence that I might now defy him, as well as the positive certitude, by this time, of the child's unconsciousness, that made me go on. "What did you take it for?"

"To see what you said about me."

"You opened the letter?"

"I opened it."

My eyes were now, as I held him off a little again, on Miles's own face, in which the collapse of mockery showed me how complete was the ravage of uneasiness. What was prodigious was that at last, by my success, his sense was sealed and his communication stopped: he knew that he was in presence, but knew not of what, and knew still less that I also was and that I did know. And what did this strain of trouble matter when my eyes went back to the window only to see

that the air was clear again and — by my personal triumph — the influence quenched? There was nothing
there. I felt that the cause was mine and that I should
surely get *all*. "And you found nothing!" — I let my
elation out.

He gave the most mournful, thoughtful little headshake. "Nothing."

"Nothing, nothing!" I almost shouted in my joy.

"Nothing, nothing," he sadly repeated.

I kissed his forehead; it was drenched. "So what
have you done with it?"

"I've burnt it."

"Burnt it?" It was now or never. "Is that what
you did at school?"

Oh what this brought up! "At school?"

"Did you take letters? — or other things?"

"Other things?" He appeared now to be thinking
of something far off and that reached him only through
the pressure of his anxiety. Yet it did reach him.
"Did I *steal?*"

I felt myself redden to the roots of my hair as well as
wonder if it were more strange to put to a gentleman
such a question or to see him take it with allowances
that gave the very distance of his fall in the world.
"Was it for that you might n't go back?"

The only thing he felt was rather a dreary little
surprise. "Did you know I might n't go back?"

"I know everything."

He gave me at this the longest and strangest look.
"Everything?"

"Everything. Therefore *did* you —?" But I
could n't say it again.

Miles could, very simply. "No. I did n't steal."

My face must have shown him I believed him utterly; yet my hands — but it was for pure tenderness — shook him as if to ask him why, if it was all for nothing, he had condemned me to months of torment. "What then did you do?"

He looked in vague pain all round the top of the room and drew his breath, two or three times over, as if with difficulty. He might have been standing at the bottom of the sea and raising his eyes to some faint green twilight. "Well — I said things."

"Only that?"

"They thought it was enough!"

"To turn you out for?"

Never, truly, had a person "turned out" shown so little to explain it as this little person! He appeared to weigh my question, but in a manner quite detached and almost helpless. "Well, I suppose I ought n't."

"But to whom did you say them?"

He evidently tried to remember, but it dropped — he had lost it. "I don't know!"

He almost smiled at me in the desolation of his surrender, which was indeed practically, by this time, so complete that I ought to have left it there. But I was infatuated — I was blind with victory, though even then the very effect that was to have brought him so much nearer was already that of added separation. "Was it to every one?" I asked.

"No; it was only to —" But he gave a sick little headshake. "I don't remember their names."

"Were they then so many?"

"No — only a few. Those I liked."

Those he liked? I seemed to float not into clearness, but into a darker obscure, and within a minute there had come to me out of my very pity the appalling alarm of his being perhaps innocent. It was for the instant confounding and bottomless, for if he *were* innocent what then on earth was I? Paralysed, while it lasted, by the mere brush of the question, I let him go a little, so that, with a deep-drawn sigh, he turned away from me again; which, as he faced toward the clear window, I suffered, feeling that I had nothing now there to keep him from. "And did they repeat what you said?" I went on after a moment.

He was soon at some distance from me, still breathing hard and again with the air, though now without anger for it, of being confined against his will. Once more, as he had done before, he looked up at the dim day as if, of what had hitherto sustained him, nothing was left but an unspeakable anxiety. "Oh yes," he nevertheless replied — "they must have repeated them. To those *they* liked," he added.

There was somehow less of it than I had expected; but I turned it over. "And these things came round — ?"

"To the masters? Oh yes!" he answered very simply. "But I did n't know they'd tell."

"The masters? They did n't — they've never told. That's why I ask you."

He turned to me again his little beautiful fevered face. "Yes, it was too bad."

"Too bad?"

"What I suppose I sometimes said. To write home."

I can't name the exquisite pathos of the contradiction given to such a speech by such a speaker; I only know that the next instant I heard myself throw off with homely force: "Stuff and nonsense!" But the next after that I must have sounded stern enough. "What *were* these things?"

My sternness was all for his judge, his executioner; yet it made him avert himself again, and that movement made *me*, with a single bound and an irrepressible cry, spring straight upon him. For there again, against the glass, as if to blight his confession and stay his answer, was the hideous author of our woe — the white face of damnation. I felt a sick swim at the drop of my victory and all the return of my battle, so that the wildness of my veritable leap only served as a great betrayal. I saw him, from the midst of my act, meet it with a divination, and on the perception that even now he only guessed, and that the window was still to his own eyes free, I let the impulse flame up to convert the climax of his dismay into the very proof of his liberation. "No more, no more, no more!" I shrieked to my visitant as I tried to press him against me.

"Is she *here?*" Miles panted as he caught with his sealed eyes the direction of my words. Then as his strange "she" staggered me and, with a gasp, I echoed it, "Miss Jessel, Miss Jessel!" he with sudden fury gave me back.

I seized, stupefied, his supposition — some sequel to what we had done to Flora, but this made me only want to show him that it was better still than that. "It's not Miss Jessel! But it's at the window — straight before us. It's *there* — the coward horror, there for the last time!"

At this, after a second in which his head made the movement of a baffled dog's on a scent and then gave a frantic little shake for air and light, he was at me in a white rage, bewildered, glaring vainly over the place and missing wholly, though it now, to my sense, filled the room like the taste of poison, the wide over-whelming presence. "It's *he?*"

I was so determined to have all my proof that I flashed into ice to challenge him. "Whom do you mean by 'he'?"

"Peter Quint — you devil!" His face gave again, round the room, its convulsed supplication. "*Where?*"

They are in my ears still, his supreme surrender of the name and his tribute to my devotion. "What does he matter now, my own? — what will he *ever* matter? *I* have you," I launched at the beast, "but he has lost you for ever!" Then for the demonstration of my work, "There, *there!*" I said to Miles.

But he had already jerked straight round, stared, glared again, and seen but the quiet day. With the stroke of the loss I was so proud of he uttered the cry of a creature hurled over an abyss, and the grasp with which I recovered him might have been that of catching him in his fall. I caught him, yes, I held him — it may be imagined with what a passion; but at the end of a minute I began to feel what it truly was that I held. We were alone with the quiet day, and his little heart, dispossessed, had stopped.

THE LIAR

I

THE train was half an hour late and the drive from the station longer than he had supposed, so that when he reached the house its inmates had dispersed to dress for dinner and he was conducted straight to his room. The curtains were drawn in this asylum, the candles lighted, the fire bright, and when the servant had quickly put out his clothes the comfortable little place might have been one of the minor instruments in a big orchestra — seemed to promise a pleasant house, a various party, talk, acquaintances, affinities, to say nothing of very good cheer. He was too occupied with his profession often to pay country visits, but he had heard people who had more time for them speak of establishments where "they do you very well." He foresaw that the proprietors of Stayes would do him very well. In his bedroom on such occasions he always looked first at the books on the shelf and the prints on the walls; these things would give in a sort the social, the conversational value of his hosts. Though he had but little time to devote to them on this occasion a cursory inspection assured him that if the literature, as usual, was mainly American and humorous the art consisted neither of the water-colour studies of the children nor of "goody" engravings. The walls were adorned with old-fash-

ioned lithographs, mostly portraits of country gentlemen with high collars and riding-gloves: this suggested — and it was encouraging — that the tradition of portraiture was held in esteem. There was
the customary novel of Mr. Le Fanu for the bedside,
the ideal reading in a country house for the hours
after midnight. Oliver Lyon could scarcely forbear
beginning it while he buttoned his shirt.

Perhaps that is why he not only found every one
assembled in the hall when he went down, but saw
from the way the move to dinner was instantly made
that they had been waiting for him. There was no
delay to introduce him to a lady, for he went out
unimportant and in a group of unmated men. The
men, straggling behind, sidled and edged as usual
at the door of the dining-room, and the *dénouement*
of this little comedy was that he came to his place
last of all. This made him suppose himself in a sufficiently distinguished company, for if he had been
humiliated — which he was not — he could n't have
consoled himself with the reflexion that such a fate
was natural to an obscure and struggling young artist. He could no longer think of himself as notably
young, alas, and if his position was n't so brilliant as
it ought to be he could no longer justify it by calling
it a struggle. He was appreciably "known" and was
now apparently in a society of the known if not of the
knowing. This idea added to the curiosity with which
he looked up and down the long table as he settled
himself in his place.

It was a numerous party — five-and-twenty people;
rather an odd occasion to have proposed to him, as

he thought. He would n't be surrounded by the quiet
that ministers to good work; however, it had never
interfered with his work to feel the human scene enclose it as a ring. And though he did n't know this,
it was never quiet at Stayes. When he was working
well he found himself in that happy state — the
happiest of all for an artist — in which things in general interweave with his particular web and make
it thicker and stronger and more many-coloured.
Moreover there was an exhilaration (he had felt it
before) in the rapid change of scene — the jump, in
the dusk of the afternoon, from foggy London and
his familiar studio to a centre of festivity in the middle of Hertfordshire and a drama half-acted, a drama
of pretty women and noted men and wonderful
orchids in silver jars. He observed as a not unimportant fact that one of the pretty women was beside
him: a gentleman sat on his other hand. But he appraised his neighbours little as yet: he was busy with
the question of Sir David, whom he had never seen
and about whom he naturally was curious.

Evidently, however, Sir David was not at dinner,
a circumstance sufficiently explained by the other
circumstance forming our friend's principal knowledge of him — his being ninety years of age. Oliver
Lyon had looked forward with pleasure to painting
a picked nonagenarian, so that though the old man's
absence from table was something of a disappointment — it was an opportunity the less to observe
him before going to work — it seemed a sign that he
was rather a sacred and perhaps therefore an impressive relic. Lyon looked at his son with the greater

interest — wondered if the glazed bloom of such a cheek had been transmitted from Sir David. That would be jolly to paint in the old man — the withered ruddiness of a winter apple, especially if the eye should be still alive and the white hair carry out the frosty look. Arthur Ashmore's hair had a midsummer glow, but Lyon was glad his call had been for the great rather than the small bearer of the name, in spite of his never having seen the one and of the other's being seated there before him now in the very highest relief of impersonal hospitality.

Arthur Ashmore was a fresh-coloured thick-necked English gentleman, but he was just not a subject; he might have been a farmer and he might have been a banker; you could scarcely paint him in character. His wife did n't make up the amount; she was a large bright negative woman who had the same air as her husband of being somehow tremendously new; an appearance as of fresh varnish — Lyon could scarcely tell whether it came from her complexion or from her clothes — so that one felt she ought to sit in a gilt frame and be dealt with by reference to a catalogue or a price-list. It was as if she were already rather a bad though expensive portrait, knocked off by an eminent hand, and Lyon had no wish to copy that work. The pretty woman on his right was engaged with her neighbour, while the gentleman on his other side looked detached and desperate, so that he had time to lose himself in his favourite diversion of watching face after face. This amusement gave him the greatest pleasure he knew, and he often thought it a mercy the human mask did interest him and that it had such a need, frequently even in spite of itself, to testify, since he was to make his living by reproducing it. Even if Arthur Ashmore would n't be inspiring to paint (a certain anxiety rose in him lest, should he make a hit with her father-in-law, Mrs. Arthur should take it into her head that he had now proved himself worthy to handle her husband); even if he had looked a little less like a page —fine as to print and margin —without punctuation, he would still be a refreshing iridescent surface. But the gentleman four persons off—what was he? Would he be a subject, or was his face only the legible door-plate of his identity, burnished with punctual washing and shaving—the least thing that was decent you might know him by?

This face arrested Oliver Lyon, striking him at first as very handsome. The gentleman might still be called young, and his features were regular: he had a plentiful fair moustache that curled up at the ends, a brilliant gallant almost adventurous air, together with a big shining breastpin in the middle of his shirt. He appeared a fine satisfied soul, and Lyon perceived that wherever he rested his friendly eye there fell an influence as pleasant as the September sun — as if he could make grapes and pears or even human affection ripen by looking at them. What was odd in him was a certain mixture of the correct and the extravagant: as if he were an adventurer imitating a gentleman with rare perfection, or a gentleman who had taken a fancy to go about with hidden arms. He might have been a dethroned prince or the war-correspondent of a newspaper: he represented both enterprise and tradition,

good manners and bad taste. Lyon at length fell into
conversation with the lady beside him — they dispensed, as he had had to dispense at dinner-parties
before, with an introduction — by asking who this
personage might be.

"Oh Colonel Capadose, don't you know?" Lyon
did n't know and asked for further information. His
neighbour had a sociable manner and evidently was
accustomed to quick transitions; she turned from her
other interlocutor with the promptness of a good cook
who lifts the cover of the next saucepan. "He has
been a great deal in India — is n't he rather celebrated?" she put it. Lyon confessed he had never
heard of him, and she went on: "Well, perhaps he
is n't; but he says he is, and if you think it that's just
the same, is n't it?"

"If *you* think it?"

"I mean if he thinks it — that's just as good, I
suppose."

"Do you mean if he thinks he has done things he
has n't?"

"Oh dear no; because I never really know the
difference between what people say —!' He's exceedingly clever and amusing — quite the cleverest
person in the house, unless indeed you 're more so.
But that I can't tell yet, can I? I only know about the
people I know; I think that's celebrity enough!"

"Enough for them?"

"Oh I see you 're clever. Enough for me! But I 've
heard of you," the lady went on. "I know your
pictures; I admire them. But I don't think you look
like them."

"They're mostly portraits," Lyon said; "and what I usually try for is not my own resemblance."

"I see what you mean. But they've much more colour. Don't you suppose Vandyke's things tell a lot about him? And now you're going to do some one here?"

"I've been invited to do Sir David. I'm rather disappointed at not seeing him this evening."

"Oh he goes to bed at some unnatural hour — eight o'clock, after porridge and milk. You know he's rather an old mummy."

"An old mummy?" Oliver Lyon repeated.

"I mean he wears half a dozen waistcoats and sits by the fire. He's always cold."

"I've never seen him and never seen any portrait or photograph of him," Lyon said. "I'm surprised at his never having had anything done — at their waiting all these years."

"Ah that's because he was afraid, you know; it was his pet superstition. He was sure that if anything were done he would die directly afterwards. He has only consented to-day."

"He's ready to die then?"

"Oh now he's so old he does n't care."

"Well, I hope I shan't kill him," said Lyon. "It was rather unnatural of his son to send for me."

"Oh they've nothing to gain — everything is theirs already!" his companion rejoined, as if she took this speech quite literally. Her talkativeness was systematic — she fraternised as seriously as she might have played whist. "They do as they like — they fill the house with people — they have *tarte blanche*."

THE LIAR

"I see — but there's still the 'title.'"

"Yes, but what's the tuppenny title ?"

Our artist broke into laughter at this, whereat his
companion stared. Before he had recovered himself
she was scouring the plain with her other neighbour.
The gentleman on his left at last risked an observation
as if it had been a move at chess, exciting in Lyon
however a comparative wantonness. This personage
played his part with difficulty: he uttered a remark as
a lady fires a pistol, looking the other way. To catch
the ball Lyon had to bend his ear, and this movement
led to his observing a handsome creature who was
seated on the same side, beyond his interlocutor. Her
profile was presented to him and at first he was only
struck with its beauty; then it produced an impression
still more agreeable — a sense of undimmed remembrance and intimate association. He had not recognised her on the instant only because he had so little
expected to see her there; he had not seen her anywhere for so long, and no news of her now ever came
to him. She was often in his thoughts, but she had
passed out of his life. He thought of her twice a week;
that may be called often, even for fidelity, when it has
been kept up a dozen years. The moment after he
recognised her he felt how true it was that only she
could carry that head, the most charming head in the
world and of which there could never be a replica.
She was leaning forward a little; she remained in profile, slightly turned to some further neighbour. She
was listening, but her eyes moved, and after a moment Lyon followed their direction. They rested on
the gentleman who had been described to him as

320

Colonel Capadose — rested, he made out, as with an habitual visible complacency. This was not strange, for the Colonel was unmistakeably formed to attract the sympathetic gaze of woman; but Lyon felt it as the source of an ache that she could let *him* look at her so long without giving him a glance. There was nothing between them to-day and he had no rights, but she must have known he was coming — it was of course no such tremendous event, but she could n't have been staying in the house without some echo of it — and it was n't natural this should absolutely fail to affect her.

She was looking at Colonel Capadose as if she had been in love with him — an odd business for the proudest, most reserved of women. But doubtless it was all right if her husband was satisfied: he had heard indefinitely, years before, that she was married, and he took for granted — as he had not heard — the presence of the happy man on whom she had conferred what she had refused to a poor art-student at Munich. Colonel Capadose seemed aware of nothing, and this fact, incongruously enough, rather annoyed Lyon than pleased him. Suddenly the lady moved her head, showing her full face to our hero. He was so prepared with a greeting that he instantly smiled, as a shaken jug overflows; but she made no response, turned away again and sank back in her chair. All her face said in that instant was "You see I'm as handsome as ever." To which he mentally subjoined: "Yes, and as much good as ever it does me!" He asked the young man beside him if he knew who that beautiful being was—the fourth person beyond him.

The young man leaned forward, considered and then said: "I think she's Mrs. Capadose."

"Do you mean his wife — that fellow's?" And Lyon indicated the subject of the information given him by his other neighbour.

"Oh is *he* Mr. Capadose?" said the young man, to whom it appeared to mean little. He admitted his ignorance of these values and explained it by saying that there were so many people and he had come but the day before. What was definite to our friend was that Mrs. Capadose was in love with her husband — so that he wished more than ever he might have married her.

"She's very fond and true," he found himself saying three minutes later, with a small ironic ring, to the lady on his right. He added that he meant Mrs. Capadose.

"Ah you know her then?"

"I knew her once upon a time — when I was living abroad."

"Why then were you asking me about her husband?"

"Precisely for that reason." Lyon was clear. "She married after that — I did n't even know her present name."

"How then do you know it now?"

"This gentleman has just told me — he appears to know."

"I did n't know he knew anything," said the lady with a crook that took him in.

"I don't think he knows anything but that."

"Then you've found out for yourself that she's

—what do you call it?—tender and true? What
do you mean by that?"

"Ah you mustn't question me—I want to put
things to *you*," Lyon said. "How do you all like her
here?"

"You ask too much! I can only speak for myself.
I think she's hard."

"That's only because she's honest and straight-
forward."

"Do you mean I like people in proportion as they
deceive?"

"I think we all do, so long as we don't find them
out," Lyon said. "And then there's something in her
face—a sort of nobleness of the Roman type, in spite
of her having such English eyes. In fact she's English down to the ground; but her complexion, her low
forehead and that beautiful close little wave in her
dark hair make her look like a transfigured Tras-
teverina."

"Yes, and she always sticks pins and daggers into
her head, to bring out that effect. I must say I like her
husband better: he *gives* so much."

"Well, when I knew her there was no comparison
that could injure her," Lyon richly sighed. "She was
altogether the most delightful thing in Munich."

"In Munich?"

"Her people lived there; they weren't rich—in
pursuit of economy in fact, and Munich was very
cheap. Her father was the younger son of some noble
house; he had married a second time and had a lot of
little mouths to feed. She was the child of the first
wife and didn't like her stepmother, but she was

charming to her little brothers and sisters. I once made a sketch of her as Werther's Charlotte cutting bread and butter while the children clustered round her. All the artists in the place were in love with her, but she would n't look at 'the likes' of us. She was too proud — I grant you that, but not stuck up nor young-ladyish, only perfectly simple and frank about it. She used to remind me of Thackeray's Ethel Newcome. She told me she must marry well: it was the one thing she could do for her family. I suppose you 'd say she *has* married well."

"She told *you?*" smiled Lyon's neighbour.

"Oh of course I proposed to her too. But she evidently thinks so herself!" he added. "I mean that it's no mistake."

When the ladies left the table the host as usual bade the gentlemen draw together, so that Lyon found himself opposite to Colonel Capadose. The conversation was mainly about the "run," for it had apparently been a great day in the hunting-field. Most of the men had a comment or an anecdote, several had many; but the Colonel's pleasant voice was the most audible in the chorus. It was a bright and fresh but masculine organ, just such a voice as, to Lyon's sense, such a "fine man" ought to have had. It appeared from his allusions that he was a very straight rider, which was also very much what Lyon would have expected. Not that he swaggered, for his points were all quietly and casually made; but they had all to do with some dangerous experiment or close shave. Lyon noted after a little that the attention paid by the company to the Colonel's remarks was not in direct proportion to the interest they seemed to offer; the result of which was that the speaker, who noticed that *he* at least was listening, began to treat him as his particular auditor and to fix his eyes on him as he talked. Lyon had nothing to do but to look sympathetic and assent — the narrator building on the tribute so rendered. A neighbouring squire had had an accident; he had come a cropper in an awkward place — just at the finish — with consequences that looked grave. He had struck his head; he remained insensible up to the last accounts : there had evidently been concussion of the brain. There was some exchange of views as to his recovery, how soon it would take place or whether it would take place at all; which led the Colonel to confide to our artist across the table that *he* should n't despair of a fellow even if he did n't come round for weeks — for weeks and weeks and weeks — for months, almost for years. He leaned forward (Lyon leaned forward to listen) and mentioned that he knew from personal experience how little limit there really was to the time a fellah might lie like a stone without being the worse for it. It had happened to him in Ireland years before; he had been pitched out of a dogcart, had turned a sheer somersault and landed on his head. They had thought he was dead, but he was n't; they had carried him first to the nearest cabin, where he lay for some days with the pigs, and then to an inn in a neighbouring town — it was a near thing they had n't put him underground. He had been completely insensible — without a ray of recognition of any human thing — for three whole months; had n't had a glimmer of consciousness of any blessed thing. It had been touch and go to that degree that they could n't come near him, could n't feed him, could scarcely look at him. Then one day he had opened his eyes — as fit as a flea!

"I give you my honour it had done me good — it rested my brain." He conveyed, though without excessive emphasis, that with an intelligence so active as his these periods of repose were providential. Lyon was struck by his story, but wanted to ask if he had n't shammed a little; not in relating it, only in keeping so quiet. He hesitated however, in time, to betray a doubt — he was so impressed with the tone in which Colonel Capadose pronounced it the turn of a hair that they had n't buried him alive. That had happened to a friend of his in India — a fellow who was supposed to have died of jungle-fever and whom they clapped into a coffin. He was going on to recite the further fate of this unfortunate gentleman when Mr. Ashmore said a word and every one rose for the move to the drawing-room. Lyon noticed that by this time no one was heeding his new friend's prodigies. These two came round on either side of the table and met while their companions hung back for each other.

"And do you mean your comrade was literally buried alive?" asked Lyon in some suspense.

The Colonel looked at him as with the thread of the conversation already lost. Then his face brightened — and when it brightened it was doubly handsome. "Upon my soul he was shoved into the ground!"

"And left there?"

"Left there till I came and hauled him out."

"*You* came?"

THE LIAR

"I dreamed about him — it's the most extraordinary story: I heard him calling to me in the night. I took on myself to dig him up. You know there are people in India — a kind of beastly race, the ghouls — who violate graves. I had a sort of presentiment that they would get at him first. I rode straight, I can tell you; and, by Jove, a couple of them had just broken ground! Crack — crack from a couple of barrels, and they showed me their heels as you may believe. Would you credit that I took him out myself? The air brought him round and he was none the worse. He has got his pension — he came home the other day. He'd do anything for me," the narrator added.

"He called to you in the night?" said Lyon, much thrilled.

"That's the interesting point. Now *what was it?* It wasn't his ghost, because he wasn't dead. It wasn't himself, because he couldn't. It was some confounded brain-wave or other! You see India's a strange country — there's an element of the mysterious: the air's full of things you can't explain."

They passed out of the dining-room, and this master of anecdote, who went among the first, was separated from his newest victim; but a minute later, before they reached the drawing-room, he had come back. "Ashmore tells me who you are. Of course I've often heard of you. I'm very glad to make your acquaintance. My wife used to know you."

"I'm glad she remembers me. I recognised her at dinner and was afraid she didn't."

"Ah I dare say she was ashamed," said the Colonel with genial ease.

"Ashamed of me?" Lyon replied in the same key.

"Was n't there something about a picture? Yes; you painted her portrait."

"Many times," Lyon said; "and she may very well have been ashamed of what I made of her."

"Well, *I* was n't, my dear sir; it was the sight of that picture, which you were so good as to present to her, that made me first fall in love with her."

Our friend lived over again for a few seconds a lost felicity. "Do you mean one with the children — cutting bread and butter?"

"Bread and butter? Bless me, no — vine-leaves and a leopard-skin. A regular Bacchante."

"Ah yes," said Lyon; "I remember. It was the first decent portrait I painted. I should be curious to see it to-day."

"Don't ask her to show it to you — she'll feel it awkward," the Colonel went on.

"Awkward?" — our artist wondered.

"We parted with it — in the most disinterested manner," the other laughed. "An old friend of my wife's — her family had known him intimately when they lived in Germany — took the most extraordinary fancy to it: the Grand Duke of Silberstadt-Schreckenstein, don't you know? He came out to Bombay while we were there and he spotted your picture (you know he's one of the greatest collectors in Europe) and made such eyes at it that, upon my word — it happened to be his birthday — she told him he might have it to get rid of him. He was perfectly enchanted — but we miss the picture."

"It's very good of you," Lyon said. "If it's in a

great collection — a work of my incompetent youth — I'm infinitely honoured."

"Oh he keeps it in one of his castles; I don't know which — you know he has so many. He sent us, before he left India — to return the compliment — a magnificent old vase."

"That was more than the thing was worth," Lyon modestly urged.

Colonel Capadose gave no heed to this observation; his thoughts now seemed elsewhere. After a moment, however, he said: "If you'll come and see us in town she'll show you the vase." And as they passed into the drawing-room he gave his fellow visitor a friendly propulsion. "Go and speak to her; there she is. She'll be delighted."

Oliver Lyon took but a few steps into the wide saloon; he stood there a moment looking at the bright composition of the lamplit group of fair women, the single figures, the great setting of white and gold, the panels of old damask, in the centre of each of which was a single celebrated picture. There was a subdued lustre in the scene and an air as of the shining trains of dresses tumbled over the carpet. At the furthest end of the room sat Mrs. Capadose, rather isolated; she was on a small sofa with an empty place beside her. Lyon could n't flatter himself she had been keeping it for him; her failure to take up his shy signal at table contradicted this, but his desire to join her was too strong. Moreover he had her husband's sanction; so he crossed the room, stepping over the tails of gowns, and stood before her with his appeal. "I hope you don't mean to repudiate me."

THE LIAR

She looked up at him with frank delight. "I'm so glad to see you. I was charmed when I heard you were coming."

"I tried to get a smile from you at dinner — but I could n't," Lyon returned.

"I did n't see — I did n't understand. Besides, I hate smirking and telegraphing. Also I'm very shy — you won't have forgotten that. Now we can communicate comfortably." And she made a better place for him on her sofa. He sat down and they had a talk that smote old chords in him; the sense of what he had loved her for came back to him, as well as not a little of the actual effect of that cause. She was still the least spoiled beauty he had ever seen, with an absence of the "wanton" or of any insinuating art that resembled an omitted faculty: she affected him at moments as some fine creature from an asylum — a surprising deaf-mute or one of the operative blind. Her noble pagan head gave her privileges that she neglected, and when people were admiring her brow she was wondering if there were a good fire in her bedroom, or at the very most in theirs. She was simple, kind and good; inexpressive but not inhuman, not stupid. Now and again she dropped something, some small fruit of discrimination, that might have come from a mind, have been an impression at first hand. She had no imagination and only the simpler feelings, but several of these had grown up to full size. Lyon talked of the old days in Munich, reminded her of incidents, pleasures and pains, asked her about her father and the others; and she spoke in return of her being so impressed with his own fame,

330

his brilliant position in the world, that she had n't
felt sure he would notice her or that his mute appeal
at table was meant for her. This was plainly a perfectly truthful speech — she was incapable of any
other — and he was affected by such humility on the
part of a woman whose grand line was unique. Her
father was dead; one of her brothers was in the navy
and the other on a ranch in America; two of her sisters
were married and the youngest just coming out and
very pretty. She did n't mention her stepmother. She
questioned him on his own story, and he described it
mainly as his not having married.

"Oh you ought to," she answered. "It's the best
thing."

"I like that — from you!"

"Why not from me? I'm very happy."

"That's just why I can't be," he returned. "It's
cruel of you to praise your state. But I've had the
pleasure of making the acquaintance of your husband.
We had a good bit of talk in the other room."

"You must know him better — you must know
him really well," said Mrs. Capadose.

"I'm sure that the further you go the more you
find. But he makes a fine show too."

She rested her good grey eyes on this recovered
"backer." "Don't you think he's handsome?"

"Handsome and clever and entertaining. You
see I'm generous."

"Yes; you must know him well," Mrs. Capadose
repeated.

"He has seen a great deal of life," said her companion.

331

THE LIAR

"Ah we've been in so many situations. You must see my little girl. She's nine years old — she's too beautiful."

Lyon rose fully to the occasion. "You must bring her to my studio some day — I should like to paint her."

"Oh don't speak of that," said Mrs. Capadose. "It reminds me of something so distressing."

"I hope you don't mean of when *you* used to sit to me — though that may well have bored you."

"It's not what you did — it's what we've done. It's a confession I must make — it's a weight on my mind! I mean on the subject of the lovely picture you gave me — it used to be so much admired. When you come to see me in London — and I count on your doing that very soon — I shall see you looking all round. I can't tell you I keep it in my own room because I love it so, for the simple reason —" It fairly pulled her up.

"Because you can't tell wicked lies," said Lyon.

"No, I can't. So before you ask for it —"

"Oh I know you parted with it — the blow has already fallen," Lyon interrupted.

"Ah then you've heard? I was sure you would! But do you know what we got for it? Two hundred pounds."

"You might have got much more," the artist smiled.

"That seemed a great deal at the time. We were in want of the money — it was a good while ago, when we first married. Our means were very small then, but fortunately that has changed rather for the better.

We had the chance; it really seemed a big sum, and I'm afraid we jumped at it. My husband had expectations which have partly come into effect, so that now we do well enough. But meanwhile the picture went."

"Fortunately the original remained. But do you mean that two hundred was the value of the vase?" Lyon asked.

"Of the vase?"

"The beautiful old Indian vase — the Grand Duke's offering."

"The Grand Duke?"

"What's his name? — Silberstadt-Schreckenstein. Your husband mentioned the transaction."

"Oh my husband!" said Mrs. Capadose; and Lyon now saw her change colour.

Not to add to her embarrassment, but to clear up the ambiguity, which he perceived the next moment he had better have left alone, he went on: "He tells me it's now in his collection."

"In the Grand Duke's? Ah you know its reputation? I believe it contains treasures." She was bewildered, but she recovered herself, and Lyon made the mental reflexion that for some reason which would seem good when he knew it the husband and the wife had prepared different versions of the same incident. It was true that he did n't exactly see Everina Brant preparing a version; that was n't her line of old, and indeed there was no such subterfuge in her eyes to-day. At any rate they both had the matter too much on their conscience. He changed the subject — said Mrs. Capadose must really bring the little girl. He sat with

333

her some time longer and imagined — perhaps too freely — her equilibrium slightly impaired, as if she were annoyed at their having been even for a moment at cross-purposes. This did n't prevent his saying to her at the last, just as the ladies began to gather themselves for bed: "You seem much impressed, from what you say, with my renown and my prosperity, and you are so good as greatly to exaggerate them. Would you have married me if you had known I was destined to success?"

"I did know it."

"*I* did n't, then!"

"You were too modest."

"You did n't think so when I proposed to you."

"Well, if I had married you I could n't have married *him* — and he's so awfully nice," Mrs. Capadose said. Lyon knew this was her faith — he had learned that at dinner — but it vexed him a little to hear her proclaim it. The gentleman designated by the pronoun came up, amid the prolonged handshaking for good-night, and Mrs. Capadose remarked to her husband as she turned away, "He wants to paint Amy."

"Ah she's a charming child, a most interesting little creature," the Colonel said to Lyon. "She does the most remarkable things."

Mrs. Capadose stopped in the rustling procession that followed the hostess out of the room. "Don't tell him, please don't," she said.

"Don't tell him what?"

"Why, what she does. Let him find out for himself." And she passed on.

"She thinks I swagger about the child — that I bore people," said the Colonel. "I hope you smoke." He appeared ten minutes later in the smoking-room, brilliantly equipped in a suit of crimson foulard covered with little white spots. He gratified Lyon's eye, made him feel that the modern age has its splendour too and its opportunities for costume. If his wife was an antique he was a fine specimen of the period of colour: he might have passed for a Venetian of the sixteenth century. They were a remarkable couple, Lyon thought, and as he looked at the Colonel standing in bright erectness before the chimney-piece and emitting great smoke-puffs he did n't wonder Everina could n't regret she had n't married *him*. All the men collected at Stayes were not smokers and some of them had gone to bed. Colonel Capadose remarked that there probably would be a smallish muster, they had had such a hard day's work. That was the worst of a hunting-house — the men were so sleepy after dinner; it was a great sell for the ladies, even for those who hunted themselves, women being so tough that they never showed it. But most fellows revived under the stimulating influences of the smoking-room, and some of them, in this confidence, would turn up yet. Some of the grounds of their confidence — not all — might have been seen in a cluster of glasses and bottles on a table near the fire, which made the great salver and its contents twinkle sociably. The others lurked as yet in various improper corners of the minds of the most loquacious. Lyon was alone with Colonel Capadose for some moments before their companions, in varied eccentricities of uniform, straggled in, and he felt how little loss of vital tissue this wonderful man had to repair.

They talked about the house, Lyon having noticed an oddity of construction in the smoking-room; and the Colonel explained that it consisted of two distinct parts, one of very great antiquity. They were two complete houses in short, the old and the new, each of great extent and each very fine in its way. The two formed together an enormous structure — Lyon must make a point of going all over it. The modern piece had been erected by the old man when he bought the property; oh yes, he had bought it forty years before — it had n't been in the family : there had n't been any particular family for it to be in. He had had the good taste not to spoil the original house — he had not touched it beyond what was just necessary for joining it on. It was very curious indeed — a most irregular rambling mysterious pile, where they now and then discovered a walled-up room or a secret staircase. To his mind it was deadly depressing, however; even the modern additions, splendid as they were, failed to make it cheerful. There was some story of how a skeleton had been found years before, during some repairs, under a stone slab of the floor of one of the passages; but the family were rather shy of its being talked about. The place they were in was of course in the old part, which contained after all some of the best rooms : he had an idea it had been the primitive kitchen, half-modernised at some intermediate period.

"My room is in the old part too then — I 'm very glad," Lyon said. "It 's very comfortable and contains all the latest conveniences, but I observed the depth of the recess of the door and the evident antiquity of the corridor and staircase — the first short one — after I came out. That panelled corridor is admirable; it looks as if it stretched away, in its brown dimness (the lamps did n't seem to me to make much impression on it) for half a mile."

"Oh don't go to the end of it!" the Colonel warningly smiled.

"Does it lead to the haunted room?" Lyon asked.

His companion looked at him a moment. "Ah you know about that?"

"No, I don't speak from knowledge, only from hope. I 've never had any luck — I 've never stayed in a spooky house. The places I go to are always as safe as Charing Cross. I want to see — whatever there is, the regular thing. *Is* there a ghost here?"

"Of course there is — a rattling good one."

"And have you seen him?"

"Oh don't ask me what *I 've* seen — I should tax your credulity. I don't like to talk of these things. But there are two or three as bad — that is, as good! — rooms as you 'll find anywhere."

"Do you mean in my corridor?" Lyon asked.

"I believe the worst is at the far end. But you 'd be ill-advised to sleep there."

"Ill-advised?"

"Until you 've finished your job. You 'll get letters of importance the next morning and take the 10.20."

"Do you mean I shall invent a pretext for running away?"

"Unless you 're braver than almost any one has ever been. They don't often put people to sleep there,

but sometimes the house is so crowded that they have
to. The same thing always happens — ill-concealed
agitation at the breakfast-table and letters of the
greatest importance. Of course it's a bachelor's room,
and my wife and I are at the other end of the house.
But we saw the comedy three days ago — the day
after we got here. A young fellow had been put there
— I forget his name — the house was so full; and the
usual consequence followed. Letters at breakfast —
an awfully queer face — an urgent call to town — so
sorry his visit was cut short. Ashmore and his wife
looked at each other and off the poor devil went."

"Ah that would n't suit me; I must do my job,"
said Lyon. "But do they mind your speaking of it?
Some people who've a good ghost are very proud of
it, you know."

What answer Colonel Capadose was on the point
of making to this query our hero was not to learn,
for at that moment their host had walked into the
room accompanied by three or four of their fellow
guests. Lyon was conscious that he was partly answered by the Colonel's not going on with the subject.
This on the other hand was rendered natural by the
fact that one of the gentlemen appealed to him for an
opinion on a point under discussion, something to do
with the everlasting history of the day's run. To Lyon
himself Mr. Ashmore began to talk, expressing his
regret for the delay of this pleasure. The topic that
suggested itself was naturally that most closely connected with the motive of the artist's visit. The latter
observed that it was a great disadvantage to him not
to have had some preliminary acquaintance with Sir

David — in most cases he found this so important. But the present sitter was so far advanced in life that there was doubtless no time to lose. "Oh I can tell you all about him," said Mr. Ashmore; and for half an hour he told him a good deal. It was very interesting as well as a little extravagant, and Lyon felt sure he was a fine old boy to have endeared himself so to a son who was evidently not a gusher. At last he got up — he said he must go to bed if he wished to be fresh for his work in the morning. To which his host replied "Then you must take your candle; the lights are out; past this hour I don't keep my servants up."

In a moment Lyon had his glimmering taper in hand, and as he was leaving the room — he did n't disturb the others with a good-night, they were absorbed in the lemon-squeezer and the soda-water cork — he remembered other occasions on which he had made his way to bed alone through a darkened country-house: such occasions had not been rare, for he was almost always the first to leave the smoking-room. If he had n't stayed at places of markedly evil repute he had, none the less — having too much imagination — sometimes found the great black halls and staircases rather "creepy": there had been often a sinister effect for his nerves in the sound of his tread through the long passages or the way the winter moon peeped into tall windows on landings. It occurred to him that if houses without supernatural pretensions could look so wicked at night the old corridors of Stayes would certainly give him a sensation. He did n't know whether the proprietors were sensitive; very often, as he had said to Colonel Capadose, people enjoyed the impeachment. What determined him to speak despite the risk was a need that had suddenly come to him to measure the Colonel's accuracy. As he had his hand on the door he said to his host: "I hope I shan't meet any ghosts."

"Any ghosts?"

"You ought to have some — in this fine old part."

"We do our best, but they're difficult to raise," said Mr. Ashmore. "I don't think they like the hot-water pipes."

"They remind them too much of their own climate? But have n't you a haunted room — at the end of my passage?"

"Oh there are stories — we try to keep them up."

"I should like very much to sleep there," Lyon said.

"Well, you can move there to-morrow if you like."

"Perhaps I had better wait," Lyon smiled, "till I've done my work." But he was to have presently the slightly humiliated sense of having been "arch" about nothing.

"Very good; but you won't work there, you know. My father will sit to you in his own apartments."

"Oh it is n't that; it's the fear of running away — like that gentleman three days ago."

"Three days ago? What gentleman?" Mr. Ashmore asked.

"The one who got urgent letters at breakfast and fled by the 10.20. Did he stand more than one night?"

"I don't know what you're talking about" — the son of Stayes was sturdy and blank. "There was no such gentleman — three days ago."

THE LIAR

"Ah so much the better," said Lyon, nodding good-night and departing. He took his course, as he remembered it, with his wavering candle, and, though he encountered a great many gruesome objects, safely reached the passage out of which his room opened. In the complete darkness it seemed to stretch away still further, but he followed it, for the curiosity of the thing, to the end. He passed several doors with the name of the room painted up, but found nothing else. He was tempted to try the last door, to look into the room his friend had incriminated; but he felt this would be indiscreet, that gentleman's warrant was somehow a document of too many flourishes. There might be apparitions or other uncanny things and there might n't; but there was surely nothing in the house so odd as Colonel Capadose.

II

Lyon found Sir David Ashmore a beautiful subject as well as the serenest and blandest of sitters. Moreover he was a very informing old man, tremendously puckered but not in the least dim; and he wore exactly the furred dressing-gown his portrayer would have chosen. He was proud of his age but ashamed of his infirmities, which however he greatly exaggerated and which did n't prevent his submitting to the brush as bravely as he might have to the salutary surgical knife. He sat there with the firm eyes and set smile of " Well, do your worst!" He demolished the legend of his having feared the operation would be fatal, giving an explanation which pleased our friend much better. He held that a gentleman should be painted but once in his life — that it was eager and fatuous to be hung up all over the place. That was good for women, who made a pretty wall-pattern; but the male face did n't lend itself to decorative repetition. The proper time for the likeness was at the last, when the whole man was there, when you got the sum of his experience. Lyon could n't reply, as he would have done in many a case, that this was not a real synthesis — you had to allow so for leakage; since there had been no crack in Sir David's crystallisation. He spoke of his portrait as a plain map of the country, to be consulted by his children in a case of uncertainty. A proper map could be drawn up only when the country had been travelled. He gave Lyon his mornings, till luncheon, and they talked of many things, not neglecting, as a stimulus to gossip, the company at Stayes. Now that he did n't "go out," as he said, he saw much less of the people in his house — processions that came and went, that he knew nothing about and that he liked to hear Lyon describe. The artist sketched with a fine point and did n't caricature, and it usually befell that when Sir David did n't know the sons and daughters he had known the fathers and mothers. He was one of those terrible old persons who keep the book of antecedents. But in the case of the Capadose family, at whom they arrived by an easy stage, his knowledge embraced two, or even three, generations. General Capadose was an old crony, and he remembered his father before him. The General was rather a smart soldier, but in private life of too speculative a turn — always sneaking into the City to put his money into some rotten thing. He had married a girl who brought him something — and with it half a dozen children. He scarcely knew what had become of the rest of them, except that one was in the Church and had found preferment — was n't he Dean of Rockingham? Clement, the fellow who was at Stayes, had apparently some gift for arms; he had served in the East and married a pretty girl. He had been at Eton with Arthur and used then to come to Stayes in his holidays. Lately, back in England, he had turned up with his wife again; that was before he — the old man — had been put to grass. He was a taking dog but had a monstrous foible.

"A monstrous foible?" Lyon echoed.

"He pulls the long bow — the longest that ever was."

Lyon's brush stopped short, while he repeated, for somehow the words both startled him and brought light: "'The longest that ever was'?"

"You're very lucky not to have had to catch him."

Lyon debated. "Well, I think I *have* rather caught him. He revels in the miraculous."

"Oh it isn't always the miraculous. He'll lie about the time of day, about the name of his hatter. It's quite disinterested."

"Well, it's very base," Lyon declared, feeling rather sick for what Everina Brant had done with herself.

"Oh it's an extraordinary trouble to take," said the old man, "but this fellow isn't in himself at all base. There's no harm in him and no bad intention; he doesn't steal nor cheat nor gamble nor drink; he's very kind — he sticks to his wife, is fond of his children. He simply can't give you a straight answer."

"Then everything he told me last night, I now see, was tarred with that brush: he delivered himself of a series of the steepest statements. They stuck when I tried to swallow them, yet I never thought of so simple an explanation."

"No doubt he was in the vein," Sir David went on. "It's a natural peculiarity — as you might limp or stutter or be left-handed. I believe it comes and goes with changes of the wind. My son tells me that his friends quite allow for it and don't pin him down — for the sake of his wife, whom every one likes."

344

"Oh his wife — his wife!" Lyon murmured, painting fast.

"I dare say she's used to it."

"Never in the world, Sir David. How can she be used to it?"

"Why, my dear sir, when a woman's fond —! And don't they mostly rather handle that instrument themselves? They're connoisseurs in the business," Sir David cackled with a harmless old-time cynicism. "They've a sympathy for a fellow performer."

Lyon wondered; he had no ground for denying that Mrs. Capadose was attached to her husband. But after a little he rejoined: "Oh not this one! I knew her years ago — before her marriage; knew her well and admired her. She was as clear as a bell."

"I like her very much," Sir David said, "but I've seen her back him up."

Lyon considered his host a moment not in the light of a sitter. "Are you very sure?"

The old man grinned and brought out: "My dear sir, you're in love with her."

"Very likely. God knows I used to be!"

"She must help him out — she can't expose him."

"She can hold her tongue," Lyon returned.

"Well, before you probably she will."

"That's what I'm curious to see." And he added privately: "Mercy on us, what he must have made of her!" He kept this reflexion to himself, for he considered that he had sufficiently betrayed his state of mind with regard to Mrs. Capadose. None the less it occupied him now immensely, the question of how such a woman would arrange herself in such a posi-

tion. He watched her with an interest deeply quickened when he mingled with the company; he had
had his own troubles in life, but had rarely been so
anxious about anything as about this question of what
the loyalty of a wife and the infection of an example
would have made of a perfectly candid mind. Oh he
would answer for it that whatever other women might
be prone to do she, of old, had stuck to the truth as a
bather who can't swim sticks to shallow water. Even
if she had n't been too simple for deviations she would
have been too proud, and if she had n't had too much
conscience would have had too little eagerness. The
lie was the last thing she would have endured or con-
doned — the particular thing she would n't have forgiven. Did she sit in torment while her husband gave
the rein, or was she now too so perverse that she
thought it a fine thing to be striking at the expense —
Lyon would have been ready to say — of one's decency? It would have taken a wondrous alchemy —
working backwards, as it were — to produce this
latter result. Besides these alternatives — that she
suffered misery in silence and that she was so much
in love that her husband's exorbitance seemed to her
but an added richness, a proof of life and talent —
there was still the possibility that she had n't found
him out, that she took his false coinage at his own
valuation. A little reflexion rendered this hypothesis
untenable; it was too evident that the account he gave
of things must repeatedly have contradicted her own
knowledge. Within an hour or two of his meeting
them Lyon had seen her confronted with that perfectly gratuitous invention about the profit they had

made of his early picture. Even then indeed she had
not, so far as he could see, smarted, and — but for the
present he could only stare at the mystery!

Even if it had n't been interfused, through his un-
eradicated interest in Mrs. Capadose, with an element
of suspense, the question would still have been attaching and worrying; since, truly, he had n't painted
portraits so many years without becoming curious of
queer cases. His attention was limited for the moment
to the opportunity the following three days might
yield, as the Colonel and his wife were going on to
another house. It fixed itself largely of course upon
the Colonel too — the fellow was *so* queer a case.
Moreover it had to go on very quickly. Lyon was at
once too discreet and too fond of his own intimate
inductions to ask other people how they answered his
conundrum — too afraid also of exposing the woman
he once had loved. It was probable indeed that light
would come to him from the talk of their companions;
the Colonel's idiosyncrasy, both as it affected his
own situation and as it affected his wife, would be a
familiar theme in any house in which he was in the
habit of staying. Lyon had n't observed in the circles
in which he visited any marked abstention from comment on the singularities of their members. It interfered with his progress that the Colonel hunted all
day, while he plied his brushes and chatted with Sir
David; but a Sunday intervened and that partly made
it up. Mrs. Capadose fortunately did n't hunt and, his
work done, was not inaccessible. He took a couple of
good walks with her — she was fond of good walks —
and beguiled her at tea into a friendly nook in the

347

hall. Regard her as he might he could n't make out to himself that she was consumed by a hidden shame; the sense of being married to a man whose word had no worth was not, in her spirit, so far as he could guess, the canker within the rose. Her mind appeared to have nothing on it but its own placid frankness, and when he sounded her eyes — with the long plummet he occasionally permitted himself to use — they had no uncomfortable consciousness. He talked to her again and still again of the dear old days — reminded her of things he had n't had (before this reunion) any sense of himself remembering. Then he spoke to her of her husband, praised his appearance, his talent for conversation, professed to have felt a quick friendship for him and asked, with an amount of "cheek" for which he almost blushed, what manner of man he was. "What manner?" she echoed. "Dear me, how can one describe one's husband? I like him very much."

"Ah you 've insisted on that to me already!" Lyon growled to exaggeration.

"Then why do you ask me again?" She added in a moment, as if she were so happy that she could afford to take pity on him: "He 's everything that 's good and true and kind. He 's a soldier and a gentleman and a dear! He has n't a fault. And he has great, great ability."

"Yes, he strikes one as having great, great ability. But of course I can't think him a dear."

"I don't care what you think him!" Everina laughed, looking still handsomer in the act than he had ever seen her. She was either utterly brazen or of a contrition quite impenetrable, and he had little prospect of extorting from her what he somehow so longed for — some avowal that she had after all better have married a man who was not a by-word for the most contemptible, the least heroic of vices. Had n't she seen, had n't she felt, the smile, the cold faded smile of complete depreciation, go round when her husband perjured himself to some particularly characteristic blackness? How could a woman of her quality live with that day after day, year after year, except by her quality's altering? But he would believe in the alteration only when he should have heard *her* lie. He was held by his riddle and yet impatient of it, he asked himself all kinds of questions. Did n't she lie, after all, when she let *his* lies pass without turning a hair? Was n't her life a perpetual complicity, and did n't she aid and abet him by the simple fact that she was n't disgusted with him? Then again perhaps she *was* disgusted and it was the mere desperation of her pride that had given her an inscrutable mask. Perhaps she protested in private, passionately; perhaps every night, in their own apartments, after the day's low exhibition, she had things out with him in a manner known only to the pair themselves. But if such scenes were of no avail and he took no more trouble to cure himself, how could she regard him, and after so many years of marriage too, with the perfectly artless complacency that Lyon had surprised in her in the course of the first day's dinner? If our friend had n't been in love with her he would surely have taken the Colonel's delinquencies less to heart. As the case stood they fairly turned to the tragical for him, even while he was sharply aware of how merely "his funny way" they were to others — and of how funny his, Oliver Lyon's, own way of regarding them would have seemed to every one.

The observation of these three days showed him that if Capadose was an abundant he was not a malignant liar and that his fine faculty exercised itself mainly on subjects of small direct importance. "He's the liar platonic," he said to himself; "he's disinterested, as Sir David said, he does n't operate with a hope of gain or with a desire to injure. It's art for art — he's prompted by some love of beauty. He has an inner vision of what might have been, of what ought to be, and he helps on the good cause by the simple substitution of a shade. He lays on colour, as it were, and what less do I do myself?" His disorder had a wide range, but a family likeness ran through all its forms, which consisted mainly of their singular futility. It was this that made them an affliction; they encumbered the field of conversation, took up valuable space, turned it into the desert of a perpetual shimmering mirage. For the falsehood uttered under stress a convenient place can usually be found, as for a person who presents himself with an author's order at the first night of a play. But the mere luxurious lie is the gentleman without a voucher or a ticket who accommodates himself with a stool in the passage.

Of one possible charge Lyon acquitted his successful rival; it had puzzled him that, irrepressible as he was, he had never got into a mess in the Service. But it was to be made out that he drew the line at the Service — over that august institution he never flapped his wings. Moreover, for all the personal pretension in his talk it rarely came, oddly enough, to swagger about his military exploits. He had a passion for the chase, he had followed it in far countries, and some of his finest flowers were reminiscences of what he had prodigiously done and miraculously escaped when off by himself. The more by himself he had been of course the bigger the commemorative nose-gay bloomed. A new acquaintance always received from him, in honour of their meeting, one of the most striking of these tributes — that generalisation Lyon very promptly made. And the extraordinary man had inconsistencies and unexpected lapses — lapses into the very commonplace of the credible. Lyon recognised what Sir David had told him, that he flourished and drooped by an incalculable law and would sometimes keep the truce of God for a month at a time. The muse of improvisation breathed on him at her pleasure and appeared sometimes quite to avert her face. He would neglect the finest open-ings and then set sail with everything against him. As a general thing he affirmed the impossible rather than denied the certain, though this too had lively exceptions. Very often, when it was loud enough — for he liked a noise about him — he joined in the reprobation that cast him out, he allowed he was trying it on and that one did n't know what had hap-pened to one till one *had* tried. Still, he never com-pletely retracted nor retreated — he dived and came up in another place. Lyon guessed him capable on occasion of defending his position with violence, though only when it was very bad. Then he might easily be dangerous — then he would hit out and not care whom he touched. Such moments as those would test his wife's philosophy — Lyon would have liked to see her there. In the smoking-room and elsewhere the company, so far as it was composed of his familiars, had an hilarious protest always at hand; but among the men who had known him long his big brush was an old story, so old that they had ceased to talk about it, and Lyon did n't care, as I have said, to bring to a point those impatiences that might have resembled his own.

The oddest thing of all was that neither surprise nor familiarity prevented the Colonel's being liked; his largest appeals even to proved satiety passed for an overflow of life and high spirits — almost of simple good looks. If he was fond of treating his gallantry with a flourish he was none the less unmistakeably gallant. He was a first-rate rider and shot, in spite of his fund of anecdote illustrating these accomplishments: in short he was very nearly as clever and brave, and his adventures and observations had been very nearly as numerous and wonderful, as the list he unrolled. His best quality however remained that indiscriminate sociability which took interest and favour for granted and about which he bragged least. It made him cheap, it made him even in a manner vulgar; but it was so contagious that his listener was more or less on his side as against the probabilities. It was a private reflexion of Oliver Lyon's that he not only was mendacious but made any charmed converser feel

as much so by the very action of the charm — of a
certain guilty submission of which no intention of ridicule could yet purge you. In the evening, at dinner
and afterwards, our friend, better placed for observation than the first night, watched his wife's face to see
if some faint shade or spasm never passed over it. But
she continued to show nothing, and the wonder was
that when he spoke she almost always listened. That
was her pride: she wished not to be even suspected of
not facing the music. Lyon had none the less an importunate vision of a veiled figure coming the next day
in the dusk to certain places to repair the Colonel's
ravages, as the relatives of kleptomaniacs punctually
call at the shops that have suffered from their depreda-
tions.

"I must apologise; of course it was n't true; I hope
no harm is done; it 's only his incorrigible —" oh to
hear that woman's voice in that deep abasement!
Lyon had no harsh design, no conscious wish to practise on her sensibility or her loyalty; but he did say to
himself that he should have liked to bring her round,
liked to see her *show* him that a vision of the dignity
of not being married to a mountebank sometimes
haunted her dreams. He even imagined the hour
when, with a burning face, she might ask *him* not to
take the question up. Then he should be almost consoled — he would be magnanimous.

He finished his picture and took his departure, after
having worked in a glow of interest which made him
believe in his success, until he found he had pleased
every one, especially Mr. and Mrs. Ashmore, when he
began to be sceptical. The party at any rate changed:

Colonel and Mrs. Capadose went their way. He was able to say to himself however that his parting with Everina was n't so much an end as a beginning, and he called on her soon after his return to town. She had told him the hours she was at home — she seemed to like him. If she liked him why had n't she married him, or at any rate why was n't she sorry she had n't? If she was sorry she concealed it too well. The point he made of some visible contrition in her on this head may strike the reader as extravagant, but something must be allowed so disappointed a man. He did n't ask much after all; not that she should love him to-day or that she should allow him to tell her that he loved her, but only that she should give him some sign she did n't feel her choice as *all* gain. Instead of this, for the present, she contented herself with exhibiting her small daughter to him. The child was beautiful and had the prettiest eyes of innocence he had ever seen: which did n't prevent his wondering if she told horrid fibs. This idea much occupied and rather darkly amused him — the picture of the anxiety with which her mother would watch as she grew older for symptoms of the paternal strain. That was a pleasant care for such a woman as Everina Brant! Did she lie to the child herself about her father — was that necessary when she pressed her daughter to her bosom to cover up his tracks? Did he control himself before the little girl — so that she might n't hear him say things she knew to be other than his account of them? Lyon scarcely thought that probable: his genius would be ever too strong for him, and the only guard for Amy would be in her being too simple for criticism. One could n't judge yet — she was too young to show. If she should grow up clever she would be sure to tread in his steps — a delightful improvement in her mother's situation! Her little face was not shifty, but neither was her father's big one; so that proved nothing.

Lyon reminded his friends more than once of their promise that Amy should sit to him, and it was now only a question of his own leisure. The desire grew in him to paint the Colonel also — an operation from which he promised himself a rich private satisfaction. He would draw him out, he would set him up in that totality about which he had talked with Sir David, and none but the initiated would know. They, however, would rank the picture high, and it would be indeed six rows deep — a masterpiece of fine characterisation, of legitimate treachery. He had dreamed for years of some work that should show the master of the deeper vision as well as the mere reporter of the items, and here at last was his subject. It was a pity it was n't better, but that was n't *his* fault. It was his impression that already no one "drew" the Colonel in the social sense more effectively than he, and he did this not only by instinct but on a plan. There were moments when he almost winced at the success of his plan — the poor gentleman went so terribly far. He would pull up some day, look at his critic between the eyes and guess he was being played upon — which would lead to his wife's guessing it also. Not that Lyon cared much for that however, so long as she failed to suppose — and she could n't divine it — that *she* was a part of his joke. He formed such a habit

355

now of going to see her of a Sunday afternoon that he was angry when she went out of town. This occurred often, as the couple were great visitors and the Colonel was always looking for sport, which he liked best when it could be had at the expense of others. Lyon would have supposed the general gregarious life, the constant presence of a gaping "gallery," particularly little to her taste, for it was naturally in country-houses that her husband came out strongest. To let him go off without her, not to see him expose himself — that ought properly to have been her relief and her nearest approach to a luxury. She mentioned to her friend in fact that she preferred staying at home, but she did n't say it was because in other people's houses she was on the rack: the reason she gave was that she liked so to be with the child. It was n't perhaps criminal to deal in such "whoppers," but it was damned vulgar: poor Lyon was delighted when he arrived at that formula. Certainly some day too he would cross the line — he would practise the fraud to which his talked "rot" had the same relation as the experiments of the forger have to the signed cheque. And in the mean time, yes, he was vulgar, in spite of his facility, his impunity, his so remarkably fine person. Twice, by exception, toward the end of the winter, when he left town for a few days' hunting, his wife remained at home. Lyon had n't yet reached the point of asking himself if the wish not to miss two of his visits might have had something to do with this course. That enquiry would perhaps have been more in place later, when he began to paint her daughter and she made a rule of coming with her. But it was n't in her to give the wrong name, to affect motives, and Lyon could see she had the maternal passion in spite of the bad blood in the little girl's veins.

She came inveterately, though Lyon multiplied the sittings: Amy was never entrusted to the governess or the maid. He had knocked off poor old Sir David in ten days, but the simple face of the child held him and worried him and gave him endless work. He asked for sitting after sitting, and it might have struck a solicitous spectator that he was wearing the little girl out. He knew better, however, and Mrs. Capadose also knew: they were present together at the long intermissions he gave her, when she left her pose and roamed about the great studio, amusing herself with its curiosities, playing with the old draperies and costumes, having unlimited leave to handle. Then her mother and their so patient friend — much more patient than her piano-mistress — sat and talked; he laid aside his brushes and leaned back in his chair; he always gave her tea. What Mrs. Capadose could n't suspect was the rate at which, during these weeks, he neglected other orders: women have no faculty of imagination with regard to a man's work beyond a vague idea that it does n't matter. Lyon in fact put off everything and made high celebrities wait. There were half-hours of silence, when he plied his brushes, during which he was mainly conscious that Everina was sitting there. She easily fell into that if he did n't insist on talking, and she was n't embarrassed nor bored by any lapse of communication. Sometimes she took up a book — there were plenty of them about; sometimes, a little way off in her chair, she watched

his progress — though without in the least advising
or correcting — as if she cared for every stroke
that was to contribute to his result. These strokes
were occasionally a little wild; he was thinking so
much more of his heart than of his hand. He was n't
more embarrassed than she, but he was more agitated:
it was as if in the sittings (for the child too was admirably quiet) something had beautifully settled itself
between them or had already grown — a tacit confidence, an inexpressible secret. He at least felt it that
way, but he after all could n't be sure she did. What
he wanted her to do for him was very little; it was n't
even to allow that she was unhappy. She would satisfy
him by letting him know even by some quite silent
sign that she could imagine her happiness with him —
well, more unqualified. Perhaps indeed — his presumption went so far — that was what she did mean
by contentedly sitting there.

III

AT last he broached the question of painting the Colonel: it was now very late in the season — there would be little time before the common dispersal. He said they must make the most of it; the great thing was to begin; then in the autumn, with the resumption of their London life, they could go forward. Mrs. Capadose objected to this that she really could n't consent to accept another present of such value. Lyon had sacrificed to her the portrait of herself of old — he knew what they had had the indelicacy to do with it. Now he had offered her this wondrous memorial of the child — wondrous it would evidently be when he should be able to bring it to a finish; a precious possession that, this time, they would cherish for ever. But his generosity and their indiscretion must stop there — they could n't be so tremendously "beholden" to him. They could n't order the picture, which of course he would understand without her explaining: it was a luxury beyond their reach, since they knew the great prices he received. Besides, what had they ever done — what above all had *she* ever done, that he should overload them with benefits? No, he was too dreadfully good; it was really impossible that Clement should sit. Lyon listened to her without protest, without interruption, while he bent forward at his work; and at last returned: "Well, if you won't take it why not let him sit just for my own pleasure and profit? Let it be a favour, a service I ask of him. All the generosity and charity will so be on your side. It will do me a lot of good to paint him and the picture will remain in my hands."

"How will it do you a lot of good?" Mrs. Capadose asked.

"Why he's such a rare model — such an interesting subject. He has such an expressive face. It will teach me no end of things."

"Expressive of what?" said Mrs. Capadose.

"Why of his inner man."

"And you want to paint his inner man?"

"Of course I do. That's what a great portrait gives you, and with a splendid comment on it thrown in for the money. I shall make the Colonel's a great one. It will put me up high. So you see my request is eminently interested."

"How can you be higher than you are?"

"Oh I'm an insatiable climber. So don't stand in my way," said Lyon.

"Well, everything in him is very noble," Mrs. Capadose gravely contended.

"Ah trust me to bring everything out!" Lyon returned, feeling a little ashamed of himself.

Mrs. Capadose, before she went, humoured him to the point of saying that her husband would probably comply with his invitation; but she added: "Nothing would induce me to let you pry into *me* that way!"

"Oh you," her friend laughed — "I could do you in the dark!"

The Colonel shortly afterwards placed his leisure at the painter's disposal and by the end of July had

paid him several visits. Lyon was disappointed
neither in the quality of his sitter nor in the degree to
which he himself rose to the occasion; he felt really
confident of producing what he had conceived. He
was in the spirit of it, charmed with his motive and
deeply interested in his problem. The only point that
troubled him was the idea that when he should send
his picture to the Academy he should n't be able to
inscribe it in the catalogue under the simple rubric
to which all propriety pointed. He could n't in short
send in the title as "The Liar" — more was the pity.
However, this little mattered, for he had now determined to stamp that sense on it as legibly — and to
the meanest intelligence — as it was stamped for his
own vision on the living face. As he saw nothing else
in the Colonel to-day, so he gave himself up to the
joy of "rendering" nothing else. How he did it he
could n't have told you, but he felt a miracle of method
freshly revealed to him every time he sat down to
work. It was in the eyes and it was in the mouth, it
was in every line of the face and every fact of the
attitude, in the indentation of the chin, in the way
the hair was planted, the moustache was twisted, the
smile came and went, the breath rose and fell. It was
in the way he looked out at a bamboozled world in
short — the way he would look out for ever. There
were half a dozen portraits in Europe that Lyon rated
as supreme; he thought of them always as immortal
things, for they were as perfectly preserved as they
were consummately painted. It was to this small exemplary group that he aspired to attach the canvas
on which he was now engaged. One of the produc-

tions that helped to compose it was the magnificent Moroni of the National Gallery — the young tailor in the white jacket at his board with his shears. The Colonel was not a tailor, nor was Moroni's model, unlike many tailors, a liar; the very man, body and soul, should bloom into life under his hand with just that assurance of no loss of a drop of the liquor. The Colonel, as it turned out, liked to sit, and liked to talk while sitting: which was very fortunate, as his talk was half the inspiration of his artist. Lyon applied without mercy his own gift of provocation; he could n't possibly have been in a better relation to him for the purpose. He encouraged, beguiled, excited him, manifested an unfathomable credulity, and his own sole lapses were when the Colonel failed, as he called it, to "act." He had his intermissions, his hours of sterility, and then Lyon knew that the picture also drooped. The higher his companion soared, the more he circled and sang in the blue, the better he felt himself paint; he only could n't make the flights and the evolutions last. He lashed his victim on when he flagged; his one difficulty was his fear again that his game might be suspected. The Colonel, however, was easily beguiled; he basked and expanded in the fine steady light of the painter's attention. In this way the picture grew very fast, astonishingly faster, in spite of its so much greater "importance," than the simple-faced little girl's. By the fifth of August it was pretty well finished: that was the date of the last sitting the Colonel was for the present able to give — he was leaving town the next day with his wife. Lyon was amply content — he saw his way so clear: he should be able to do at leisure the little that remained, in respect to which his friend's attendance would be a minor matter. As there was no hurry, in any case, he would let the thing stand over till his own return to London, in November, when he should come back to it with a fresh eye. On the Colonel's asking him if Everina might have a sight of it next day, should she find a minute — this being so greatly her desire — Lyon begged as a special favour that she would wait: what he had yet to do was small in amount, but it would make all the difference. This was the repetition of a proposal Mrs. Capadose had made on the occasion of his last visit to her, and he had then recommended her not coming till he should be himself better pleased. He had really never been, at a corresponding stage, better pleased; and he blushed a little for his subtlety.

By the fifth of August the weather was very warm, and on that day, while the Colonel sat at his usual free practice Lyon opened for the sake of ventilation a little subsidiary door which led directly from his studio into the garden and sometimes served as an entrance and an exit for models and for visitors of the humbler sort, and as a passage for canvases, frames, packing-boxes and other professional gear. The main entrance was through the house and his own apartments, and this approach had the charming effect of admitting you first to a high gallery, from which a winding staircase, happily disposed, dropped to the wide decorated encumbered room. The view of this room beneath them, with all its artistic ingenuities and the objects of value that Lyon had collected, never failed to elicit exclamations of delight from persons stepping into the gallery. The way from the garden was plainer and at once more practicable and more private. Lyon's domain, in Saint John's Wood, was not vast, but when the door stood open of a summer's day it offered a glimpse of flowers and trees, there was a sweetness in the air and you heard the birds. On this particular morning the side-door had been found convenient by an unannounced visitor, a youngish woman who stood in the room before the Colonel was aware of her, but whom he was then the first to see. She was very quiet — she looked from one of the men to the other. "Oh dear, here's another!" Lyon exclaimed as soon as his eyes rested on her. She belonged in fact to the somewhat importunate class of the model in search of employment, and she explained that she had ventured to come straight in, that way, because very often when she went to call upon gentlemen the servants played her tricks, turned her off and would n't take in her name.

"But how did you get into the garden?" Lyon asked.

"The gate was open, sir — the servants' gate. The butcher's cart was there."

"The butcher ought to have closed it," said Lyon.

"Then you don't require me, sir?" the lady continued.

Lyon continued to paint; he had given her a sharp look at first, but now his eyes were only for his work. The Colonel, however, examined her with interest. She was a person of whom you could scarcely say whether being young she looked old or old looked young; she had at any rate clearly rounded several of the corners of life; she had a face that was rosy, yet that failed to suggest freshness. She was nevertheless rather pretty and even looked as if at one time she might have sat for the complexion. She wore a hat with many feathers, a dress with many bugles, long black gloves encircled with silver bracelets, and very bad shoes. There was something about her not exactly of the governess out of place nor completely of the actress seeking an engagement, but that savoured of a precarious profession, perhaps even of a blighted career. She was perceptibly soiled and tarnished, and after she had been in the room a few moments the air, or at any rate the nostril, became acquainted with a vague alcoholic waft. She was unpractised in the *h*, and when Lyon at last thanked her and said he did n't want her — he was doing nothing for which she could be useful — she replied in rather a wounded manner: "Well, you know you *'ave* 'ad me!"

"I don't remember you," Lyon protested.

"Well, I dare say the people who saw your pictures do! I have n't much time, but I thought I'd look in."

"I'm much obliged to you."

"If ever you should require me and just send me a postcard —"

"I never send postcards," said Lyon.

"Oh well, I should value a private letter! Anything to Miss Geraldine, Mortimer Terrace Mews, Notting 'ill —"

"Very good; I'll remember," said Lyon.

Miss Geraldine lingered. "I thought I'd just stop on the chance."

"I'm afraid I can't hold out hopes, I'm so busy with portraits," Lyon continued.

"Yes; I see you are. I wish I was in the gentleman's place."

. "I'm afraid in that case it would n't look like the gentleman," the Colonel sociably laughed.

"Oh of course it could n't compare — it would n't be so 'andsome! But I do hate them portraits!" Miss Geraldine declared. "It's so much bread out of our mouths."

"Well, there are many who can't paint them," Lyon suggested for comfort.

"Oh I've sat to the very first — and only to the first! There's many that could n't do anything without me."

"I'm glad you're in such demand." Lyon's amusement had turned to impatience and he added that he would n't detain her — he would send for her in case of need.

"Very well; remember it's the Mews — more's the pity! You don't sit so well as *us* !" Miss Geraldine pursued, looking at the Colonel. "If *you* should require me, sir —"

"You put him out; you embarrass him," said Lyon.

"Embarrass him, oh gracious!" the visitor cried with a laugh that diffused a fragrance. "Perhaps *you* send postcards, eh ?" she went on to the Colonel; but she retreated with a wavering step. She passed out into the garden as she had come.

"How very dreadful — she's drunk!" said Lyon.

366

He was painting hard, but looked up, checking himself: Miss Geraldine, in the open doorway, had thrust in her head again.

"Yes, I do hate it — that sort of thing!" she cried with an explosion of mirth which confirmed Lyon's charge. On which she disappeared.

"What sort of thing — what does she mean?" the Colonel asked.

"Oh my painting you when I might be painting her."

"And have you ever painted her?"

"Never in the world; I've never seen her. She's quite mistaken."

The Colonel just waited; then he remarked: "She was very pretty — ten years ago."

"I dare say, but she's quite ruined. For me the least 'drop too much' spoils them; I should n't care for her at all."

"My dear fellow, she's not a model," the Colonel laughed.

"To-day, no doubt, she's not worthy of the name; but she has done her time."

"*Jamais de la vie!* That's all a pretext."

"A pretext?" Lyon pricked up his ears — he wondered what now would come.

"She did n't want you — she wanted *me*."

"I noticed she paid you some attention. What then does she want of you?"

"Oh to do me an ill turn. She hates me — lots of women do. She's watching me — she follows me."

Lyon leaned back in his chair — without a single grain of faith. He was all the more delighted with what he heard and with the Colonel's bright and candid manner. The story had shot up and bloomed, from the dropped seed, on the spot. "My dear Colonel!" he murmured with friendly interest and commiseration.

"I was vexed when she came in — but I was n't upset," his sitter continued.

"You concealed it very well if you were."

"Ah when one has been through what I have! To-day, however, I confess I was half-prepared. I've noticed her hanging about — she knows my movements. She was near my house this morning — she must have followed me."

"But who is she then — with such charming 'cheek'?"

"Yes, she has plenty of cheek," said the Colonel; "but as you observe she was primed. Still, she carried it off as a cool hand. Oh she's a bad 'un! She is n't a model and never was; no doubt she has known some of those women and picked up their form. She had hold of a friend of mine ten years ago — a young jackanapes who might have been left to be plucked but whom I was obliged to take an interest in for family reasons. It's a long story — I had really forgotten all about it. She's thirty-seven if she's a day. I was able to make a diversion and let him get off — after which I sent her about her business. She knew it was me she had to thank. She has never forgiven me — I think she's off her head. Her name is n't Geraldine at all and I doubt very much if that's her address."

"Ah what *is* her name?" Lyon was all participation. He had always noted that when once his friend was launched there was no danger in asking; the more you asked the more abundantly you were served.

"It's Pearson — Harriet Pearson; but she used to call herself Grenadine — was n't that a rum notion? Grenadine — Geraldine — the jump was easy." Lyon was charmed with this flow of facility, and his interlocutor went on: "I had n't thought of her for years — I had quite lost sight of her. I don't know what her idea is, but practically she's harmless. As I came in I thought I saw her a little way up the road. She must have found out I come here and have arrived before me. I dare say — or rather I'm sure — she's waiting for me there now."

"Had n't you better have protection?" Lyon asked with amusement.

"The best protection 's five shillings — I 'm willing to go that length. Unless indeed she has a bottle of vitriol. But they only throw vitriol on the fellows who have 'undone' them, and I never undid her — I told her the first time I saw her that it would n't do. Oh if she 's there we 'll walk a little way together and talk it over, and, as I say, I 'll go as far as five shillings."

"Well," said Lyon, "I 'll contribute another five." He felt this little to pay for what he was getting.

That entertainment was interrupted, however, for the time, by the Colonel's departure. Lyon hoped for some sequel to match — a report, by note, of the next scene in the drama as his friend had met it, but this genius apparently did n't operate with the pen. At any rate he left town without writing — they had taken a tryst for three months later. Oliver Lyon always passed the holidays in the same way; during the first weeks he paid a visit to his elder brother, the happy possessor, in the south of England, of a rambling old house with formal gardens, in which he delighted, and then he went abroad — usually to Italy or Spain. This year he carried out his custom after taking a last look at his all but finished work and feeling as nearly pleased with it as decency permitted, the translation of the idea by the hand appearing always to him at the best a pitiful compromise. One yellow afternoon in the country, as he smoked his pipe on one of the old terraces, he was taken with a fancy for another look at what he had lately done, and with that in particular of doing two or three things more to it: he had been much haunted with this unrest while he lounged there. The provocation was not to be resisted, and though he was at any rate so soon to be back in London he was unable to brook delay. Five minutes with his view of the Colonel would be enough — it would clear up questions that hummed in his brain; so that the next morning, to give himself this luxury, he took the train for town. He sent no word in advance; he would lunch at his club and probably return into Sussex by the 5.45.

In Saint John's Wood the tide of human life flows at no time very fast, and in the first days of September Lyon found mere desolation in the straight sunny roads where the little plastered garden-walls, with their incommunicative doors, looked feebly Oriental. There was definite stillness in his own house, to which

he admitted himself by his pass-key, it being a matter
of conscience with him sometimes to take his servants
unawares. The good woman set in authority over
them and who cumulated the functions of cook and
housekeeper was, however, quickly summoned by his
step, and — as he cultivated frankness of intercourse
with his domestics — received him without the confusion of surprise. He reassured her as to any other
effect of unpreparedness — he had come up but for a
few hours and should be busy in the studio. She
announced that he was just in time to see a lady and a
gentleman who were there at the moment — they had
arrived five minutes before. She had told them he
was absent but they said it was all right; they only
wanted to look at a picture and would be very careful
of everything. "I hope it's all right, sir," this informant concluded. "The gentleman says he's a sitter and he gave me his name — rather an odd name;
I think it's military. The lady's a very fine lady, sir;
at any rate there they are."

"Oh it's all right" — Lyon read the identity of his
visitors. The good woman could n't know, having
when he was at home so little to do with the comings
and goings; his man, who showed people in and out,
had accompanied him to the country. He was a good
deal surprised at the advent of Mrs. Capadose, who
knew how little he wished her to see the portrait unfinished, but it was a familiar truth to him that she was
a woman of a high spirit. Besides, perhaps the lady
was n't Everina; the Colonel might well have brought
some inquisitive friend, a person who perhaps wanted
a portrait of *her* husband. What were they doing in

371

town, in any case, at that moment? Lyon made his
way to the studio with a certain curiosity; he wondered
vaguely what his friends were "up to." He laid his
hand upon the curtain draping the door of communication, the door opening upon the gallery constructed
for relief at the time the studio was added to the house;
but with his motion to slide the tapestry on its rings
arrested in the act. A singular startling sound reached
him from the room beneath; it had the appearance of
a passionate wail, or perhaps rather a smothered
shriek, accompanied by a violent burst of tears. Oliver
Lyon listened intently and then passed in to the balcony, which was covered with an old thick Moorish
rug. His step was noiseless without his trying to keep
it so, and after that first instant he found himself pro-
fiting irresistibly by the accident of his not having at-
tracted the attention of the two persons in the studio,
who were some twenty feet below him. They were in
truth so deeply and strangely engaged that their unconsciousness of observation was explained. The
scene that took place before Lyon's eyes was more
extraordinary than any he had ever felt free to over-
look. Delicacy and the failure to understand kept him
at first from interfering — what he saw was a woman
who had thrown herself in a flood of tears on her companion's bosom; after which surprise and discretion
gave way to a force that made him step back behind
the curtain. This same force, further — the force of
a *need* to know — caused him to avail himself for
better observation of a crevice formed by his gathering together the two halves of his swinging tapestry.
He was perfectly aware of what he was about — he

was for the moment an eavesdropper and a spy; but he was also aware that something irregular, as to which his confidence had been trifled with, was on foot, and that he was as much concerned with the reasons of it as he might be little concerned with the taken form. His observation, his reflexions, accomplished themselves in a flash.

His visitors were in the middle of the room; Mrs. Capadose clung to her husband, weeping; she sobbed as if her heart would break. Her distress was horrible to Oliver Lyon, but his astonishment was greater than his horror when he heard the Colonel respond to it by the vehement imprecation "Damn him, damn him, damn him!" What in the world had happened? why was she sobbing and whom was he damning? What had happened, Lyon saw the next instant, was that the Colonel had finally rummaged out the canvas before which he had been sitting — he knew the corner where the artist usually placed it, out of the way and its face to the wall — and had set it up for his wife on an empty easel. She had looked at it a few moments and then — apparently — what she saw in it had produced an explosion of dismay and resentment. She was too overcome, and the Colonel too busy holding her and re-expressing his wrath, to look round or look up. The scene was so unexpected to Lyon that all impulse failed in him on the spot for a proof of the triumph of his hand — of a tremendous hit: he could only wonder what on earth was the matter. The idea of the triumph was yet to come. He could see his projected figure, however, from where he stood; he was startled with its look of life — he had n't supposed the force of the thing could so prevail. Mrs. Capadose flung herself away from her husband — she dropped into the nearest chair, leaned against a table, buried her face in her arms. The sound of her woe diminished, but she shuddered there as if overwhelmed with anguish and shame. Her husband stood a moment glaring at the picture, then went to her, bent over her, took hold of her again, soothed her. "What is it, darling—what the devil is it?"

Lyon fairly drank in her answer. "It's cruel — oh it's too cruel!"

"Damn him, damn him, damn him!" the Colonel repeated.

"It's all there — it's all there!" Mrs. Capadose went on.

"Hang it, what's all there?"

"Everything there ought n't to be — everything he has seen. It's too dreadful!"

"Everything he has seen? Why, ain't I a good-looking fellow? I'll be bound to say he has made me handsome."

Mrs. Capadose had sprung up again; she had darted another glance at the painted betrayal. "Handsome? Hideous, hideous! Not that — never, never!"

"Not *what*, in heaven's name?" the Colonel almost shouted. Lyon could see his flushed bewildered face.

"What he has made of you — what you know! *He* knows — he has seen. Every one will, every one know and see. Fancy that thing in the Academy!"

"You're going wild, darling; but if you hate it so it need n't go," the poor branded man declared.

"Ah he'll send it — it's so good! Come away — come away!" Mrs. Capadose wailed, seizing her husband.

"It's so good?" the victim cried.

"Come away — come away," she only repeated, and she turned toward the staircase that ascended to the gallery.

"Not that way — not through the house in the state you're in," Lyon heard her companion object. "This way — we can pass," he added; and he drew his wife to the small door that opened into the garden. It was bolted, but he pushed the bolt and opened the door. She passed out quickly, but he stood there looking back into the room. "Wait for me a moment!" he cried out to her; and with an excited stride he re-entered the studio. He came up to the picture again — again he covered it with his baffled glare. "Damn him — damn him — damn him!" he broke out once more. Yet it was n't clear to Lyon whether this malediction had for object the guilty original or the guilty painter. The Colonel turned away and moved about as if looking for something; Lyon for the moment wondered at his intention; saying to himself the next, however, below his breath: "He's going to do it a harm!" His first impulse was to raise a preventive cry, but he paused with the sound of Everina Brant's sobs still in his ears. The Colonel found what he was looking for — found it among some odds and ends on a small table and strode back with it to the easel. At one and the same moment Lyon recognised the object seized as a small Eastern dagger and saw that he had plunged it into the canvas. Animated as with a sudden

fury and exercising a rare vigour of hand, he dragged
the instrument down — Lyon knew it to have no very
fine edge — making a long and abominable gash.
Then he plucked it out and dashed it again several
times into the face of the likeness, exactly as if he were
stabbing a human victim : it had the most portentous
effect — that of some act of prefigured or rehearsed
suicide. In a few seconds more the Colonel had tossed
the dagger away — he looked at it in this motion as
for the sight of blood — and hurried out of the place
with a bang of the door.

The strangest part of all was — as will doubtless
appear — that Oliver Lyon lifted neither voice nor
hand to save his picture. The point is that he did n't
feel as if he were losing it or did n't care if he were, so
much more was he conscious of gaining a certitude.
His old friend *was* ashamed of her husband, and he
had made her so, and he had scored a great success,
even at the sacrifice of his precious labour. The revelation so excited him — as indeed the whole scene did
— that when he came down the steps after the Colonel had gone he trembled with his happy agitation ; he
was dizzy and had to sit down a moment. The portrait had a dozen jagged wounds — the Colonel literally had hacked himself to death. Lyon left it there
where it grimaced, never touched it, scarcely looked
at it ; he only walked up and down his studio with a
sense of such achieved success as nothing finished and
framed, varnished and delivered and paid for had ever
given him. At the end of this time his good woman
came to offer him luncheon ; there was a passage under
the staircase from the offices.

"Ah the lady and gentleman have gone, sir? I did n't hear them."

"Yes; they went by the garden."

But she had stopped, staring at the picture on the easel. "Gracious, how you *'ave* served it, sir!"

Lyon imitated the Colonel. "Yes, I cut it up — in a fit of disgust."

"Mercy, after all your trouble! Because they were n't pleased, sir?"

"Yes; they were n't pleased."

"Well, they must be very grand! Blest if I would!"

"Have it chopped up; it will do to light fires," Lyon magnificently said.

He returned to the country by the 3.30 and a few days later passed over to France. There was something he found himself looking for during these two months on the Continent; he had an expectation — he could hardly have said of what; of some characteristic sign or other on the Colonel's part. Would n't he write, would n't he explain, would n't he take for granted Lyon had discovered the way he had indeed been "served" and hold it only decent to show some form of pity for his mystification? Would he plead guilty or would he repudiate suspicion? The latter course would be difficult, would really put his genius to the test, in view of the ready and responsible witness who had admitted the visitors the day of the ravage and would establish the connexion between their presence and that perpetration. Would the Colonel proffer some apology or some amends, or would any word from him be only a further expression of that exasperated wonder which our friend

had seen his wife so suddenly and so fatally communicate? He would have either to take oath that he
had n't touched the picture or to admit that he had,
and in either case would be at costs for a difficult version. Lyon was impatient for this probably remarkable story, and as no letter came was disappointed at
the failure of the exhibition. His impatience however
was much greater in respect to Mrs. Capadose's inevitable share in the report, if report there was to be;
for certainly that would be the real test, would show
how far she would go for her husband on the one side
or for himself on the other. He could scarcely wait
to see what line she would take — whether she would
simply adopt the Colonel's, whatever it might be. It
would have met his impatience most to draw her out
without waiting, to get an idea in advance. He wrote
to her, to this end, from Venice, in the tone of their
established friendship, asking for news, telling her of
his movements, hoping for their reunion in London
and not saying a word about the picture. Day followed day, after the time, and he received no answer;
on which he reflected that she could n't trust herself
to write — was still too deeply ruffled, too disconcerted, by his "betrayal." Her husband had espoused
her resentment and she had espoused the action he
had taken in consequence of it; the rupture was therefore complete and everything at an end. Lyon was
frankly rueful over this prospect, at the same time
that he thought it deplorable such charming people
should have put themselves so grossly in the wrong.
He was at last cheered, though little further enlightened, by the arrival of a letter, brief but breathing

good humour and hinting neither at a grievance nor at a bad conscience. The most interesting part of it to him was the postscript, which ran as follows: "I have a confession to make to you. We were in town for a couple of days, early in September, and I took the occasion to defy your authority: this was very bad of me but I could n't help it. I made Clement take me to your studio — I wanted so dreadfully to see what you had done with him, your wishes to the contrary notwithstanding. We made your servants let us in and I took a good look at the picture. It is really wonderful!" "Wonderful" was non-committal, but at least with this letter there was no rupture.

The third day after his return was a Sunday, so that he could go and ask Mrs. Capadose for luncheon. She had given him in the spring a general invitation to do so and he had several times profited by it. These had been the occasions, before his sittings, when he saw the Colonel most familiarly. Directly after the meal his host disappeared (went out, as he said, to call on *his* women) and the second half-hour was the best, even when there were other people. Now, in the first days of December, Lyon had the luck to find the pair alone, without even Amy, who appeared but little in public. They were in the drawing-room, waiting for the repast to be announced, and as soon as he came in the Colonel broke out: "My dear fellow, I'm delighted to see you! I'm so keen to begin again."

"Oh do go on; it's so beautiful," Mrs. Capadose said as she gave him her hand.

Lyon looked from one to the other; he did n't know

what he had expected, but he had n't expected this. "Ah then you think I 've got something?"

"You 've got everything." And Mrs. Capadose smiled from her golden-brown eyes.

"She wrote you of our little crime?" her husband asked. "She dragged me there — I had to go." Lyon wondered for a moment whether he meant by their little crime the assault on the canvas; but his friend's next words made this impossible. "You know I like to sit—you want me animated, and it leaves me so to wag my tongue. And just now I 've time."

"You must remember how near I had got to the end," Lyon returned.

"So you had. More 's the pity. I should like you to begin again."

"My dear fellow, I shall have to begin again!" laughed the painter with his eyes on Mrs. Capadose. She did n't meet them — she had got up to ring for luncheon. "The picture has been smashed," Lyon continued.

"Smashed? Ah what did you do that for?" cried Everina, standing there before him in all her clear rich beauty. Now that she did look at him she was impenetrable.

"I did n't — I found it so — with a dozen holes punched in it!"

"I say!" cried the Colonel —"what a jolly shame!"

Lyon took him in with a wide smile. "I hope *you* did n't go for it?"

"Is it done for?" the Colonel earnestly asked. He was as brightly true as his wife and he looked simply as if Lyon's question could n't be serious. "For the love of sitting to you? My dear fellow, if I had thought of it I would!"

"Nor you either?" the painter demanded of Mrs. Capadose.

Before she had time to reply her husband had seized her arm as if a lurid light had come to him. "I say, my dear, that woman — that woman!"

"That woman?" Mrs. Capadose repeated; and Lyon too wondered what woman he meant.

"Don't you remember when we came out, she was at the door — or a little way from it? I spoke to you of her — I told you about her. Geraldine — Grenadine — the one who burst in that day," he explained to Lyon. "We saw her hanging about — I called Everina's attention to her."

"Do you mean she got at my picture?"

"Ah yes, I remember," said Mrs. Capadose with a vague recovery.

"She burst in again — she had learned the way — she was waiting for her chance," the Colonel continued. "Ah the horrid little brute!"

Lyon looked down; he felt himself colouring. This was what he had been waiting for — the day the Colonel should wantonly sacrifice some innocent person. And could his wife be a party to that final atrocity? He had reminded himself repeatedly during the previous weeks that when her husband perpetrated his misdeed she had already quitted the room; but he had argued none the less — it was a virtual certainty — that he had on rejoining her at once mentioned his misdeed. He was in the flush of performance; and even if he had n't reported what he had done

381

she would have guessed it. Lyon did n't for an instant
believe poor Miss Geraldine to have been hovering
about his door, nor had the account given by the
Colonel the summer before of his relations with this
lady affected him as in the least convincing. Lyon
had never seen her till the day she planted herself
in his studio, but he knew her and classified her as if
he had made her. He was acquainted with the London model in all her feminine varieties — in every
phase of her development and every step of her decay.
When he entered his house that September morning
just after the arrival of his two friends there had been
no symptoms whatever, up and down the road, of
Miss Geraldine's reappearance. That fact had been
fixed in his mind by his recollecting the vacancy of the
prospect when his cook told him that a lady and a
gentleman were in his studio: he had wondered there
was neither carriage nor cab at his door. Then he had
reflected that they would have come by the underground railway; he was near the Marlborough Road
station and he knew the Colonel, repeating his pil-
grimage so often, habitually made use of that convenience. "How in the world did she get in ?" He
addressed the question to his companions indifferently.

"Let us go down to luncheon," said Mrs. Capadose, passing out of the room.

"We went by the garden — without troubling
your servant — I wanted to show my wife." Lyon
followed his hostess with her husband, and the Colonel
stopped him at the top of the stairs. "My dear fellow,
I *can't* have been guilty of the folly of not fastening
the door ?"

"I'm sure I don't know, Colonel," Lyon said as they went down. "It was a very determined hand that did the deed — in the spirit of a perfect wild-cat."

"Well, she *is* a wild-cat — confound her! That's why I wanted to get him away from her."

"But I don't understand her motive."

"Well, she's practically off her head — and she hates me. That was her motive."

"But she does n't hate me, my dear fellow!" Lyon amusedly urged.

"She hated the picture — don't you remember she said so? The more portraits, the less employment for such as her."

"Yes; but if she's not really the model she pretends to be, how can that hurt her?" Lyon asked.

The question baffled the Colonel an instant — but only an instant. "Ah she's so bad she goes it blind. She does n't know where she is."

They passed into the dining-room, where Mrs. Capadose was taking her place. "It's too low, it's too horrid!" she said. "You see the fates are against you. Providence won't let you be so disinterested — throwing off masterpieces for nothing."

"Did *you* see the woman?" Lyon put to her with something like a sternness he could n't mitigate.

She seemed not to feel it, or not to heed it if she did. "There was a person, not far from your door, whom Clement called my attention to. He told me something about her, but we were going the other way."

"And do you think she did it?"

"How can I tell? If she did she was mad, poor wretch."

"I should like very much to get hold of her," said Lyon. This was a false plea for the truth: he had no desire for any further conversation with Miss Geraldine. He had exposed his friends to his own view, but without wish to expose them to others, and least of all to themselves.

"Oh depend upon it she'll never show again. You're all right *now!*" the Colonel guaranteed.

"But I remember her address — Mortimer Terrace Mews, Notting Hill."

"Oh that's pure humbug. There isn't any such place."

"Lord, what a practised deceiver!" said Lyon.

"Is there any one else you suspect?" his host went on.

"Not a creature."

"And what do your servants say?"

"They say it wasn't *them*, and I reply that I never said it was. That's about the substance of our interviews."

"And when did they discover the havoc?"

"They never discovered it at all. I noticed it first — when I came back."

"Well, she could easily have stepped in," said the subject of Miss Geraldine's pursuit. "Don't you remember how she turned up that day like the clown in the ring?"

"Yes, yes; she could have done the job in three seconds, except that the picture wasn't out."

"Ah my dear fellow," the Colonel groaned, "don't utterly curse me! — but of course I dragged it out."

"You didn't put it *back?*" Lyon tragically cried.

384

"Ah Clement, Clement, did n't I tell you to?" Mrs. Capadose reproachfully wailed.

The Colonel almost howled for compunction; he covered his face with his hands. His wife's words were for Lyon the finishing touch; they made his whole vision crumble — his theory that she had secretly kept herself true. Even to her old lover she would n't be so! He was sick; he could n't eat; he knew how strange he must have looked. He attempted some platitude about spilled milk and the folly of crying over it — he tried to turn the talk to other things. But it was a horrid effort and he wondered how it pressed upon *them*. He wondered all sorts of things: whether they guessed he disbelieved them — that he had seen them of course they would never guess; whether they had arranged their story in advance or it was only an inspiration of the moment; whether she had resisted, protested, when the Colonel proposed it to her, and then had been borne down by him; whether in short she did n't loathe herself as she sat there. The cruelty, the cowardice of fastening their unholy act upon the wretched woman struck him as monstrous — no less monstrous indeed than the levity that could make them run the risk of her giving them, in her righteous indignation, the lie. Of course that risk could only exculpate her and not inculpate them — the probabilities protected them so perfectly; and what the Colonel counted on — what he would have counted upon the day he delivered himself, after first seeing her, at the studio, if he had thought about the matter then at all and not spoken from the pure spontaneity of his genius —

was simply that Miss Geraldine must have vanished
for ever into her native unknown. Lyon wanted so
much to cut loose, in his disgust, that when after a
little Mrs. Capadose said to him "But can nothing
be done, can't the picture be repaired? You know
they do such wonders in that way now," he only made
answer: "I don't know, I don't care, it's all over,
n'en parlons plus!" Her hypocrisy revolted him.
And yet by way of plucking off the last veil of her
shame he broke out to her again, shortly afterwards:
"And you *did* like it, really?" To which she returned, looking him straight in his face, without a
blush, a pallor, an evasion: "Oh *cher grand maître*, I
loved it!" Truly her husband had trained her well.
After that Lyon said no more, and his companions
forbore temporarily to insist, like people of tact and
sympathy aware that the odious accident had made
him sore.

When they quitted the table the Colonel went away
without coming upstairs; but Lyon returned to the
drawing-room with his hostess, remarking to her
however on the way that he could remain but a moment. He spent that moment — it prolonged itself
a little — standing with her before the chimney-piece.
She neither sat down nor asked him to; her manner
betrayed some purpose of going out. Yes, her husband had trained her well; yet Lyon dreamed for a
moment that now he was alone with her she would
perhaps break down, retract, apologise, confide, say
to him: "My dear old friend, forgive this hideous
comedy — you understand!" And then how he
would have loved her and pitied her, guarded her,

386

helped her always! If she were n't ready to do something of that sort why had she treated him so as a dear old friend; why had she let him for months suppose certain things — or almost; why had she come to his studio day after day to sit near him on the pretext of her child's portrait, as if she liked to think what might have been? Why had she come so near a tacit confession if she was n't willing to go an inch further? And she was n't willing — she was n't; he could see that as he lingered there. She moved about the room a little, rearranging two or three objects on the tables, but she did nothing more. Suddenly he said to her: "Which way was she going when you came out?"

"She — the woman we saw?"

"Yes, your husband's strange friend. It's a clue worth following." He did n't want to scare or to shake her; he only wanted to communicate the impulse that would make her say: "Ah spare me — and spare *him!* There was no such person."

Instead of this Everina replied: "She was going away from us — she crossed the road. We were coming toward the station."

"And did she appear to recognise the Colonel — did she look round?"

"Yes; she looked round, but I did n't notice much. A hansom came along and we got into it. It was n't till then that Clement told me who she was: I remember he said that she was there for no good. I suppose we ought to have gone back."

"Yes; you'd have saved the picture."

For a moment she said nothing; then she smiled.

THE LIAR

"For you, *cher maître*, I'm very sorry. But you must remember I possess the original!"

At this he turned away. "Well, I must go," he said; and he left her without any other farewell and made his way out of the house. As he went slowly up the street the sense came back to him of that first glimpse of her he had had at Stayes — of how he had seen her gaze across the table at her husband. He stopped at the corner, looking vaguely up and down. He would never go back — he could n't. Nor should he ever sound her abyss. He believed in her absolute straightness where she and her affairs alone might be concerned, but she was still in love with the man of her choice, and since she could n't redeem him she would adopt and protect him. So he had trained her.

THE TWO FACES

I

THE servant, who, in spite of his sealed stamped look, appeared to have his reasons, stood there for instruction in a manner not quite usual after announcing the name. Mrs. Grantham, however, took it up — "Lord Gwyther?" — with a quick surprise that for an instant justified him even to the small scintilla in the glance she gave her companion, which might have had exactly the sense of the butler's hesitation. This companion, a shortish fairish youngish man, clean-shaven and keen-eyed, had, with a promptitude that would have struck an observer — which the butler indeed was — sprung to his feet and moved to the chimney-piece, though his hostess herself meanwhile managed not otherwise to stir. "Well?" she said as for the visitor to advance; which she immediately followed with a sharper "He's not there?"

"Shall I show him up, ma'am?"

"But of course!" The point of his doubt made her at last rise for impatience, and Bates, before leaving the room, might still have caught the achieved irony of her appeal to the gentleman into whose communion with her he had broken. "Why in the world not —? What a way —!" she exclaimed as Sutton felt beside his cheek the passage of her eyes to the glass behind him.

"He was n't sure you 'd see any one."

"I don't see 'any one,' but I see individuals."

"That's just it — and sometimes you don't see them."

"Do you mean ever because of *you?*" she asked as she touched into place a tendril of hair. "That's just his impertinence, as to which I shall speak to him."

"Don't," said Shirley Sutton. "Never notice anything."

"That's nice advice from you," she laughed, "who notice everything!"

"Ah but I speak of nothing."

She looked at him a moment. "You're still more impertinent than Bates. You'll please not budge," she went on.

"Really? I must sit him out?" he continued as, after a minute, she had not again spoken — only glancing about, while she changed her place, partly for another look at the glass and partly to see if she could improve her seat. What she felt was rather more than, clever and charming though she was, she could hide. "If you're wondering how you seem I can tell you. Awfully cool and easy."

She gave him another stare. She was beautiful and conscious. "And if you're wondering how *you* seem —"

"Oh I'm not!" he laughed from before the fire. "I always perfectly know."

"How you seem," she retorted, "is as if you did n't!"

Once more for a little he watched her. "You're

looking lovely for him — extraordinarily lovely, within the marked limits of your range. But that's enough. Don't be clever."

"Then who *will* be ?"

"There you are !" he sighed with amusement.

"Do you know him ?" she asked as, through the door left open by Bates, they heard steps on the landing.

Sutton had to think an instant, and produced a "No" just as Lord Gwyther was again announced, which gave an unexpectedness to the greeting offered him a moment later by this personage — a young man, stout and smooth and fresh, but not at all shy, who, after the happiest rapid passage with Mrs. Grantham, put out a hand with a straight free "How d' ye do ?"

"Mr. Shirley Sutton," Mrs. Grantham explained.

"Oh yes," said her second visitor quite as if he knew; which, as he could n't have known, had for her first the interest of confirming a perception that his lordship would be — no, not at all, in general, embarrassed, only was now exceptionally and especially agitated. As it is, for that matter, with Sutton's total impression that we are particularly and almost exclusively concerned, it may be further mentioned that he was not less clear as to the really handsome way in which the young man kept himself together and little by little — though with all proper aid indeed — finally found his feet. All sorts of things, for the twenty minutes, occurred to Sutton, though one of them was certainly not that it would, after all, be better he should go. One of them was that their hostess was doing it in perfection — simply, easily, kindly, yet with something the least bit queer in her wonderful eyes; another was that if he had been recognised without the least ground it was through a tension of nerves on the part of his fellow guest that produced inconsequent motions; still another was that, even had departure been indicated, he would positively have felt dissuasion in the rare promise of the scene. This was in especial after Lord Gwyther not only had announced that he was now married, but had mentioned that he wished to bring his wife to Mrs. Grantham for the benefit so certain to be derived. It was the passage immediately produced by that speech that provoked in Sutton the intensity, as it were, of his arrest. He already knew of the marriage as well as Mrs. Grantham herself, and as well also as he knew of some other things; and this gave him doubtless the better measure of what took place before him and the keener consciousness of the quick look that, at a marked moment — though it was not absolutely meant for him any more than for his companion — Mrs. Grantham let him catch.

She smiled, but it had a gravity. "I think, you know, you ought to have told me before."

"Do you mean when I first got engaged? Well, it all took place so far away, and we really told, at home, so few people."

Oh there might have been reasons; but it had not been quite right. "You were married at Stuttgart? That wasn't too far for *my* interest, at least, to reach."

"Awfully kind of you — and of course one knew

you *would* be kind. But it was n't at Stuttgart; it was over there, but quite in the country. We should have managed it in England but that her mother naturally wished to be present, yet was n't in health to come. So it was really, you see, a sort of little hole-and-corner German affair."

This did n't in the least check Mrs. Grantham's claim, but it started a slight anxiety. "Will she be — a — then German ?"

Sutton knew her to know perfectly what Lady Gwyther would "be," but he had by this time, while their friend explained, his independent interest. "Oh dear no ! My father-in-law has never parted with the proud birthright of a Briton. But his wife, you see, holds an estate in Würtemberg from *her* mother, Countess Kremnitz, on which, with the awful condition of his English property, you know, they 've found it for years a tremendous saving to live. So that though Valda was luckily born at home she has practically spent her life over there."

"Oh I see." Then, after a slight pause, "Is Valda her pretty name ?" Mrs. Grantham asked.

"Well," said the young man, only wishing, in his candour, it was clear, to be drawn out — "well, she has, in the manner of her mother's people, about thirteen; but that's the one we generally use."

Mrs. Grantham waited but an instant. "Then may *I* generally use it ?"

"It would be too charming of you; and nothing would give her — as I assure you nothing would give *me* — greater pleasure." Lord Gwyther quite glowed with the thought.

"Then I think that instead of coming alone you might have brought her to see me."

"It's exactly what," he instantly replied, "I came to ask your leave to do." He explained that for the moment Lady Gwyther was not in town, having as soon as she arrived gone down to Torquay to put in a few days with one of her aunts, also her godmother, to whom she was an object of great interest. She had seen no one yet, and no one — not that *that* mattered — had seen her; she knew nothing whatever of London and was awfully frightened at facing it and at what (however little) might be expected of her. "She wants some one," he said, "some one who knows the whole thing, don't you see? and who's thoroughly kind and clever, as you would be, if I may say so, to take her by the hand." It was at this point and on these words that the eyes of Lord Gwyther's two auditors inevitably and wonderfully met. But there was nothing in the way he kept it up to show he caught the encounter. "She wants, if I may tell you so, a real friend for the great labyrinth; and asking myself what I could do to make things ready for her, and who would be absolutely the best woman in London — "

"You thought naturally of *me?*" Mrs. Grantham had listened with no sign but the faint flash just noted; now, however, she gave him the full light of her expressive face — which immediately brought Shirley Sutton, looking at his watch, once more to his feet.

"She *is* the best woman in London!" He addressed himself with a laugh to the other visitor, but offered his hand in farewell to their hostess.

THE TWO FACES

"You're going?"

"I must," he said without scruple.

"Then we do meet at dinner?"

"I hope so." On which, to take leave, he returned with interest to Lord Gwyther the friendly clutch he had a short time before received.

II

THEY did meet at dinner, and if they were not, as it happened, side by side, they made that up afterwards in the happiest angle of a drawing-room that offered both shine and shadow and that was positively much appreciated, in the circle in which they moved, for the favourable "corners" created by its shrewd mistress. Mrs. Grantham's face, charged with something produced in it by Lord Gwyther's visit, had been with him so constantly for the previous hours that, when she instantly challenged him on his "treatment" of her in the afternoon, he was on the point of naming it as his reason for not having remained with her. Something new had quickly come into her beauty; he could n't as yet have said what, nor whether on the whole to its advantage or its loss. Till he should see this clearer, at any rate he would say nothing; so that he found with sufficient presence of mind a better excuse. If in short he had in defiance of her particular request left her alone with Lord Gwyther it was simply because the situation had suddenly turned so exciting that he had fairly feared the contagion of it — the temptation of its making him, most improperly, put in his word.

They could now talk of these things at their ease. Other couples, ensconced and scattered, enjoyed the same privilege, and Sutton had more and more the profit, such as it was, of feeling that his interest in

Mrs. Grantham had become — what was the luxury
of so high a social code — an acknowledged and protected relation. He knew his London well enough to
know that he was on the way to be regarded as her
main source of consolation for the trick Lord Gwyther
had several months before publicly played her. Many
persons had not held that, by the high social code in
question, his lordship could have "reserved the right"
to turn up that way, from one day to another, engaged to be married. For himself London took, with
its short cuts and its cheap psychology, an immense
deal for granted. To his own sense he was never —
could in the nature of things never be — any man's
"successor." Just what had constituted the pre-
decessorship of other men was apparently that they
had been able to make up their mind. He, worse
luck, was at the mercy of her face, and more than
ever at the mercy of it now, which meant moreover
not that it made a slave of him, but that it made, dis-
concertingly, a sceptic. It was the absolute perfection of the handsome, but things had a way of coming
into it. "I felt," he said, "that you were there together at a point at which you had a right to the ease
the absence of a listener would give. I was sure that
when you made me promise to stay you had n't
guessed —"

"That he could possibly have come to me on such
an extraordinary errand? No, of course I had n't
guessed. Who *would?* But did n't you see how little
I was upset by it?"

Sutton demurred. Then with a smile: "I think *he*
saw how little."

"You yourself did n't then?

He again held back, but not, after all, to answer. "He was wonderful, was n't he?"

"I think he was," she returned after a moment. To which she added: "Why did he pretend that way he knew you?"

"He did n't pretend. He somehow felt on the spot that I was 'in it.'" Sutton had found this afterwards and found it to represent a reality. "It was an effusion of cheer and hope. He was so glad to see me there and to find you happy."

"Happy?"

"Happy. Are n't you?"

"Because of *you?*"

"Well — according to the impression he received as he came in."

"That was sudden then," she asked, "and unexpected?"

Her companion thought. "Prepared in some degree, but confirmed by the sight of us, there together, so awfully jolly and sociable over your fire."

Mrs. Grantham turned this round. "If he knew I was 'happy' then — which, by the way, is none of his business, nor of yours either — why in the world did he come?"

"Well, for good manners, and for his idea," said Sutton.

She took it in, appearing to have no hardness of rancour that could bar discussion. "Do you mean by his idea his proposal that I should grandmother his wife? And if you do is the proposal your reason for calling him wonderful?"

Sutton laughed. "Pray what's yours?" As this was a question, however, that she took her time to answer or not to answer — only appearing interested for a moment in a combination that had formed itself on the other side of the room — he presently went on. "What's *his?* — that would seem to be the point. His, I mean, for having decided on the extraordinary step of throwing his little wife, bound hands and feet, into your arms. Intelligent as you are, and with these three or four hours to have thought it over, I yet don't see how that can fail still to mystify you."

She continued to watch their opposite neighbours. "'Little,' you call her. Is she so very small?"

"Tiny, tiny — she *must* be; as different as possible in every way — of necessity — from you. They always *are* the opposite pole, you know," said Shirley Sutton.

She glanced at him now. "You strike me as of an impudence —!"

"No, no. I only like to make it out with you."

She looked away again and after a little went on. "I'm sure she's charming, and only hope one is n't to gather he's already tired of her."

"Not a bit! He's tremendously in love, and he'll remain so."

"So much the better. And if it's a question," said Mrs. Grantham, "of one's doing what one can for her, he has only, as I told him when you had gone, to give me the chance."

"Good! So he *is* to commit her to you?"

"You use extraordinary expressions, but it's settled that he brings her."

"And you'll really and truly help her?"

"Really and truly?" said Mrs. Grantham with her eyes again on him. "Why not? For what do you take me?"

"Ah is n't that just what I still have the discomfort, every day I live, of asking myself?"

She had made, as she spoke, a movement to rise, which, as if she was tired of his tone, his last words appeared to determine. But, also getting up, he held her, when they were on their feet, long enough to hear the rest of what he had to say. "If you do help her, you know, you'll show him you've understood."

"Understood what?"

"Why, his idea — the deep acute train of reasoning that has led him to take, as one may say, the bull by the horns; to reflect that as you might, as you probably *would*, in any case, get at her, he plays the wise game, as well as the bold one, by treating your generosity as a real thing and placing himself publicly under an obligation to you."

Mrs. Grantham showed not only that she had listened, but that she had for an instant considered. "What is it you elegantly describe as my getting 'at' her?"

"He takes his risk, but puts you, you see, on your honour."

She thought a moment more. "What profundities indeed then over the simplest of matters! And if your idea is," she went on, "that if I do help her I shall show him I've understood them, so it will be that if I don't —"

"You'll show him" — Sutton took her up — "that

you have n't? Precisely. But in spite of not wanting to appear to have understood *too* much —"

"I may still be depended on to do what I can? Quite certainly. You'll see what I may still be depended on to do." And she moved away.

III

IT was not, doubtless, that there had been anything in their rather sharp separation at that moment to sustain or prolong the interruption; yet it definitely befell that, circumstances aiding, they practically failed to meet again before the great party at Burbeck. This occasion was to gather in some thirty persons from a certain Friday to the following Monday, and it was on the Friday that Sutton went down. He had known in advance that Mrs. Grantham was to be there, and this perhaps, during the interval of hindrance, had helped him a little to be patient. He had before him the certitude of a real full cup — two days brimming over with the sight of her. He found, however, on his arrival that she was not yet in the field, and presently learned that her place would be in a small contingent that was to join the party on the morrow. This knowledge he extracted from Miss Banker, who was always the first to present herself at any gathering that was to enjoy her, and whom moreover — partly on that very account — the wary not less than the speculative were apt to hold themselves well-advised to engage with at as early as possible a stage of the business. She was stout red rich mature universal — a massive much-fingered volume, alphabetical wonderful indexed, that opened of itself at the right place. She opened for Sutton instinctively at G——, which happened to be re-

markably convenient. "What she's really waiting
over for is to bring down Lady Gwyther."

"Ah the Gwythers are coming?"

"Yes; caught, through Mrs. Grantham, just in time.
She'll be the feature — every one wants to see her."

Speculation and wariness met and combined at
this moment in Shirley Sutton. "Do you mean — a
— Mrs. Grantham?"

"Dear no! Poor little Lady Gwyther, who, but
just arrived in England, appears now literally for the
first time in her life in any society whatever, and
whom (don't you know the extraordinary story? you
ought to — *you!*) she, of all people, has so wonderfully taken up. It will be quite — here — as if she
were 'presenting' her."

Sutton of course took in more things than even
appeared. "I never know what I ought to know; I
only know, inveterately, what I ought n't. So what *is*
the extraordinary story?"

"You really have n't heard —?"

"Really," he replied without winking.

"It happened indeed but the other day," said
Miss Banker, "yet every one's already wondering.
Gwyther has thrown his wife on her mercy — but
I won't believe you if you pretend to me you don't
know why he should n't."

Sutton asked himself then what he *could* pretend.
"Do you mean because she's merciless?"

She hesitated. "If you don't know perhaps I
ought n't to tell you."

He liked Miss Banker and found just the right tone
to plead. "*Do* tell me."

"Well," she sighed, "it will be your own fault —!
They had been such friends that there could have
been but one name for the crudity of his original
procédé. When I was a girl we used to call it throwing
over. They call it in French to *lâcher*. But I refer not
so much to the act itself as to the manner of it, though
you may say indeed of course that there's in such
cases after all only one manner. Least said soonest
mended."

Sutton seemed to wonder. "Oh he said too much ?"

"He said nothing. That was it."

Sutton kept it up. "But was *what?*"

"Why, what she must, like any woman in her
shoes, have felt to be his perfidy. He simply went
and *did* it — took to himself this child, that is, without
the preliminary of a scandal or a rupture — before
she could turn round."

"I follow you. But it would appear from what you
say that she *has* turned round now."

"Well," Miss Banker laughed, "we shall see for
ourselves how far. It will be what every one will try
to see."

"Oh then we've work cut out!" And Sutton certainly felt that he himself had — an impression that
lost nothing from a further talk with Miss Banker in
the course of a short stroll in the grounds with her
the next day. He spoke as one who had now considered many things.

"Did I understand from you yesterday that Lady
Gwyther's a 'child'?"

"Nobody knows. It's prodigious the way she has
managed."

"The way Lady Gwyther has — ?"

"No, the way May Grantham has kept her till this hour in her pocket."

He was quick at his watch. "Do you mean by 'this hour' that they're due now?"

"Not till tea. All the others arrive together in time for that." Miss Banker had clearly, since the previous day, filled in gaps and become, as it were, revised and enlarged. "She'll have kept a cat from seeing her, so as to produce her entirely herself."

"Well," Sutton mused, "that will have been a very noble sort of return —"

"For Gwyther's behaviour? Very. Yet I feel creepy."

"Creepy?"

"Because so much depends for the girl — in the way of the right start or the wrong start — on the signs and omens of this first appearance. It's a great house and a great occasion, and we're assembled here, it strikes me, very much as the Roman mob at the circus used to be to see the next Christian maiden brought out to the tigers."

"Oh if she *is* a Christian maiden —!" Sutton murmured. But he stopped at what his imagination called up.

It perhaps fed that faculty a little that Miss Banker had the effect of making out that Mrs. Grantham might individually be, in any case, something of a Roman matron. "She has kept her in the dark so that we may only take her from her hand. She'll have formed her for us."

"In so few days?"

"Well, she'll have prepared her — decked her for the sacrifice with ribbons and flowers."

"Ah if you only mean that she'll have taken her to her dressmaker —!" And it came to Sutton, at once as a new light and as a check, almost, to anxiety, that this was all poor Gwyther, mistrustful probably of a taste formed by Stuttgart, might have desired of their friend.

There were usually at Burbeck many things taking place at once; so that wherever else, on such occasions, tea might be served, it went forward with matchless pomp, weather permitting, on a shaded stretch of one of the terraces and in presence of one of the prospects. Shirley Sutton, moving, as the afternoon waned, more restlessly about and mingling in dispersed groups only to find they had nothing to keep him quiet, came upon it as he turned a corner of the house — saw it seated there in all its state. It might be said that at Burbeck it was, like everything else, made the most of. It constituted immediately, with multiplied tables and glittering plate, with rugs and cushions and ices and fruit and wonderful porcelain and beautiful women, a scene of splendour, almost an incident of grand opera. One of the beautiful women might quite have been expected to rise with a gold cup and a celebrated song.

One of them did rise, as happened, while Sutton drew near, and he found himself a moment later seeing nothing and nobody but Mrs. Grantham. They met on the terrace, just away from the others, and the movement in which he had the effect of arresting her might have been that of withdrawal. He quickly saw, however, that if she had been about to pass into the house it was only on some errand — to get something or to call some one — that would immediately have restored her to her public. It somehow struck him on the spot — and more than ever yet, though the impression was not wholly new to him — that she felt herself a figure for the forefront of the stage and indeed would have been recognised by any one at a glance as the *prima donna assoluta*. She caused, in fact, during the few minutes he stood talking to her, an extraordinary series of waves to roll extraordinarily fast over his sense, not the least mark of the matter being that the appearance with which it ended was again the one with which it had begun. "The face — the face," as he kept dumbly repeating; that was at last, as at first, all he could clearly see. She had a perfection resplendent, but what in the world had it done, this perfection, to her beauty? It was her beauty doubtless that looked out at him, but it was into something else that, as their eyes met, he strangely found himself looking.

It was as if something had happened in consequence of which she had changed, and there was that in this swift perception that made him glance eagerly about for Lady Gwyther. But as he took in the recruited group — identities of the hour added to those of the previous twenty-four — he saw, among his recognitions, one of which was the husband of the person missing, that Lady Gwyther was not there. Nothing in the whole business was more singular than his consciousness that, as he came back to his interlocutress after the nods and smiles and hand-waves he had launched, she knew what had been his thought. She knew for whom he had looked without success; but why should this knowledge visibly have hardened and sharpened her, and precisely at a moment when she was unprecedentedly magnificent? The indefinable apprehension that had somewhat sunk after his second talk with Miss Banker and then had perversely risen again — this nameless anxiety now produced on him, with a sudden sharper pinch, the effect of a great suspense. The action of that, in turn, was to show him that he had n't yet fully known how much he had at stake on a final view. It was revealed to him for the first time that he "really cared" whether Mrs. Grantham were a safe nature. It was too ridiculous by what a thread it hung, but something was certainly in the air that would definitely tell him.

What was in the air descended the next moment to earth. He turned round as he caught the expression with which her eyes attached themselves to something that approached. A little person, very young and very much dressed, had come out of the house, and the expression in Mrs. Grantham's eyes was that of the artist confronted with her work and interested, even to impatience, in the judgement of others. The little person drew nearer, and though Sutton's companion, without looking at him now, gave it a name and met it, he had jumped for himself at certitude. He saw many things — too many, and they appeared to be feathers, frills, excrescences of silk and lace — massed together and conflicting, and after a moment also saw struggling out of them a small face that